Stuffed!

Why there is now no hope for England and the English; why we are doomed to generations of penury, depression and social strife; who is to blame and why the only solution to our nation's woes is a revolution.

Vernon Coleman

Blue Books

Dedication

To Donna Antoinette, my love, my wife, my friend, my life. Without you the world would be cold and dark, cruel and pointless. With you there is hope and purpose. Amidst the chaos, uncertainty, injustice, frustration and despair there is beauty, love and happiness because I share my days with you.

Note 1

People around the world use `England' when they are referring to Britain or the United Kingdom. This is particularly true of Americans. And so, given the fact that a good many Scots want to leave the United Kingdom, and regularly profess their hatred of the English, I have chosen, in this book, to use the word `England' when tradition might suggest that the use of the other names might be considered appropriate. As a pleasant side effect this may well annoy a few rabid Scottish nationalists. To them I say simply: totter ye off and enjoy your precarious, penurious and spurious independence.

Note 2

All opinions, predictions and ramblings found in this book are aired in public purely as entertainment. I certainly do not recommend that any reader makes any decisions of any kind based on any of the material in this book.

Disclaimers invariably go on to insist that readers who rely on anything in the book they are reading do so at their own risk. These warnings are included because the world is now full of lawyers and litigants who, under the often misguided impression that there might be money to be made, will leap at every opportunity to gouge lolly out of anyone who can be blamed for fate's little tricks. And so, as author and publisher, I feel that I must follow fashion and warn readers that if they act on any of the alleged facts in this book, or decide to follow any advice which has crept, uninvited, onto the pages therein, they do so entirely at their own risk. I recommend that advice and opinions should be disregarded or treated with great suspicion. Any reader who believes the alleged facts in this book, or follows any advice the book may accidentally include, does so entirely at their own risk. Moreover, I would also like to make it clear that books can be dangerous objects and should not be dropped, thrown or otherwise projected into areas where people or delicate objects might be damaged. In other words, dear reader, drop this book onto a passing health and safety official and you're on your own.

Contents

Preface

A reader wrote to me recently to tell me how much he had enjoyed my book *2020* and how much fun he was having watching the predictions come true. He had, he wrote, told many friends about the book and had been surprised by the response of one. 'Why would you want a book that tells you what might happen? What's the point?'

My reader was puzzled by this response. It seemed to him to be enormously valuable to have some sort of idea of what the future may bring. We are living in a time of great change. Very little stays the same for more than a few months and many aspects of life which we took for granted just a year or two ago have changed beyond recognition.

There are, of course, many reasons for wanting to have some idea of what might happen next, and how those developments might affect our daily lives. For a start, it is difficult to plan any sort of future for yourself and your family unless you have some idea of the nature of the world in which you will be living. It seems clear to me that unless you have a rough idea of the possibilities it is impossible to make decisions about where to live, how to live and how to invest.

It is not, of course, possible to predict the future with 100% accuracy. The last few years have reminded us that all sorts of strange things can, and do, happen. But it is possible to assess many of the possibilities and, by understanding how politicians work, and why they do the things they do, it is possible to make some useful guesses.

In some ways this is a depressing book (to write as well as to read) because we are living through a time when expectations must be kept low. Our present and future lives are shaped by lobbyists, self-interest and hidden agendas. (To some extent this makes it easier, not harder, to predict the future. All we must do is work out which lobbyists, whose self-interest and which hidden agendas are likely to take precedence.)

There are two ways to be a successful forecaster without actually making any accurate forecasts. The first is to produce a barrage of forecasts (preferably contradictory) and then promote the ones you got right. Organisations such as banks manage this by allowing named individuals or subsidiaries to make opposing predictions. The bank can then draw attention to the ones that came true. The other way to be successful is to forecast so far into the future that no one will remember what you predicted. If you make predictions about what is going to happen in 2050 then the chances are that many of the people who read your predictions will be dead and the rest will have long ago forgotten everything you said.

I have always eschewed these two safe ways to forecast; preferring to take my chances on the tightrope by making specific, fairly short-term predictions. And, I'm relieved to say, my success rate to date has been high enough to encourage me to carry on a little longer.

A growing number of people now agree with a position I have held for a number of years concerning our economy. Thanks to the egregious and wilful incompetence of politicians and bankers the future promises endless chaos and disappointments.

But this book deals with far, far more than the economic problems we face. In this book I have described the underlying problems, the reasons why our society is going to have to change dramatically; why things are never again going to be the way they used to be.

I believe that the views in this book are fairly cautious and certainly not extreme. I know of people who have bought a lot of gold, a good many guns and rolls of razor wire and retired to far away homes. (It may well be that they were the sensible ones). I prefer to hang around on the fringe of civilisation for a while, protect the Princess and myself as best I can, and see how things work out.

I chose to write this book in the style of *England Our England*, packaging the information in relatively small sections, because I feel it helps to define and draw attention to the salient facts. It's a style which I first used for my book *England Our England* (which has sold well over 40,000 copies, which isn't bad for a book on politics in general and for a book on English nationalism in particular, especially since advertisements were widely banned and the book received no national newspaper coverage whatsoever). This style has been rudely attacked by the few people who have ever bothered to review my political books (and by more who have criticised them but haven't bothered to read them) but I would point out that this format isn't new. It is, after all, the style in which The Bible is written.

I wrote this book for the small number of faithful readers who have been kind enough to read my books for the last few years. The print run will be limited to 750 copies and the book will not be reprinted. When the 750 have gone there will be no more. I want to share the thoughts in this book with my readers so that they may share my ideas of the future that awaits us. This book will not be offered for review or for general sale and so it will have no influence on the world at large. But I offer it to my loyal readers because I believe everything in it is true and everything in it is important.

The truth is that I now find myself in the position of that gentle man who used to parade up and down Oxford Street holding a placard announcing that *The end is nigh*. (He would not, today, be allowed to make such a prognosis in public. I suspect that he would be arrested for some breach of the peace as defined by the European Union.)

And to what end are we nigh?

That's simple.

The end of our country, our culture, our history. The end of ambition, entrepreneurship, respect, honesty, integrity in public life. The end of growth. The end of house prices rising indefinitely. The end of secure employment. The end of safe pensions. The end of equity market growth.

We aren't all going to die. It isn't that sort of end. The world is not going to implode overnight because of global warming. We aren't all going to boil to death as glaciers melt and coastal towns flood. Those, if they are real, are relatively trivial problems; exaggerated and promoted to distract us from more serious issues and to explain and excuse energy policies designed to hide from the mass of people the fact that the oil (and just about everything else) is running out.

And, as with most ends, it is also a beginning.

The beginning of widespread poverty. The beginning of lawlessness and street fighting and frustration and unrest. The rise, rise and rise of crimes against property and crimes against people. The beginning of the first steps towards a revolution. The beginning of the return of nationalism.

This is, at last, my final book on politics, economics, the state of the nation and the future of our world. It is the last because the factors described in this book aren't going to change in my lifetime. You and I know that things shouldn't be like this. But they are. And until the people are ready for a revolution we can do nothing but learn how to survive.

My remaining books will, I promise you faithfully, dear and loyal reader, be more fun than this one.

Vernon Coleman Summer 2012

Prologue

`These are the times that try men's souls.' - Thomas Paine, Englishman

There is a widespread feeling (particularly popular on the financial pages and in investment magazines) that this is just another bust (following a boom) and that everything will soon be tickety boo again.

Wrong.

The planet's future is very bleak indeed. And I'm sorry to have to tell you that the future for England is particularly gloomy. Our country has lived beyond its means for decades, living on borrowed money and with governments dependant upon people buying lots of stuff they didn't need with money they didn't have. And, with money raised and borrowed, governments also spent wildly; throwing money around on vote-winning benefits programmes, disguising debts and ignoring long-term liabilities such as the Ponzi scheme that is State employee pension liabilities (whereby future liabilities are ignored and left to be paid by future generations).

The world (or, more specifically, the Western world) also has a massive debt problem. Our apparent wealth has been built on credit. The money we have used to enrich our nations and ourselves was created out of thin air by greedy bankers. Our monetary system is based entirely on debt, and servicing the massive debts requires constant economic growth. Governments need more and more money to pay for all the salaries and pensions of their public employees and to pay the debts they have incurred in building huge bureaucracies and huge buildings in which to house the bureaucrats. Companies need more and more money to pay for the pensions and bonuses to which their employees have become accustomed and to pay the interest on the loans they took out to buy over-priced property. And individual families need growth to pay back the debts they incurred in buying houses, cars and television sets they could not afford.

Everyone needs growth.

But there isn't any. And (unless the politicians decide to start a major war to trigger manufacturing growth in the armaments industry) there probably isn't going to be any. Japan has been stagnating for decades. An elderly population, overpriced real estate and huge debts have left the country forever doomed to deal with yesterday.

Greece isn't the only Western economy to have been built on deceit, fraud, corruption and debt. But it is probably the only Western economy that will be bailed out and allowed to default on its debts at someone else's expense. There isn't enough money left to bail out America, England, Italy, Spain, France and all the other heavily indebted superpowers. It sounds like a cliché but it really is different this time.

The only global solution to this global problem is inflation. State organised, State controlled and State endorsed inflation.

And that is why the English and American governments have been busy printing money and devaluing their currencies. They simply do not care about the consequences for the prudent and the sensible; they care nothing about the consequences for pensioners, widows and orphans. Our economic policy is specifically, deliberately designed to transfer wealth from the middle classes (the hard-working, taxpaying savers) to the imprudent, the reckless and the lazy. (The rich will not be affected because they will receive special treatment and very special advice and will either move their money or themselves offshore.) The vaguely disguised (but never admitted) reason for this transfer of wealth is to eradicate debt (both private and government) and so, ultimately, to encourage growth. The programme isn't going to work because the debt is simply too huge and because the need to cut costs will never be matched by the will or (in the face of political opposition from public sector unions jealously guarding the absurd rights of their over-fatted, over-indulged members) the ability.

But I want to go further and examine other, deeper problems which will, I believe, ensure that England (and, indeed, the rest of the United Kingdom) remains in decline for the foreseeable future (by which I mean for at least another two or three generations, taking us well into the second half of the 21st century).

We aren't facing World War III or the Great Plague (well, at least as far as I know, we're not). And I have no reason to suspect that the fellow who used to wander the streets with a placard warning of the end of the world is going to be saying `I told you so' anytime soon. But we are facing the end of the superior sort of lifestyle to which those of us in the so-called developed countries have grown accustomed and which we've grown to like very much indeed. We are coming to the end of a way of life. Things are going to change a great deal and they're going to change permanently.

We've had the rise, now comes the fall.

It would have eventually come anyway but it was brought forward and made worse by Brown, the Bank of England and a legion of greedy bankers (many of them foreign). The economic crash was caused by governments and people spending money they didn't have on stuff they didn't need.

The other problems we face were caused or exacerbated by inequality, greed, corruption, globalisation, multiculturalism, State imposed targets, political correctness, regulatory nonsenses emanating from a fascist bureaucracy and institutional thuggery. Even charity shops now exist to rip off local communities (by charging high prices for low quality goods) so that overpaid executives in fancy offices can receive undeserved bonuses and over-generous pensions. (Charities in general have become infamous for self-aggrandisement and luxury living for staff members. In 2008, something called *The One Foundation*, started by a tax exile and pop singer called Bono, was alleged to have raised £9.5 million but to have spent just £118,000 on 'good causes'. Over half the money raised apparently went on `running costs'. And, surprisingly, some charities are now no more than Government funded pressure groups running campaigns to influence public opinion and change laws. For example, the anti-smoking group ASH is funded by various Government bodies and then uses the money the Government gives it to influence public policy. (So the Government gives our money to a charity which spends the money lobbying the Government.) The Government also now uses charities to campaign for unpopular causes - such as greater State power. The theory is that the Government can then announce that it is merely responding to public opinion.

I confess that I have been pessimistic about our world for some years. When I wrote *Why Everything Is Going To Get Worse (Before It Gets Better)* I added the last bit to the title simply so that the book didn't sound too gloomy. I did not, I'm afraid, really believe that things were about to get better. (And many readers wrote to tell me that they didn't either.)

We know in our hearts that we are living through an unprecedented crisis and that we live in a world without values and meaning. We live in a world where the elderly are unwilling to go into hospital because they will, they know, be killed or allowed to die (and there is no difference). We know that most of our problems are caused by stupid politicians and bureaucrats deliberately making life more difficult for us because that makes life easier for them; they pretend they are protecting us but that's as ingenuous and dishonest as a supermarket manager claiming that he is in business to provide the community with good healthy comestibles at prices they can afford.

We live in a world where we are refugees with no sense of place or presence or significance or importance. We know that if the State were a human being even those fervently opposed to capital punishment would vote to hang it. But the State controls all. We struggle to survive in a bureaucratic society where it is the form filler, the networker, the lobbyist, the creep, who succeeds; anyone truly original and daring is oppressed by the system. We live in a world where the individuals fêted, enriched and honoured are bureaucrats, bankers, politicians and tawdry, hollow celebrities whose fame and fortune is built upon shallow, shifting sands. We live in a world scarred by the incessant vulgarity of S. Cowell, W. Rooney, G. Ramsey and the Beckhams. We live in a world where cruelty is accepted as humour and entertainment, in the same way that throwing Christians to the lions was considered good entertainment in a fading empire 2,000 years ago. We live in an insensitive world where millions are obsessed by the tawdry excesses of celebrities famous for little more than being famous, sleeping with someone famous or being prepared to spend their days on the operating table and their evenings displaying the results. It's impossible to avoid the comparison with the final days of Rome: self-indulgence, corruption and superficiality.

We live in a Statist country where everyone is exhausted by the little things which have joined together to become big things: the red tape, the forms, the rules. We are worn out by frustration, disappointment and the searing knowledge that we are surrounded by cruelty and injustice; worn out by constant battling against casual lies, deliberate deceit and incompetence. Tired of, and frustrated by, a world in which the law is what we live with and justice is now just our hope and aspiration. We live lives flecked with disappointment and we have constantly to fight the tendency to become bitter and angry. We know that in our inexhaustibly corrupt society standing by your convictions will get you nowhere, except convictions (the best way to get convicted is to stand by your convictions). We are confused by a modern world which is run by politically correct fanatics who are enraged if a man is crass enough to hold a door open for a woman because to them good manners are worse than no manners. We are bewildered by a world in which the establishment, and the individuals in it, always take longer than seems possible to recognise and accept obvious truths. We are weary of expecting courtesy and constantly being disappointed, weary of change without purpose, weary of believing that truth will always prevail, if only it is given a chance to breathe, walk about and meet people, but knowing that any truth considered damaging or embarrassing to those in authority will be forever suppressed. We all depend on one another more than ever. But we have been encouraged by the system to be ever more selfish.

We live in a world where the breakdown of family and community has led to almost universal depression, loneliness and despair and where the never-ending onslaught of laws (disguised as rules and regulations) have added fear to the mixture.

We despair at living in a world where the weak and powerless (the mentally ill, the aged, animals) are abused, taken advantage of and mistreated by the people who are trusted (and paid) to look after them. We live in confusion because it seems as though the structure of society has been disassembled and reassembled the wrong way. Politicians, bureaucrats, judges, doctors, nurses, teachers, lawyers, bankers, journalists and editors no longer do what they are supposed to do but do what will benefit themselves.

Our leaders have, through incompetence, greed and dishonesty, betrayed us and created a political system which combines the worst of fascism, the worst of a dictatorship and the worst aspects of communism. We have the worst of everything. We are bewildered by a world in which respect and loyalty are regarded as signs of weakness; where national pride is a sin if you are English but a virtue if you are anything else.

These days corruption among senior politicians is the rule rather than the exception. In the wake of the parliamentary expenses scandal I cannot name a single modern politician whom I would not describe as fundamentally `corrupt'. Elliot Morley, a former Government Minister, was jailed for 16 months for claiming over £30,000 in bogus mortgage payments while he was an MP. The judge said that Morley avoided a longer jail sentence because of the lack of sophistication of his fraud. Since it seems fair to assume that Morley isn't entirely stupid one can only assume that he hadn't even bothered to be `clever' in his deceit. The leader of the Opposition, Ed Miliband, recently pretended to be ill in order to avoid a public engagement which he didn't want to attend. (He was due to talk about boring health care). He was spotted at a Hull football match. Was he so arrogant and stupid that he thought he would get away with it? Or did he simply not care? He did not offer to resign. It can hardly be surprising that millions of people now routinely take time off work so that they can attend sporting events or watch television programmes. It is common for presenters working for the BBC to advise listeners to stay at home in order to watch particular programmes.

Politicians today don't even start off with real passion and purpose. They start off expecting to be corrupted and hoping to be corrupted. They are ready to be corrupted and I suspect that they will be disappointed if they aren't corrupted. To today's politicians politics is a business, a career, an alternative to a lifetime spent working in a windowless office in some huge State bureaucracy. Modern politicians don't care about anything except themselves. I doubt if there is more than a handful of people in the Palace of Westminster with anything that could be described as a vocation. Honour and integrity are now simply words in history books. Government leaders routinely bestow favours on particular businesses or individuals - usually in return for political or financial support. That isn't capitalism, it's corruption. And socialists, who tend to be greedier than conservatives, are invariably more open to corruption. If they cannot get what they want by deception and intrigue they will get it by brute force - using the police and the army. Politicians no longer resign, however terrible their crime, because being a politician is all that they know what to do. They know nothing else. Only after several years in the job, some fame (or, more likely, notoriety) and a thick contacts book full of names and e-mail addresses of people for whom favours were done can there be another life and can the financial rewards for all these years of misplaced service really begin to accumulate. Most disturbing of all, perhaps, is the fact that politicians tell barefaced lies so often that voters actually expect them to lie. When, I wonder, will an aggrieved voter sue a politician for fraudulently making a promise which he has broken? Why should politicians be exempt from the sort of legal requirements which govern the ordinary person's life? If a tradesman or businessman broke promises so blatantly he would undoubtedly be found guilty of fraud. Why should politicians be immune to the laws they force the rest of us to obey?

Our society has encouraged gross dishonesty. Just 55% of the over 65s say that they would never lie on a job application form. But among those under the age of 25 only 30% would never lie on a job application form - which means that 70% would and, since no one can tell who is lying, all job application forms are, therefore, effectively worthless. How can we be surprised by this when Tony Blair is, it seems to me, now largely remembered by many for his lying?

Not surprisingly, corruption and dishonesty have spread through society and are now commonplace rather than unusual. Morality has been replaced by box-ticking, bureaucratic pseudo-compliance. Dishonesty is now normal in every aspect of English public life. Doctors lie. Policemen lie. Journalists lie. Civil servants lie as though born to it. Justice is a forgotten concept. Estate agents lie so much they wouldn't know the truth if it were chiselled onto their stony hearts. Our society sometimes seems to encourage greed and dishonesty. `You cannot have morality without community,' said G. K. Chesterton but there cannot be much sense of community in a world where people spend their days stealing from one another.

In February 2011, the magazine *Readers Digest* contained an article entitled *Skive, but don't get caught*. According to *Readers Digest* (a magazine which used to respect and promote strong, honest principles) the first Monday in February is National Sickie Day `the high point of the year for people calling work to say they're ill.' And then *Readers Digest*, in what must be the most irresponsible piece of writing ever published, gave a number of tips for people wanting to pretend they are ill and avoid going to work. `Join the duvet-day legion with these tips on fooling your boss.' The tips include: `Sound genuinely concerned about having to take time off' and `give lots of gory details about your illness. Cough loudly.'

No wonder the country is in a mess.

A rather pompous and self-righteous newspaper called the *Guardian* ran an article telling its readers how to circumvent the *Times's* pay-to-read policy for its website. (In short, telling readers how to steal.) Subsequently, the *Financial Times* suggested that the *Times* might consider running an article telling readers how to nick copies of the *Guardian* from W.H. Smith.

Some insurance companies have stopped offering cover for mobile phone theft. It was revealed that approximately 40% of mobile phone claims are fraudulent. Most of the fraudsters are pretty stupid. People ring up on Monday and say: `Will I be covered if I drop my phone out of a train window?' They are told they will. Then on Wednesday they ring up and report that they have dropped their phone out of a train window. Corruption, deceit, thoughtlessness and uncaring behaviour are commonplace. Desperate shoppers at a store sale stepped over a man who had collapsed with a heart attack (he died). When does such behaviour stop being simple rudeness and start being criminal behaviour?

Corruption is rife within the scientific community too. The difficulty with science these days is in finding any scientist without a personal financial interest in supporting the relevant industry. Most scientists (and I include medical doctors in that generalisation) are paid lobbyists, professional whores. Global warming may well be happening (though there isn't any convincing scientific evidence for the theory) but if it is then whether or not it is man-made is just a guess. It would be just as scientific to say it was caused by Martians pointing big flaming torches in the direction of our planet. Professional science journalists support genetic engineering and global warming and deny that vaccination could ever do any harm, let alone be responsible for problems such as autism, because they are blind, ill-informed, prejudiced and bought by the relevant industries.

We are ruled by, and surrounded by, people who have absolutely no interest in our health or well-being and who will, for their own ends (or the ends of the organisation they serve) oppress, suppress and cheat. We now go through life expecting to be ignored, treated unfairly, abused, accused, suspected and mistreated. In these things we are rarely disappointed. Values, principles and respect are largely forgotten. In our curiously distorted society serious corruption is largely ignored while the authorities are relentless in their persecution of politically incorrect trivialities. Until there is more intolerance of corrupt and greedy officials the country will continue to be run by corrupt and greedy officials. Corruption, lobbying and fraud are endemic and, in varying proportions, now embedded in politics, the civil service, banking, medicine, utilities, pension fund management and every other area of public life and big business.

When the people who are paid and trusted to lead are shamelessly corrupt (and largely get away with it) the lesson percolates down through society, and it is hardly surprising if corruption becomes regarded as `normal' and `acceptable'. Nothing will change until our senior politicians and our top civil servants are honest, honourable and trustworthy. And that isn't likely to happen soon.

Ironically, as the population of cheats and fraudsters has rocketed so has the number of people prepared to cooperate with the authorities and to sneak on friends and neighbours as well as strangers. There are, of course, financial incentives for sneaking. (And people who are being investigated by the tax authorities may receive friendlier treatment if they provide the names and addresses of suitable targets). But much of the dobbing in is, it seems, done by folk who do it merely for the joy of the thing. Yesterday, while performing an entirely legal U turn on a deserted road a man on the pavement glared and wrote down my car number. At a garage where I had spent £98 on diesel fuel and logs the attendant told me that my broken taillight was illegal and that I could be fined £300. He was clearly about to pick up his telephone and ring the authorities when I pointed out that the piece which was broken was merely an outer piece of irrelevant plastic. He made a disapproving noise and did nothing. He was foreign and spoke English the way I speak French but he knew all about dobbing in and doubtless thought he might receive a reward or bonus of some kind.

I'm afraid that everything in our rotting civilisation is going to get worse, much worse. And then, eventually, things may get a little better and the gloom may lift a little. But things will never get back to the way they used to be and they will certainly never arrive at the place where today's young people expect them to be. Moreover, the improvement will only occur after a huge, painful, social, political and economic revolution.

The underlying difficulty is that our current crisis isn't just caused by financial problems. The crisis we are facing is one which is caused by underlying, deep-rooted, social, cultural and political problems. Our whole society has gone bad. And politicians and economists are so blinkered, so confined in their thinking, that they have been unable to see the truth. Most don't even recognise the existence of these problems, let alone plan to do anything about them. The few who do see at least some of these hazards are too frightened of the beneficiaries of the problems to do anything much to deal with them. Our so-called leaders don't look at the big picture and they never ask the right questions. When they do make decisions they can invariably be relied upon to make the wrong decisions. If they can screw up they will; even if it involves doing things the very difficult way. (This is, indeed, the one thing that we can rely upon. It has, as I have pointed out in other books, long been a foundation stone of my investment philosophy. As an investor, one can always rely upon the people in charge, the ones who make the important decisions, to do the wrong thing and make the wrong decisions.) Our world is constantly changing in ways most people cannot understand or control. Worse still our world is constantly changing in ways our leaders cannot understand or control.

Today, the big issues are ignored and suppressed and those who raise them are dismissed as lunatics, heretics or fanatics. Anyone who dares to spread the truth, or raise questions about perceived truths, will be subjected to smear campaigns. Our liberty and our freedom of speech have been strangled by cross party consensus and an obedient media. Politicians and commentators concentrate their efforts on narrow, specific questions. The big questions, the important questions, the fundamental questions, are never asked. And so, not surprisingly, no answers are forthcoming. As Texan congressman and USA Presidential Candidate Ron Paul put it: 'truth is treason in the empire of lies'.

The end result is that no one is attempting to deal with the real underlying problems - the problems which helped create the mess in the first place. And so the problems are still there, real and untouched and getting worse by the day. Although there are very simple answers to these very serious, very complex problems, nothing will be done about them until we, the people, decide that something has to be done. Until then we are utterly, completely, totally and permanently stuffed. Expect the worst and be prepared for it. Everything is now going to get very, very bad.

The problems which we are ignoring or suppressing are serious structural faults which are causing irreparable damage to our society. In exactly the same way that a bridge will collapse (or a family will break up) if there are fundamental problems with the structure, so our society will implode if we do nothing to repair the serious faults which exist.

What do I mean by `implode'?

Remember what happened in Egypt, Libya and other Middle Eastern countries?

Riots. The oppressive use of force by the police and, when they cannot cope, the military.

We're heading for a revolution.

And it's really not very far away.

To use a motoring analogy we're sitting in a motor car which is careering downhill at an increasing speed. The steering doesn't work. The brakes don't work. And the driver is sending a text message to his garage complaining that the interior light doesn't work properly.

That's the sort of mess we're in.

Only worse. Much worse.

As long as the basic problems are ignored (or made worse rather than better) the world in which we live will become increasingly violent; there will be more anger, frustration and resentment and our lives will in every conceivable way become worse. We cannot do anything to change any of this until a majority of the voters know and understand this truth. Curiously, the problems we face are simpler, more specific and easier to deal with than our politicians and commentators admit. But that does not, of course, mean that they will take the necessary action. And so, in the meantime, all we can do is know what is happening, understand why it is happening and use our knowledge to help us survive.

Things aren't going to get better because the people making the decisions, and pulling our strings, aren't tackling the real problems. And they aren't tackling the real problems because when they recognise them (which is rare) they know them to be fundamental and to require huge, brave decisions which will be unpopular with the millions in our society (public sector workers and those on benefits) who are soft, flabby and spoiled and who expect and demand that they continue to be mollycoddled. The obvious improvements are not going to be made because there are too many people who have a vested interest in maintaining the status quo. And so all the problems I have defined in this book will remain, unaltered. Sadly, I no longer expect anyone in authority to care about me or those I care about: I don't expect to see any change for the better and I don't expect those in power to be subjective to effective control. None of the problems I outline in this book will be dealt with. Our politicians and civil servants are not going to put things right. For heaven's sake, they never even manage to sort out minor problems successfully. And the problems I've defined in this book are certainly not minor problems. Our 'leaders' will fail because they are too short-sighted, too narrow-minded, too unoriginal and too beholden to a variety of vested interests. It doesn't help that they are also cowardly and stupid. Even if they recognise the enormity and significance of these problems there is little or no chance that they will look for any solutions and no chance at all that they will find them.

In that marvellous old movie *Mr Smith Goes To Washington*, James Stewart plays an ordinary guy who confronts the politicians with some simple truths. `Either I'm dead right,' he says, `Or I'm crazy.'

You decide.

Chapter 1

An Economy In Tatters

Introduction

When, a couple of decades ago, I pointed out that the Government's old age pension programme was (it still is) a Ponzi scheme the remark seemed to cause much amusement. There are, today, still those who do not believe me and who genuinely believe that the money they pay in national insurance is invested for them and will be paid back to them when they retire.

The problem is that in the same way that most people cannot imagine that anyone could be as crooked as Ponzi was so there are also many who believe that things cannot be as bad as all that because the smart men and women in suits at the central banks, and the smooth politicians in positions of power, must know what they are doing.

Well, I have news for them.

The people in charge have absolutely no idea what they are doing. They don't know how things got into the mess they're in. And they certainly don't know how to deal with the problems. Their sole concern is looking after themselves, their salaries, their pensions, their perks, their bonuses and their reputations.

The result of this potent mixture of ignorance, selfishness and greed is that things are worse than most people imagine them to be.

The indefensible printing of money by the Bank of England (without the authority of the people) has destroyed our currency, created inflation, increased our national debt and deliberately impoverished the prudent and the elderly. If there were gold medals for the `World's Most Indebted Country', England would win them all.

Thanks largely to the imprudent policies of Gordon Brown we are now in debt in a slightly absurd, almost unbelievable, South American sort of way. It was Gordon Brown who destroyed this country's economy. Between 2000 and 2010 our Government's real expenditure increased by 53%. Welfare costs alone rose by 40% between 2002 and 2007 and welfare now consumes a third of all State expenditure. (All these costs will be difficult to reverse but they must be. There is going to be much unhappiness.)

The economic crisis that Brown's policies created was made a thousand times worse when the bad-tempered Scotsman decided to bail out incompetently run Scottish banks in order to preserve Scottish banking jobs and Scottish bankers' bonuses. (The only other people protected by Brown's bailouts were largely foreign bank creditors. If you or I invest badly, but honestly, we lose our money. But Brown bailed out fools and crooks because they were Scottish - when he should have been putting them in prison. I suspect that to him the people paying all the bills were the enemy: English taxpayers.)

Thanks to Brown, private debts became public debts. And Brown's banker chums were able to continue paying themselves huge, undeserved salaries and bonuses. Brown has weakened England so much that we are going to be vulnerable, and in recession, for many, many years. In fact, to be precise, our recession is going to become a depression. It gives me no pleasure at all to say that I forecast this some years ago. (I started buying gold when Gordon Brown was selling it.) Brown really didn't have a clue about what he was doing. According to Alastair Darling, who was Chancellor of the Exchequer when Brown was Prime Minister, the hapless Scottish son of the manse predicted that the global financial crisis would all blow over in six months. (The Bank of England has recently estimated that the global crisis will cost between £40 trillion and £70 trillion. Give or take a trillion or ten.)

We think we have a capitalist society but we don't. We have a crony capitalist society, we have a corrupt version in which insiders help themselves and their pals to everything they can grab.

The State is far too big and has far too many functionaries and far too much power. We have far too many regulators and far too many regulations. We have an incomprehensible, over complicated and unfair tax system. But now the spenders and scroungers have pretty well run out of other people's money. And so things are going to get really nasty.

And, finally, there's another aspect to our problems. We are part of the planet earth. And, as you may have noticed, there isn't a country in the developed, Western world which isn't in rather a mess. The global financial crisis (which involves America, Europe, Japan and just about anywhere else you can think of) is pretty well out of control. What happens to us depends to a large extent on what happens everywhere else. That isn't good news because although there is, thankfully, only one Gordon Brown, there are a good many other incompetent buffoons out there still busily creating chaos.

1

In Brown's years most people spent every penny they earned and saved nothing. They felt rich because their homes kept rising in value. Brown's government spent every penny they could gouge out of people. They didn't spend it building new hospitals or roads or repairing our Victorian water and sewage systems. They didn't invest in boring infrastructure because that is as dull as buying paint to preserve the fence when you could be spending your money on chocolate and Sky television. Brown spent billions on hiring expensive consultants to teach people how to blow their noses and these were, of course, long-term commitments which came with a whole host of responsibilities not including pension commitments. Every one who has ever run a business knows that buying a new computer is a one off cost which can be defined but that hiring a new employee has always been something more substantial and is now, thanks to rules and regulations which make it damned near impossible to sack anyone, a massive long-term financial commitment. And Brown, who seemed to me to know nothing about anything except supporting Scotland and making sure that the Scots made as much money as possible out of the English, sent billions up North so that he could prove to the Scottish voters that he loved them dearly and that when he signed the Scottish Claim of Rights he meant it. And, because he was (and probably still is) a complete moron he also spent more money introducing new laws and regulations designed to really bugger up business. Many of these came from the EU, of course, but some he actually managed to think up all by his Scottish selfness. And he hired loads more stormtroopers to enforce the new laws. Businesses stagnated as legislation piled up so thick and fast that no one could keep track of what was legal or not legal and effectively it soon became easier to assume that anything that wasn't compulsory was probably illegal. Overwhelmed by taxes and rules, wages in the private sector stagnated. And just to make things worse (and acquire yet more money to give to the Scots) Brown destroyed private pension schemes. Unemployment continued but was, like everything else, relabelled and millions of hoodies suddenly found that instead of being unemployed they were actually on training schemes.

Why does no one now blame Brown for all this? The moron screwed up big time.

None of Brown's spending delivered a boom except among public sector workers, the unemployed and the Scots (many of whom were the same person). Much money was spent on expensive 22-year-old consultants, hired to tell people how to measure the amount of insulation in their airing cupboards. They were sent on six week courses, given diplomas and licences and made to feel very, very important and they generally buggered up people's lives very nicely. None of the money was spent on helping industry. Manufacturing, which had been enfeebled for years, collapsed.

Generally, folk thought everything was still OK because borrowing money was easy and cheap and house values kept going up and so the middle classes were merry enough. Even people who didn't know Bernie Madoff or Allen Stanford could get rich.

Manufacturing was screwed, of course, because productivity had gone up in other parts of the world (it hadn't gone up much in England because the unions insisted on no one starting work until they had at least three cups of tea, and health and safety regulations insisted that two men be hired to ensure that the teapot was protected with a knitted cosy at all times so that no one could burn themselves if they stumbled and came into contact with it) and employment of the sort not requiring more than half a dozen neurones was pretty well down everywhere but particularly in England. The uneducated, who used to work in factories, where they were often well-paid, suddenly found that the only jobs they could get were in McDonalds, Tescos, phone shops, the Royal Bank of Scotland or call centres for banks and insurance companies. The jobs were very low paid (except for the ones at the Royal Bank of Scotland where even half-wits were given so much money that they had to hire men with wheelbarrows to take it all to a proper bank) and even duller than factory jobs where people could at least see that they had made something and could have a laugh and a joke with the person sitting next to them on the production line stamping out tail lights or kettle lids. And most of the call centres were either in Scotland or the Philippines or just outside Delhi and it's a real bugger to get to any of these godforsaken places on a bus because the bus services have largely disappeared and the ones still running charge an arm and a leg and are about as reliable as a politician's expenses sheet. The result was that people preferred to go on the dole and let the foreigners take the miserable jobs that were available because the dole paid better, offered better career prospects and meant that they could get up late, sit at home, watch Sky television and do a little black market moonlighting to pay for the second car and the foreign holidays. And they quickly learned that if they acquired an illness of some nebulous kind (stress soon overtook backache as the general favourite) they could claim even more money and so move up the career structure very quickly.

Some of this had happened in the 1930s in the USA when agriculture was destroyed by combine harvesters and fertilisers. Redundant farm workers couldn't do anything else (phone shops hadn't been invented) and couldn't sell their houses and move somewhere else because no one wanted a house in the middle of 20,000 acres of bleak and boring farmland where the only excitement was the occasional visit of a combine harvester.

The USA Government screwed things up really well (as all governments do) by introducing legislation to 'solve' the problem and hold back the sea. Roosevelt's new laws kept agricultural wages high so that the agricultural workers wouldn't suddenly find themselves facing pay cuts. Of course, what Roosevelt hadn't realised was that by insisting that wages be kept high he was destroying even more jobs and making fertilisers and combine harvesters an even better bet. Politicians always feel a desperate need to interfere and they always muck things up. It is the one uncertainty in a desperately confusing world and if you understand it well enough you can use it to help you make quite a lot of money.

Our current lot of politicians (led by Brown but quickly followed by the terrible Cameron and the even worse Clegg) should have let the banks go bust and let the boil burst. There would have been pus everywhere for a while and things would have been unpleasant and messy but we would, by now, be better off than we are. (If you doubt this consider Iceland. They couldn't bail out their banks because the banks owed more money than the country could raise and so the politicians couldn't do anything other than sit around polishing their glasses and going harumph a lot. The result is that Iceland, which had mega problems, is now recovering very nicely and should be able to buy sweets and comics again any time soon.)

The one thing that wasn't Brown's fault (and it is tempting to try to blame him for this but we must be fair) was globalisation. He did however get excited about it and enthuse about it almost as much as he enthused about multiculturalism, means testing, targets and giving loads of money to Scotland. Globalisation meant that instead of television sets being made in Wales they were made in Japan (by robots of course) and then, when Japan discovered commercial hubris and stopped being fashionable, in China.

Politicians everywhere shouted about the virtues of globalisation and a flat earth and a level playing field and all working together and then went mad when they realised that globalisation meant that China was going to win all the medals and eat all the ice cream. England was left with a financial services industry which was run by and for a bunch of self-serving crooks and thieves, and a massive `State'.

Here are the basic facts about our nation's financial crisis:

i. The whole thing was originally caused by bankers in America doing draft and greedy things. A bunch of get-very-rich-very-quickly crooks set up what were effectively Ponzi schemes disguised as investments. They used customers' money, heavily leveraged, and should have all ended up in prison but instead all ended up very rich. English bankers (or, more accurately, bankers working in England) joined in the Ponzi scheme and although many of them became multi-millionaires some of their banks went bust as a result. None of the bankers has been sent to prison. None of them has been fined. Most of them still have all the money they made. And most of them are still in business, still making exactly the same mistakes and still taking home huge, undeserved and unsupportable salaries and bonuses. Guys on multi million pound salaries claimed that they weren't a `substantive part of the decision making process'. Or they blame computer software. Or they blame the collegiate process or excuse themselves with the `collective responsibility' argument so popular with Labour Party politicians who are now terrified of facing a war crimes tribunal. These guys have loads of money and the best lawyers and, by a curious coincidence, they also have the best excuses. If a teenager breaks a window he will, if caught, be fined. He may even be sent to prison (one young man was, not long ago, given 14 years in prison for damaging a butcher's van) but bankers who have cost taxpayers billions remain unpunished.

ii. There was little or no regulation of the banks in America or in England. There are lots of highly paid regulators. But, although the regulators enjoyed lovely, big bonuses, they were stupid, cowardly and too busy counting their bonuses to do anything to stop the damage.

iii. The banks could have just gone bust, with bankers losing their jobs, but Brown decided to bail them out. In England, Brown's Government took over the debts of Scottish banks for political reasons. Gordon Brown had, after all, signed The Scottish Claim of Rights. The Scottish Claim of Rights states: `We...do hereby declare and pledge that in all our actions and deliberations (the) interests (of the Scottish people) shall be paramount.' The result was that England was left with debts which were equal to the nation's Gross Domestic Product.

iv. When governments take on debts it is sometimes thought that they have access to money of their own. They don't. When a government is in debt, it is the taxpayers who will have to pay the bills. Our governments have borrowed huge sums of money in order to bail out banks and bankers. Whenever a government borrows money it is saddling the next generation with these debts. This is acceptable if the country is fighting a war for survival. (Wars can be expensive. It is worth mentioning that the Government has not yet paid off the debts it acquired when fighting the First World War.) But it is not acceptable when the debts are accumulated in order to protect the interests of a small group of bankers. Such activity is, in my view, immoral. In a just and decent world Brown (and those who let him do what he did) would now be serving a very long prison sentence instead of giving highly paid lectures to the bankers whose world he helped protect.

v. England was already in a terrible financial state when it took on financial responsibility for the bankrupt Scottish banks. Gordon Brown's imprudent policies had impoverished the nation. He had behaved like a financially incontinent pools winner and his spend, spend, spend policies had done permanent damage to the economy.

vi. When the Coalition Government was elected (after Brown's inevitable defeat) it announced that it would introduce a programme of austerity to pay off the nation's debts. However, the Coalition has not cut Government spending (they merely cut the rate at which the spending was increasing). In an attempt to deal with the problem they raised taxes and fees and forced private individuals and companies to pay off the debt. Public spending continued to rise before Osbourne's March 2012 budget and it continued to rise after it. Tax receipts are falling because people are poorer, or have given up work because of higher taxes. (The Government did, however, lower tax rates for the wealthiest of Gordon Brown's banker friends, thereby saving Brown's chum Fred Goodwin huge amounts of money.) It is salutary to note that our Government debt doubled between 2007 and 2011. And in May 2012, in the same week that the Chancellor announced that he had changed his mind about three tax increases, doctors and teachers announced that they were going on strike in protest about proposed modest amendments to their pensions.

vii. The bankers have not changed their ways at all. They have continued to behave recklessly, using their clients' money for their own gambling and insisting on paying themselves indecently large and completely undeserved salaries and bonuses.

viii. The current financial problem is global. A number of countries (including the USA, Japan, Italy, Spain,

Ireland, Portugal and Greece) would be bankrupt if they were people. The global mess has been caused by greedy, incompetent and reckless bankers, complacent and incompetent regulators and venal, self-serving, dishonest politicians. England is probably in a worse state than any other country on the planet.

2

It is worth repeating that Chancellor Obsorne hasn't cut the deficit and he hasn't reduced Government spending. He has slowed the rate at which the deficit is growing by increasing taxes. Total Government spending in 2011-12 was £22.6 billion higher than in 2008-9 (that's 2.4% higher). Taxes have increased by £30 billion since 2009-11. The Government's austerity programme has been aimed at the wrong people - businesses and taxpayers. Check out the figures if you don't believe me

3

`A Ponzi scheme is an investment fraud that involves the payment of purported returns to existing investors from funds contributed by new investors. Ponzi scheme organisers often solicit new investors by promising to invest funds in opportunities claimed to generate high returns with little or no risk. In many Ponzi schemes, the fraudsters focus on attracting new money to make promised payments to earlier-stage investors and to use for personal expenses, instead of engaging in any legitimate investment activity.' - US Securities and Exchange Commission

4

England's national debt is currently around £1 trillion. If the Cameron-Clegg Alliance carries on the way it is going then within five years the debt will have risen to £1.5 trillion. (The interest on the debt just keeps growing.) In cash terms Government expenditure was 4% higher in May 2012 than it was at the end of Labour's disastrous term of office. That's some austerity programme.

5

The Government employs forecasters who live in la la land and the Government's financial planning is based on the predictions of these la la land dwellers. Their predictions are invariably optimistic. So, for example, the forecasters are claiming that growth will rise, unemployment will fall, inflation will fall and tax revenue will rise. (Those are pretty much the standard official forecasts). The Government's plans are based on these la la land expectations. That would be fine except for the rather annoying fact that the forecasters are always wrong. They are not just wrong a bit of the time. History shows us that they are always wrong. But the Government keeps the la la land residents on the staff and keeps listening to what they say because what they say is always optimistic. (The latest figures show just how wrong the forecasters are. HMRC's tax income fell by 3.9% as earnings were down just about everywhere and VAT fell because people were spending less. The only thing that went up was central government spending.)

6

'The price of this financial crisis is being borne by people who absolutely did not cause it. Now is the period when the cost is being paid. I'm surprised that the degree of public anger has not been greater than it has.' - Mervyn King, Bank of England Governor, speaking at the House of Commons Treasury Select Committee in spring 2011. King went on to say that the impact on living standards would be 'long-term and severe' and to predict that 'we may not get the lost output back for very many years, if ever.'

7

There has been an oil fired super boom for half a century or more. For a variety of reasons (not least the fact that the days of cheap oil are over) the super boom is now finished. For a number of glorious years investors believed that they were automatically entitled to an annual profit (after tax and inflation) of 10% on their investments. For the last ten years most investors have had to make do with no gain on their investments. Investors who still have the money they started off with are lucky for many investment funds have succeeded in losing money. High fees mean that on average, money which was put into a pension fund or unit trust ten years ago is now worth less than it was worth when it was invested. The ravages of inflation (and tax) mean that, in real terms, the wealth of those investors has, in many cases, more than halved. Just about the only people who've been making money have been the fund managers. (If you consider a million quid a year satisfactory then they've been doing nicely thank you.) In real terms, after inflation, the Dow Jones Index in the USA is still 17% below its 1999 peak. In other words, if you bought the American index in 1999, you are, after a decade and a quarter, 17% poorer than you were when you started.

8

The problems haven't been solved and aren't going to go away. Reckless fiscal policies, mixed with lies, incompetence and greed, will lead to regular, recurring crises for the foreseeable future. We aren't going to get out of this mess through growth for several reasons. First, the banks aren't interested in lending money because they are still too busy playing silly gambling games. Second, the size of our national (and private) debt is so great that any potential growth will be stunted by our debts and the interest on our debts. Third, the red tape created by the European Union (and gold plated by successive Parliaments) means that our industry has no chance of making decent profits - let alone growing. Finally, we no longer have much of a manufacturing industry. We import most of the things we buy.

9

Individuals and companies are deleveraging but the public sector is borrowing and spending more than ever. Despite their austerity claims, the Cameron-Clegg Government has been throwing money at civil servants with even more enthusiasm than the infamous Brown-Darling duo. The Government seems to be under the misapprehension that if they allow the public sector to keep spending, while they cut the private sector and put up taxes, the country will grow its way out of debt and recession. Unfortunately, things don't quite work like that. The public sector is a huge leech, sucking the blood and the life out of the nation. Civil servants don't make anything and don't bring any money into the country. They are always an expense and never a source of profit.

10

Many of our current problems were caused by unwarranted Government interference. For example, if the Government had not deliberately encouraged the constant rise in house prices there would not have been a bubble. And many of our future problems are being created by Government policies. If the Government had allowed house prices to fall gently and naturally when they were too high the eventual crash would have been smaller. As it is house prices have been kept artificially high. They are falling artificially (as inflation rises) but there is still a bubble and there is still a crash to come. My guess is still that house prices are 30% too high and could, therefore, still fall by 50%. (Prices which have risen too high always fall too far when they eventually fall.) When the crash eventually arrives it will be harder and last longer because of the Government's actions.

11

Many English companies are struggling to survive and will undoubtedly fail within the next year or two. They are being kept alive by the fact that the Government is putting pressure on banks not to allow companies to fail. And so companies which are constantly at the limit of their overdraft facility, and which are building up bigger and bigger debts, are kept alive artificially. They will fail eventually, of course. But in the meantime those companies are taking business from other, healthier companies which may, as a result, also fail. Government interference almost always makes things worse.

12

It wasn't just State functionaries who became addicted to Brown's spend, spend, spend philosophy. Millions of individuals also became accustomed to spending for no good reason, becoming obsessed with bed cushions and scented candles. As a result, tens of millions won't have their personal debts under control for another decade at least. Most of those people will be hit hard when interest rates go up and when inflation pushes up the cost of food, energy and petrol.

13

Half the population is now totally or partly dependent on the State and the situation is getting worse. England is also responsible for looking after Scotland, Wales and Northern Ireland. A relatively small number of weary, English taxpayers are expected to pay all the bills.

14

The Government has insisted that banks go easy on homeowners who borrowed too much and (even with interest rates at an all time low) cannot pay it back. When interest rates eventually go up there will be millions of people who will suddenly find that they really do have to sell up and move. The Government's `ostrich' plan is merely delaying things and will make the eventual crash even more painful.

15

The USA has, for years, been regarded as the power-house of the world. But things are bad in America too. Like England, the USA is leveraging up. It is borrowing more and more money so that it can pay the interest on its debts. (Although the dullards working for the European Union seem to believe that you can solve your debt problems by borrowing more money this really isn't a sound economic theory and must eventually lead to tears.) And America is, like the rest of the Western world, very vulnerable. Investors have been receiving 3% to 5% on

USA bonds since around 1850. They are now receiving a fraction of that. If the American Government suddenly had to pay 5% interest it would be paying out £500 billion a year in interest charges. That is equivalent to the military budget. It's around a third of the total USA tax revenue.

16

Many of the world's leading politicians, regulators and bankers now follow the teachings of an economist called Joseph A. Schumpeter. Let me tell you about Schumpeter. First, he made a fortune as an investment banker (not difficult) but lost it all (not easy). Second, he wrote that Marx was wrong to believe that capitalism would result in a greater divide between the very rich and the poor. He was wrong about that. Although he was an economist and had no medical training he claimed that victories over cancer (and other disorders) were just around the corner. He was wrong about that too. Schumpeter, who started life as an Austrian and ended it as an American, was, like most modern economists, a buffoon. I'm not surprised that many of the people now trying to run the world regard him as a wise man.

17

In a desperate attempt to keep house prices high the Government is using taxpayers' money to guarantee loans of up to £500,000 to people wanting to buy houses but unable to afford or obtain a mortgage. Once again prudent savers are being punished to help the imprudent, the reckless and the greedy. Around 100,000 lucky people (probably mostly Romanians) will be given these taxpayer guaranteed loans.

18

John Maynard Keynes believed that during any sort of slump a government should borrow money and spend it on public works - employing the unemployed to build roads and so on. This philosophy is enormously popular with politicians because they love spending other people's money. (Friedrich Hayek, on the other hand, was always opposed to politicians spending money. He wanted to cut back the power of the State. He was not terribly popular with politicians.)

19

The clear and consistent message from Gordon Brown and his successors is to `spend spend spend'. It has repeatedly been made clear to citizens that if they save, their Government will punish them but that if they spend every penny they earn then they will be rewarded with benefits and credits and loans and cheap money. The result is that in old age the standard of living of the wastrels and the spendthrifts now easily matches, and often surpasses, that of the prudent and the fiscally responsible.

20

Our economic problems were started when the USA and England deregulated and globalised the financial markets. We were told by the self-styled experts that this was a good thing which would lead to wealth for everyone. But the globalisation we were sold was a fraud and deregulating the markets merely left everything open to abuse by pinstriped crooks and fraudsters, who proceeded to take over the financial system.

Ever since they were first invented financial markets have generated financial crises and the crises have only ever been solved when the authorities had the courage to regulate the banks and stamp on the sneaky fingers of the greediest bankers and usurists.

The problem in 2007, 2008 and 2009 was that the authorities, the regulators, had been taken over by bankers who naturally wanted to protect their chums. So, for example, the man in America charged with sorting out the crisis was the newly appointed US Secretary of the Treasury, Henry M. Paulson.

Paulson, who was George W. Bush's Secretary of the Treasury from July 2006 until January 2009 had spent the previous 32 years working at the world's most evil and socially irresponsible company: Goldman Sachs. As an employer of the world's worst company Paulson had become enormously rich. And a lot of his chums were bankers who had also become enormously rich. (Goldman Sachs has been responsible for a lot of very bad things. It was Goldman Sachs who helped the Greeks lie about their debts. And so it was Goldman Sachs which has impoverished millions of Europeans. Bernie Madoff was a misunderstood angel compared to the Goldman Sachs Gang. Wherever there is deceit will be found the cold, clammy hand of Goldman Sachs.)

So it was no real surprise when the authorities, led by Paulson, responded to the problem by protecting the bankers rather than investors or taxpayers.

Bubbles usually go bang and the people who lose out are usually the greedy bastards who caused the bubbles. This time was different. In both the USA and England the people who had caused the bubble (and done all the damage) were protected and everyone else paid the price.

This wasn't the first time that a bubble (and the bubble makers) had been protected. When the dot-com bubble burst early in the 21st century a dolt called Alan Greenspan kept interest rates so low for so long that America had a housing boom. The housing boom peaked in 2006 and, because in the end it wasn't an ordinary housing boom, it helped create the crises and crash that followed shortly thereafter. Very low interest rates may seem attractive to home buyers but they always cause problems. They encourage inflation (the debtor's friend), they encourage unwise and unproductive investment (the money is so cheap how can we lose?) and they create asset priced bubbles which always burst.

The housing bubble was different from other bubbles in that it brought with it a whole host of seemingly sophisticated risk management techniques which were based on a nutty piece of financial nonsense called the efficient market hypothesis. Mortgages were converted into Collateralized Debt Obligations (CDOs). The half-witted bankers who thought these up believed that real estate prices never fall everywhere at once and that their new financial instruments would reduce risk through geographic diversification. Other idiot bankers (many of them in England) believed this obvious nonsense and bought the CDOs by the barrow load.

Within months there had been an explosion in the demand for these damned things. There were more CDOs than mortgages. In order to keep the whole Ponzi scheme going bankers and brokers were (almost literally) throwing money at people who wanted to buy homes. If you were an unemployed alcoholic with no savings and no hope you would still find bankers eager for you to borrow $500,000 and buy a six bedroom house with three garages. `Don't worry about paying back the loan. We'll make the payments real easy.'

And when the bust came (as it was bound to do) the entire international banking system fell apart. Bankers and regulators, who had been taken in by this nonsense, seemed genuinely surprised to find that the magician doesn't really saw the lady in half.

Then, as the crisis developed the authorities (many of them alumni of Goldman Sachs) in England and the USA found new and exciting ways to make things worse. Gordon Brown put his underpants on over his trousers and announced himself ready, willing and able to save the world. Both in England and America the authorities sent lorry loads of cash round to the banks and turned commercial losses into State losses. Many of the politicians were good pals with the bankers (it was, don't forget Gordon Brown who gave Fred Goodwin a knighthood for services to banking) and wanted to do everything they could to rescue their chums.

21

According to Mitch Feierstein, writing in his book *Planet Ponzi* 'The United Kingdom and Japan are currently duking it out for the title of World's Most Indebted Country.' Our total indebtedness is close to 500% of GDP. Our indebtedness as a percentage of GDP doubled during the dark years of Brown. We have a net 'international investment position' of minus £180 billion. Thanks to the banks we will have to sell the Queen, Stonehenge and the Isle of Wight if we want to avoid bankruptcy. (Actually, I'd much rather we sold Scotland which is, after all, the cause of most of our troubles.)

22

The Government doesn't manage its accounts like anyone else. Here's an example. In April 2012, the English public sector posted a surplus of £16.5 billion. Now how, you might ask, could the civil service make such a decent sized profit? That's almost enough to buy a Premier League footballer. Are all those civil servants now moonlighting at their local supermarket and handing their wages over to the Government? Sadly, no. The surplus comes from the fact that the Royal Mail transferred its £28 billion pension plan to the Government so that the Government can sell the damned organisation to some foreigners who will doubtless demand that second class stamps cost a fiver and insist that anyone not living within 100 yards of their local sorting office collect their own mail. This transfer means, of course, that the Government (in this case aka taxpayers, because when there are debts around that is what the word 'Government' means) will be responsible for paying out massive pensions to around 82 million postmen and postwomen. That's another massive cost for the next generation to worry about. But meanwhile, let's celebrate because the Government made a profit this month.

23

The world is changing. America's exceptional status as originator of the world's reserve currency is coming to an end. The USA is about to come face to face with its own huge debts and the deficit which has been building rapidly since the 1980s will bite America hard. Globalisation allowed the USA to consume more than it produced and to live on the backs of the workers of the rest of the world. Every time the financial system seemed at risk the authorities (staffed largely by former bankers) removed more and more regulations, intervening whenever the bankers looked as if they might be at risk.

Everything got out of hand when new financial products became so complex that no one (not even the people who had invented them) understood them or comprehended the consequences of their inventions. The banks relied on what the inventors of these arcane financial weapons told them. Worst still, so did the ratings agencies. No one took the responsibility they were paid to take. Everyone simply assumed that things would turn out well. And a great many people thought they were much cleverer than they were and that because they were taking home £20 million a year they must be cleverer than everyone else.

Eventually the banks stopped trusting each other and the world's financial system looked as if it was about to grind to a halt. And that's when the politicians made a bad situation worse. Instead of allowing the banks to go bust and forcing them to separate their basic banking facilities from their investment banking gambling, morons like Brown simply bailed out the banks and allowed them to carry on as before - this time gambling with taxpayers' money instead of money loaned to them by depositors.

The result of this will be a global realignment. The USA will continue to decline. China (and to a lesser extent India) will rise, rise and rise again.

24

The USA controls the World Bank and the International Monetary Fund and insists that all countries (with one exception) follow strict market discipline. The exception, of course, is the USA, which has built up a massive current account deficit.

25

Once the Government had bailed out the banks (with taxpayers' money) taxpayers were surprised to see that the banks were pushing up the interest rates they were charging for overdrafts and, at the same time, introducing a mass of new fees. Public anger was fuelled by the knowledge that the bankers had been bailed out with taxpayers' money and were still giving one another huge bonuses and carrying on as though there had never been a crisis. As the absurdities of the situation created yet more anger, both bankers and politicians called for an end to banker bashing and said how unfair it was. Some of the best paid bankers threatened to leave their jobs and quit the country. They did not say what they would do or where they would go.

26

Prudence has become the new paedophilia. A woman on benefits who was worried about surviving in her old age, and who scrimped and saved and managed to save £20,000 out of her benefit money (by living an incredibly frugal existence) has apparently been arrested, told to give all her savings to the Government, fined £6,000 for not spending her money and threatened with imprisonment. And, of course, savers everywhere have to make do with 0.1% interest on their money while banks routinely charge 17% or more on overdrafts.

27

England has come to terms with the fact that it is no longer a global force. America is still in denial. The future belongs to China and the global currency system, and the global economy, are now linked inextricably to the Chinese currency and the Chinese economy. It will not be long before it is the Chinese yuan, rather than the American dollar, which is the world's reserve currency. When that happens America will fall fast and far. The so-called `special relationship' which our politicians have nurtured will become an even greater drag on our reputation and our economy.

28

`The issuers may have, and in the case of a government paper, always have, a direct interest in lowering the value of the currency, because it is the medium in which their own debts are computed.' - John Stuart Mill, 1848, The Principles of Political Economy

29

Balancing the budget by cutting spending or raising interest rates would penalise those who are employed by the public sector, those in debt and those receiving benefits. Those are now the voters who control the politicians and so what needs to be done will not be done. As I have previously pointed out, those who earn and pay tax are now in a minority. They have, therefore, been disenfranchised.

30

It is widely believed by economists that credit is essential to make an economy function because without debt businesses can't grow. This is, of course, dangerous nonsense. Economists spend their lives thinking about money and dealing with money. If they are so clever why aren't they all rich?

31

The English Government now owes over £1,000,000,000. That's a trillion pounds. And that figure doesn't include the cost of paying pensions to civil servants as they retire. Nor does it include the cost of providing health care and social security and benefits for the millions of retired and `disabled' citizens who rely upon the State for their food and shelter.

32

When you borrow money you are importing your imagined (and hoped for) future into the present. When you borrow money in order to increase your investment risks you are buying a hoped for prosperity that hasn't been earned and that can easily be taken away. These simple truths are not understood. Many people now have the gall to complain that they borrowed money because they were offered it and so it wasn't their fault and it is unfair that they are now in trouble.

33

The Bank of England, the Federal Reserve in the USA and the European Central Bank (for the European Union) have made things far, far worse than they were and have turned an acute problem into a chronic one. We are now entering an economic depression which will last for generations. The people running these institutions have proved themselves to be incompetent, dishonest and reckless. For several years the Bank of England has regularly expressed surprise at the way inflation keeps rising. They usually say that the inflation is temporary or a result of factors entirely outside England's control (such as the price of oil or the price of food) but either the people running the Bank of England are too stupid to be running a village hall or they are deliberately using inflation to get rid of our debts and, in the process, to rob savers and investors and private sector pensioners of what little wealth they may have managed to secure. Now, the Bank of England is about to be given even greater powers. The staff of the Bank of England are accountable to the public but have never shown any signs of understanding this. The people of England would be in a far better financial state if we dumped the Bank of England and let the market decide interest rates.

34

Consumer debt rose by 66% in the last decade. Much of this debt was created when people bought houses they couldn't possibly afford and shouldn't have been allowed to buy.

35

In 1988, in my book *Health Scandal* I forecast that we would have real problems when the number of people working, earning and paying tax fell below the number of people dependent on the Government. I forecast that the real problems would come to a head in the year 2020. (I obviously picked the date because it has a nicer ring to it than 2019 or 2021. But I still think that forecast was pretty accurate.) We are heading for more big bankruptcies, for apparently never ending crashes and turmoil and the worst financial crisis in history. Whenever G7 and G20 ministers meet it is obvious that they don't have the foggiest idea what to do about the problems. (The G20 is, I confess, something of a curiosity in that it consists of 19 proper countries and someone representing the European Union.) They mess around rearranging the flowers while the roof caves in and an uncontrollable fire rages in the west wing. Reality awaits and will win. The next bull market won't be for quite a while.

36

England's debts are unlikely to be repaid in real terms. (In other words, with money which has the same purchasing power as the money had when it was borrowed). The politicians have three choices: inflation, default and (the Japanese solution) stagnation.

The politicians are unlikely to want to default (that is embarrassing) and although they are so far following the Japanese route they will soon find that humiliating (Japan has been in decline for two decades) so they are likely to take the easy way out and to get rid of the debt by inflating it away.

Actually, there is a fourth choice: staying out of the way and allowing market forces to take over (which means allowing the grotesquely indebted to go bust). That is the only method that would really work but it would mean doing nothing and no politician will do that.

37

When Queen Elizabeth II asked why no one had foreseen the coming problem no one knew what to say. Sadly, she asked the wrong people. She asked the people who had created the problem, or who had stood by while it happened and who had not, of course, seen what was coming.

38

A third of England's adult working age population is now unemployed, non-earning, non-tax paying (that includes people who are sick, who are on benefits, who are unemployed and who are studying). But if you then add in children and pensioners (including civil service pensioners who retired at 60, 55 or 50) and you add on the millions who are employed by the Government, councils or quangos (and who are therefore, by definition, non-productive workers) it is clear that the country is being held together by a hard-working minority. It is also clear that this state of affairs is unsustainable.

39

England is now paying £43 billion a year in interest on the £1 trillion we owe in debt. And our debt is rising at the rate of £120 billion a year. In other words, despite the best efforts of our Coalition Government, the debt is getting bigger not smaller. A third of our new debt is interest on the old debt. And of course, thanks to the wonders of compound interest we pay interest on the interest. Meanwhile, the much-publicised Government cuts haven't started yet.

40

The Labour Party stayed in power by making sure that house prices kept rising. People borrowed more than they could afford to spend and were delighted when the value of their homes rose (as they were bound to do). The rising value of their homes made them feel rich beyond their wildest dreams. Many were earning far more from their homes than from their jobs. `I earned £500 this week but my house went up by double that!' `The house made £1,000 this week so if we spend just £500 on DVDs, meals out and toys we are still ahead.' Millions of the new rich borrowed against their ever more valuable homes and spent the money the banks gave them on wide screen television sets and second cars. As they borrowed so the banks made more money and as they spent so the Government's tax income rose. Everyone, it seemed, was getting richer. But the wealth was based on debt and it was all a trick.

41

The Bank of England's official solution to our problems has been quantitative easing - an Orwellian term which simply means printing more money and devaluing the currency. The official aim of quantitative easing is to make more money available so that banks can lend it out to companies so that they can employ more people and make more things. Naturally, however, the banks have been keeping the virtually free money they've been given because they realise that if they simply lend it back to other governments they can make free profits without actually doing anything. The whole idea of quantitative easing was flawed from the start because it was always pretty damned obvious that even if the plan had worked it would have had to stop one day. And when it stopped things would go wrong again: falling house prices and rising unemployment being the obvious consequences. Quantitative easing was an attempt to keep the whole crumbling financial edifice standing for longer. It was an attempt to protect the bankers from their own idiotic and venal behaviour. It is not surprising that it was also popular in America. Politicians and central bankers there are as much in the pockets of the bankers as are the politicians and central bankers in England. The people who devised this barmy solution to our problems must surely have been aware that government actions and interventions helped create the problem and have consistently made things far, far worse. The credit crisis developed because of too much debt (encouraged by too much irresponsible lending), reckless Statist overspending, waste everywhere, absurdly inflated expectations and wildly overgenerous monetary policies. Or maybe they weren't aware of any of this. Maybe they had all spent the last few decades in a holiday camp on Mars.

The combination of quantitative easing (QE) and low interest rates has devastated the living standards of the retired and destroyed the value of the savings of the prudent. Quantitative easing takes money from the cautious, the hard-working and the poor and gives it in bucketfuls to the reckless, the greedy and the very, very rich. The whole idea is wicked beyond belief. The Government prints more money and then uses the money to buy its own gilts. That's a financial plan? The Bank of England now owns a third of all gilts. So the Government prints them and then buys them. What's the *future* plan? Is it going to keep its own gilts or destroy them and pretend they never existed? QE was designed to bring gilt yields down and has resulted in a slump in annuity rates. Those who retire now, and who are dependent upon a private pension, as opposed to a civil service pension, will be locked into a pitifully low return on their pension savings. The people who decided to introduce QE are, of course, immune to these bad effects. Quantitative easing has dramatically reduced the income available to pensioners who are taking money from their private pension, forced investors seeking income to take huge risks for little reward and hastened the death of defined-benefit pensions. All this is being done in a vain attempt to clear up the mess Gordon Brown left behind; a decade of uncontrolled, debt-fuelled consumption. Quantitative easing is a shameful and morally repugnant policy: it is nothing more than a State-controlled mugging of the elderly, the careful and the responsible.

Company pensions are being battered too. When gilt yields are low it is harder for fund managers to match their income with their expenditure and so they are closing down pension schemes completely.

The promoters of QE claim that increasing the amount of money in circulation makes it easier for companies to borrow and grow. This would be very nice if it were true. But it isn't. QE has resulted in the banks acquiring vast amounts of money at virtually no cost, thereby enabling them to maintain their absurdly obscene bonus levels. But the low interest rates, and the billions of new money, have not filtered through into the real economy. Entrepreneurs and company owners who can borrow money are paying 20% interest rates (or more) as the bankers who caused the recession take advantage of the recession to boost their own bonuses still more. The banks' shareholders (which in the case of RBS and Lloyds means taxpayers) have not benefitted from this lunacy since the profits have been scooped up by senior bankers greedily grabbing multi-million pound bonuses for themselves. When you make more of anything, you damage the value of whatever it is you are making. If a baker produces twice as many loaves then the price per loaf will inevitably fall. If a nation prints more money then the perceived and real value of the currency on the international market will fall. Even the Chancellor and the Governor of the Bank of England should know that.

The real truth (never admitted) is that politicians and central bankers devised and chose to introduce QE and low interest rates in a deliberate attempt to boost inflation. They want to inflate away the significance of the Government's debt, to help those who had bought houses they couldn't afford and to keep the bankers happy. (Gordon Brown's love affair with the bankers is well-known - and was a major factor in the destruction of England - but the love affair between politicians and bankers is not over. The leaders of the Coalition Government are just as desperate as Brown was to please the bankers.)

The big beneficiaries of QE have been the bankers and the borrowers. The big losers have been the people who have `done the right thing', saved their money, invested carefully and saved for their retirement. The prudent have been severely punished and have now no doubt realised that they would have been better off if they'd spent their earnings on folderols and fripperies. QE transfers money from savers to borrowers. The lesson for the young is clear and simple: spend, spend, spend. Do not, under any circumstances, save or trust your Government.

No one in the Government or at the Bank of England had the courtesy to ask the taxpayers whether they wanted debts and savings to be destroyed by deliberate inflation (which will be very difficult to control once it gets going properly).

42

The leading advocate of quantitative easing in England is not, an Englishman. But he is not, rather surprisingly perhaps, Scottish. The man promoting QE in England is called Adam Posen. He is an American economist, described by the *Jewish Chronicle* as an important Jewish policy-maker. Just what he is doing deciding what happens to our economy is beyond me.

43

The Government (and its spokesidiots) claim (with no regard whatsoever for the truth) that the people who are suffering most from its austerity policies are the people who gained most from the years of over-borrowing, over-spending and over-indulgence. Even for politicians this is a lie of Brobdigean proportions. The people who over-consumed are not suffering at all because their debts are being reduced by inflation and made palatable by the lowest interest rates in history. The people who did not over-consume, the individuals who were sensible and cautious, are the ones being deliberately destroyed by the Government's policies. The Bank of England and the Government have proved that they have no respect for electors or their money and in the long-term their policies will encourage workers to spend every penny they earn.

44

Central banks are supporting the banks at the expense of ordinary taxpayers. The cost of this support will grow and grow as inflation leaps higher (and eventually goes out of control) and as jobs are lost because of the long-term depression the policies will create. The deliberately engineered rise in inflation will lead to massive rises in the price of imported fuel and food and this will hurt the hard-working poor (whose travel costs will soar) and damage growing businesses (many of which will falter and fail as a direct result). Instead of making things better (as we were promised) QE has created huge short-term problems for the poor, the elderly and the prudent. And it will create massive medium and long-term problems. Only the bankers have been helped.

45

Most of us are poorer than we think we are. And will get poorer. Our houses are worth less than we think they are. Our pensions are worth less than we think they are (and nowhere near as reliable). Our investments will probably soon be worth less than their current prices. It isn't our fault that the country is in a mess. The politicians and the bankers caused the problems. But we are paying the price and they are not.

46

We are so broke that the Government is toying with the idea of flogging off some of our assets. They're trying to get a price for things like Stonehenge and Westminster Palace. They will then presumably flog them off to the highest bidding Sovereign fund. Nothing, it seems, is not for sale. How much could we get for the Isle of Wight? And the Royal Family? Maybe we could flog off the Queen? Or one of the Princes? Lots of countries love our royalty. The French would love to have a queen. Or a king. We could get a damned decent price for William and probably a pretty decent price for Harry. Maybe we could even flog off their uncle Edward? Well, perhaps not. Maybe that's a prince too far.

47

The politicians and central bankers have continually intervened to protect the greedy from their greed and to protect the bankers from their stupidity. In doing so they have prevented the healing, financial catharsis which we need. And so when the pain comes, which it will, it will last longer and be chronic; rather than being sudden and acute and nasty it will last generations and cause enormous damage. How can anyone with a functioning cortical matter regard spending, borrowing and printing as a solution to the worst economic crisis in our history?

48

Today, the only growth industry in England consists of groups of Eastern Europeans washing cars (for cash) on otherwise deserted garage forecourts.

49

Central banks have enormous power over printing, money managing interest rates, controlling the value of the currency and keeping inflation under control. The Bank of England has increased the money supply by 400% over the last decade; they mortgaged our future (and our children's future and our grandchildren's future) so that Brown could spend billions on projects which the nation didn't need and certainly couldn't afford.

Let me remind you, that Brown signed The Scottish Claim of Rights. That is why so much English money has headed north of the border. Let me remind you that The Scottish Claim of Rights states: `We...do hereby declare and pledge that in all our actions and deliberations (the) interests (of the Scottish people) shall be paramount.'

Gordon Brown, former Prime Minister of Great Britain, signed that.

50

The way quantitative easing works is like this: the Bank of England gives money to anyone who wants to sell gilts (banks and pension funds and other institutions). The plan is that the people who sell their gilts will then use the money they've been given to buy shares and bonds, thereby giving money to companies which can grow. This is such an utterly stupid idea that it is difficult to believe that anyone with an IQ bigger than their shoe size actually thought it up. In reality QE is just a welfare state for bankers. It pushes up corporate bond prices and makes banks richer. It hasn't encouraged bank lending in practice. The sole *real* purpose of quantitative easing (an absurd euphemism for `printing money and therefore devaluing the currency') has been to create inflation and get rid of the nation's private and sovereign debts. And all this has been done by a bunch of employed civil servants and advisors. These were major political decisions (probably the most significant decisions made for decades) which will affect the lives of everyone. And the decisions were made by State employees without debate, without discussion, without contradiction, without supervision and without any public mandate. It would have made more sense to allow traffic wardens to create the law.

It was, of course, Gordon Brown (the main architect of our misery) who gave the Bank of England these powers. Maybe he did so hoping that his newly empowered public sector workers would help him destroy the hard-working English and devalue the English currency with a massive currency printing exercise. Before you dismiss this notion as fanciful we should remember, as always, that Gordon Brown was a signatory to The Scottish Claim of Rights.

Still think it an entirely fanciful notion?

51

There have been 122 stimulative policy initiatives from central banks in the recent months. That means that on 122 occasions, governments have printed more money in order to inflate away their debts. Not one government on the planet has yet decided to get to grips with the idea of spending less and borrowing less.

52

It is estimated that in 2011 quantitative easing took an additional £90 billion out of corporate pension schemes (affecting shareholders as well as employees). Quantitative easing did not, of course, affect in any way the pensions given to politicians, public sector workers or Bank of England employees.

53

When the Bank of England prints more currency the value of the pound goes down in the international markets. And so the cost of our imports goes up. Oil becomes more expensive. Food becomes more expensive. And then the Governor of the Bank of England has the gall to say that inflation is caused by international factors outside the Bank's control.

54

Our current problems were caused by too many people and governments buying things they didn't need with money they didn't have. Simple.

55

Economic chaos is common within the European Union. The only countries in Europe whose economies are growing are Poland, Latvia and Finland. The next best countries are Lithuania, Slovakia, Estonia, Germany and Norway. The rest are either in a bit of trouble, a lot of trouble or (like us) dire straits.

56

In February 2012, India said it didn't want any more aid from England. Since India is now growing far faster than we are, and is an extremely rich and powerful country, I can understand their embarrassment at our continuing to dump money on them like an impoverished maiden aunt insisting on stuffing fivers into her banker nephew's pocket at Christmas.

Those who still believe that we should send money to India might like to know that most of the money is dribbled away on the flimsiest of projects. For example, we gave £118,000 to the city of Bhopal so that it could fit its buses and dustcarts with GPS satellite tracking systems. Hundreds of thousands of pounds of taxpayers' money was spent on delivering 7,000 television sets to Indian schools.

India has a £6 billion space programme, nuclear weapons and an aid programme of its own. India is buying $11 billion worth of American fighter jets. They are presumably using the foreign aid we are giving them to help pay for these.

And still we send them billions every year.

We give money to China too. Giving money to India and China is like sending money to the Queen so that she can have a nice Christmas.

57

It is fashionable to regard globalisation as a new phenomenon, a 21st century innovation which will transform our lives.

But globalisation really began with the growth of the English Empire in the 17th century. (Everything of note started in England. And the English invented globalisation.). English sailors and English merchants took gold (earned by bringing sugar and tobacco from the Americas) and used it to buy silks in India. It was the gold standard which helped create globalisation. England had a navy protecting trade routes, a sound currency in sterling and a willingness to invest overseas. Steamships enabled England to import wheat and meat from across the Atlantic and freed up agricultural workers to take employment in factories, enabling the industrial revolution to get going.

Globalisation isn't new.

But the idea, propagated by wide-eyed liberals, that globalisation will somehow benefit everyone and create a world of people living in joyful harmony is new. And it's a crazy idea - particularly since the era of cheap energy is rapidly coming to an end.

Globalisation means that we are now all dependent on one another.

We have, of course, been becoming more reliant on others (for heat and food, etc.) for years. Just a few generations ago people in England grew their own food, found their own wood for their hearth and dealt with their own rubbish. They made their own clothes and, indeed, often made their own furniture and household equipment too. For years we've been reliant on others for everything in our lives. This has meant that a strike, a protest or a slow down in another part of the country could cause great disruption.

But now that we've become a global economy our lives are likely to be affected by things happening thousands of miles away. The number of people upon whom we rely totally has increased dramatically. We rely on the Middle East for oil. We rely on Russia for gas. We rely on China for the goods we seem to need. We rely on farmers all around the world for the food we eat. Our local industries and local farmers simply cannot compete with industries and farmers operating in countries where the cost of living is much lower, wages are much lower and regulations are almost non-existent. Huge ships constantly move between China and England. The ships bringing stuff over are packed with television sets and dishwashers. The ships going back are full of our recyclables. We pay the Chinese to take them off our hands and then they dump them. They must think we're mad; a failing, doomed segment of civilisation. (We do import some rubbish. We take America's nuclear waste.)

Globalisation may have enabled the lucky few to make fortunes out of clever financial juggling but it has increased our dependence and our vulnerability and it is time to end the myth that it's good for us.

58

The size of England's national debt is now so great that every man, woman, child, scrounger, pensioner and civil servant in the country owes around £20,000. Each. And the interest on that means that the debt is rising by the minute. You'd think that as a nation we would be rich. After all, we seem to own a lot of stuff: buildings, roads, and so on. But we've mortgaged just about everything.

59

The bankers and politicians who caused our economic mess sometimes seem to be the only people in our society who are not being expected to pay the price of dealing with the chaos. Indeed, shameless fools who helped cause the mess (and who should now either be bankrupt or in prison or both) now generously offer advice on how we should reform the banks and our world.

60

Economics is almost alone in being the only profession never to have solved any of the problems its practitioners struggle so unsuccessfully to define. There are university departments, books and magazines devoted to economics but the world's economic position is in a worst state than ever and the economists (who never successfully predict anything) have no answers. There were 60 recessions around the world between 1989 and 1998 and economists forecast just three of them.

61

Am I the only one to think it dotty that governments should try to solve debt problems by issuing more debt? Am I crazy or are they? It seems to me that the people who insist on handing out more cheap money to countries and individuals who cannot afford to pay their old debts are ignoring democracy, reality and common sense.

62

England is twice as much in debt as any other EU nation. The total extent of our debt is difficult to measure. But it's a lot. Our Government claims to be putting straight the mess created by Gordon Brown but government spending is still more than government earnings and none of the cutbacks announced so far will solve the debt or the interest on the debt.

63

Whenever there is doubt about the state of the economy, or the abilities of politicians to put right what they have put wrong, then there is no doubt.

64

Our manufacturing industry is a third of the size it was just 30 years ago. And yet it is a nation's manufacturing sector which gives a nation wealth by bringing money into the country (it is, for example, difficult to export hairdressing). Our entire manufacturing industry would now not pay the nation's benefits bill.

65

The Government is pushing banks to lend more money to businesses. But people running businesses don't want to borrow money. They don't want to borrow because they don't trust the Government (which, they suspect, will introduce yet more destructive legislation); they don't trust the banks (which, they fear, will suddenly demand the repayment of loans at an inconvenient moment) and they don't trust suppliers or buyers (all of whom might well go bust). So, why on earth would they borrow any money?

66

Most people in England are aware that the Greek economy is pretty well stuffed. But how many realise that we owe three times as much money as they do?

67

After the 2012 Budget, bankers enjoyed a cut in their tax rate whereas pensioners found themselves left with a tax rise. After the Budget, caviar (a favourite of bankers) was taxed at 0% but hot pasties (favourites among shop assistants, tramps and impoverished pensioners) were taxed at 20%. Clegg's wife, reputed to be earning £600,000 a year as a political lobbyist (she apparently helped the nasty Kraft take over iconic English chocolate maker Cadbury) enjoyed a tax cut which must have saved her far more than the average national wage.

68

Usually, when a Ponzi scheme is running, someone gets very rich. Usually, the money sticks to quite a lot of people.

Our Government (and most other western governments are pretty well as bad) has been running a complicated Ponzi scheme for years. The debts have been mounting and each new generation pays off the debts of the previous generations.

But who has been getting rich? If we now owe a trillion pounds or more, and the American people owe endless trillions of dollars, who has been getting rich?

It's a hypothetical question, of course.

You already know the answer.

It's the people who have been hiring the lobbyists to persuade the Government to treat them kindly. It's the people who run the drug companies, the arms companies and all the other companies which own parliamentarians.

But mostly it's the bankers and the people working in what is usually summarised as 'the finance industry'.

Nick Clegg's wife is a lobbyist.

Nick Clegg's dad? Banker.

David Cameron's father? Stock broker.

Keep it in the family, eh?

69

The Organisation for Economic Cooperation and Development has warned that the current austerity programme will not bring down the level of debt. Despite the Coalition Government's five-year programme of spending cuts and tax increases, the national debt is still rising rapidly and will reach £1.5 trillion by 2016. To bring this down to a manageable and sustainable level will require years of severe cuts (far more severe than anything suggested). The Government needs to cut another £120-£150 billion off the annual bill (just under 10% of the economy) and that can really only come by sacking unnecessary public sector workers, reducing public sector pensions and cutting State benefits. (Around 30% of all public sector spending goes on salaries for public sector workers.) It isn't possible to raise taxes any further without doing serious damage to the economy. People need to be encouraged to work and save and overtaxing and grabbing more money from people's savings and private pensions is exactly the wrong thing to do. Just to make things worse we have an ageing population and (thanks to EU rules) a massive and unstoppable influx of immigrants who want to take advantage of our absurdly over generous benefits system. Just as we need to cut costs so our costs will rise remorselessly.

70

George Osbourne increased the national debt by 60% in his first parliament alone. Austerity, anyone?

71

The number of people who are dependent on the State is now greater than the number of people working, earning and paying tax. (It happened eight years earlier than I predicted in my book *The Health Scandal*.)

72

If the crisis had been allowed to do what crises are supposed to do then the knaves working at places like Goldman Sachs and the Royal Bank of Scotland would all be looking for proper jobs instead of having been bailed out by taxpayers.

73

Before 2030, England will need to increase the breadth and depth of its austerity programme. Only the USA, Japan and Ireland have a more worrying demographic problem. Few, if any, countries are embedded as deeply in the mire as England is. But then no other country had Gordon the Moron holding the national wallet. Actually it wasn't the holding that did the damage, so much as the constant opening.

74

Here's another way of summing up what went wrong. Appallingly ignorant people borrowed too much and appallingly ignorant people lent too much.

75

All over Europe people are voting out politicians who have tried to deal with their nation's debts by introducing mild austerity measures. In most of those countries the measures were far too mild to have any real effect. In the May elections in France, for example, Sarkozy was rejected for merely suggesting an increase in the official retirement age from 60 to 62. In England, the Coalition was thrashed by Labour in local elections even though Cameron, Clegg and Company had done so little that the nation's debt was greater than it had been when they had started, but even these modest measures were far too painful for the majority of voters to accept. People will always vote for the bread and the circuses even though they surely know that they are destroying their children's futures. The inevitable result must be that the financial crisis will now continue for decades - and there will be more crashes to come. In my more pessimistic moments I can see England remaining in recession permanently. We will not escape from it without some form of economic or political revolution. People have become accustomed to being able to spend more than they earn and they want to carry on living the very good life without actually having to work hard enough to earn the money to pay for it. The euro will go bust (and the EU will break up) because the austerity measures necessary to correct the EU's financial problems will not be accepted either by EU bureaucrats or by voters. The pound will merely remain in an unstoppable decline.

76

Politicians are encouraged by the party system, and the voting system, to penalise the diligent and to subsidise the feckless. They have done so with rare enthusiasm. Low interest rates, high taxes on savings and a constant hailstorm of legislation designed to punish those stupid enough to save their money, rather than spend it, have disappointed the current generation of savers and made it perfectly clear to future generations that there is absolutely no point at all in saving, investing or putting money into any sort of pension fund. And then the politicians pretend to wonder why we are in a mess. If they had wanted to destroy our nation's economic stability they could not have done so more efficiently.

77

The Government knows that our nation's debts and our personal debts will last for generations (and possibly for ever) unless they are inflated away. And so that is what they are doing. Of course, when you deliberately devalue the currency by printing money, lowering interest rates and doing everything you can to encourage inflation (while at the same time expressing certainty that inflation will soon be under control and surprise when it is not) you will knowingly destroy the savings of the daft souls who, not having a public sector pension to look forward to, have prudently put aside a chunk of their earnings so that they can look after themselves in their old age.

78

EU countries (except England and Czech Republic) have signed an agreement to keep government debt to below 60% of GDP and to reduce it if it breaches this level, or face a fine of up to 0.1% of GDP. (I love rules like this. If a country is in deep financial trouble the EU will take more money from it so that it goes into deeper financial trouble. But at least the EU bureaucrats get more funding for long lunches and even longer holidays.) Of the countries which signed the agreement the following were (at the time) in breach of it: Portugal, Spain, Italy, Greece, Netherlands, Germany, France, Hungary, Ireland, Austria, Malta, Cyprus. Naturally, England was also in breach. The really stupid thing about this is that those countries signed a document knowing that they were in breach, knowing that they would remain in breach for the forseeable future and knowing that their nations would be fined huge sums of money until the sky started raining down money and they were able to buy their way out of their mess.

79

Central banks are now preventing the prices of property, bonds and shares from falling to their natural levels. Markets are regulated, controlled and artificially inflated by governments. The State now controls the housing market and the price of bonds and shares (though not, of course, their true value).

80

Companies and households are deleveraging. They are scared and they are cutting back on discretionary spending. (They worry, for example, about what heating and petrol prices are going to be next winter.) This will lead to lower corporate profits and a lower tax take for the Government.

81

Governments need money to pay their debts but dare not cut the public sector as much as they should and so they will push up taxes and introduce a mass of new fees and fines. These will damage business and households and push up unemployment.

82

Central banks are printing money to try to get people borrowing and spending in the utterly insane belief that debt problems can be solved by spending more money. (This is what I call Brownian Economics - which I define as 'economic theory devised by a moron'.) Everyone working at the Bank of England should be locked up or, ideally, executed for a new offence called treasonous stupidity. The plan isn't working (and won't work) because the commercial banks aren't lending because they are too frightened of not getting their money back. And they need the money to pay off their own debts and to satisfy barking new EU rules about solvency. And even if they wanted to lend money no one wants to borrow.

83

The Government and the EU now force pension funds to invest most of their money in gilts. (The Government also wants the pension funds to invest in infrastructure funds but they are not allowed to do this by the EU.) At the same time the Government is buying vast amounts of gilts. The result is that the price of gilts is rising and the yields obtained are falling. This is very bad for pensioners because their pensions are directly linked to gilt yields.

84

Retailers usually make their money out of consumers aged between 18 and 34 but for most manufacturers and retailers the current generation are a dead loss. They simply don't have the money to spend. Those who have been to university have huge debts, little or no net worth and, unless they've been lucky enough to obtain work as investment bankers, barely enough cash to buy food and shelter. Many have either never left home or have had to go back home in order to survive. Most have already had to cut back their expenditure. They have had to postpone marriage. Many have huge credit card debts. They take boring, low paid jobs to try to pay some of their bills. The two things they still spend money on are clothes and mobile phones. Self-image is important. And when you're broke and facing a bleak future it is pretty well all there is left. The young dress well, text well and surf well. But they store up problems for the future by eating crappy food and cheap booze.

85

In 2010, just 29 people were declared bankrupt in Ireland. In contrast, in England and Wales there were 135,089 bankruptcies and in Scotland there were 20,323. The difference? In Ireland it takes 12 years to be discharged. In England, Wales and Scotland it takes just 12 months and bankrupts can hold onto their homes, cars and mobile telephones. Bankruptcy in England is now no big deal and under an IVA (individual voluntary arrangement) the court which decides what a borrower can afford to pay allows him money for essentials such as a mobile phone contract and a satellite TV subscription. Corporate bankruptcies are even worse. Companies go bust and then reappear within minutes with all the previous creditors furious but legally stuffed and the borrower free to carry on regardless. It is hardly surprising that people from all over Europe are now coming to England to go bust. England has become known as the bankruptcy centre of the world; people flock to England for their debts to be forgiven and forgotten.

86

Much of the personal debt crisis which will hold back the economy for generations to come was caused by the availability of easy credit - available through banks and credit cards. Banks have stopped offering easy credit but credit cards are booming and old-fashioned cash is in decline. In Sweden only around 3% of all transactions involve cash, and Canada has just decided to phase out the penny (one cent) coin, telling retailers to round up their transactions. (This is a tax on the poor because it is the poor who tend to use cash most often for small purchases). In late July 2012, a Government minister actually announced that it was immoral to pay tradesmen in cash. He was presumably unaware that cheques bounce and that credit card companies charge crippling levels of commission.

Governments claim that manufacturing coins is expensive and banks hate cash, partly because moving money around is expensive and partly because cash is anonymous. Plus, there is the advantage that credit card companies can charge both retailers and consumers huge fees for the privilege of using their plastic. These days every financial institution is jumping onto the bandwagon and producing their own cash replacements. Barclays has devised a system which allows mobile phone owners to pay for stuff by swiping a sticker on their phones. As if to help them the EU has insisted that nations introduce strict limits on the amount of cash that can be used in any one transaction. (They argue, naturally, that cash is being phased out to stop terrorism, money laundering and, for all I know, the spread of fungal infections.) All this is rather sad because cash does have many advantages. It is anonymous, secure (the most you can lose is the amount you are carrying) and, most important of all, it imposes a discipline on the user. If you don't have the cash you can't spend it. Credit and debit cards encourage spending and they encourage over spending.

87

I try desperately hard to avoid any feelings of paranoia but is it possible that the plan is just to kill off the middle classes for political reasons? To weaken the one group of people who might start a real revolution (all real revolutions begin not with the dispossessed but with the middle classes) and to give strength to the principles of the statist branch of fascism espoused by the EU? The Government and the EU have already done everything they can to damage marriage (one of the most important strengtheners for individuals and one which turns weak, nervous individuals into strong, determined couples) but are they now planning to kill off the middle classes (and particularly those middle classes who are, by their work, independent of the State) by removing their wealth? Private pension funds have been steadily and deliberately destroyed over recent years. (Gordon Brown started the process but he has not been the only culprit.) Investment money has been steadily transferred away from the middle classes by rapacious governments and fund managers. And now, by devaluing savings, by encouraging inflation, the Government is destroying the financial independence of those wary souls who saved and put their spare pennies into a sock under the bed.

88

All investing is now gambling because everything that affects stock and bond prices, interest rates and inflation, is political and is, therefore, decided by selfish, irrational psychopaths. Investors who do not understand and accept this truth will lose their money. (My investment philosophy is contained in my book *Moneypower*.)

89

When it was clear that the world was facing a huge economic crisis (back in 2007) governments would have been wise to stand clear. Bad banks should have been allowed to go bust. Bad bankers should have been allowed to lose their mansions, town houses, yachts and private jets. Bad companies should have gone out of business. Greedy house buyers who bought more than they could afford should have been allowed to lose their homes. There would have been a lot of pain. Many hedge fund managers and investment managers would have gone bust. Millions of people would have got poorer. Millions would have lost their jobs. There would have been a Great Correction. And by now everything would be much better. There would be sunshine on the horizon. We would have a growing economy. New businesses would be springing up.

But the politicians couldn't leave things alone. They had to interfere. And, inevitably, the Gordon Browns of this world made things much, much worse. The politicians failed to understand the basic principle of money: you need to balance your outgoings with your income. Mr Micawber understood it. Most housewives and entrepreneurs understand it. But politicians, Treasury officials and bankers don't think it applies to them in their official capacity (though they probably accept it in their private capacity). The outgoings and the incomings have to be managed and balanced. There is no other way. It's really quite simple. But hubris clearly overwhelms the Browns and Goodwins of this world.

Conclusion

Many middle class citizens have lost their jobs, their homes, their pensions, their standards of living and their hopes. The rich bankers have got richer and the politicians have acquired ever more money and power.

The Treasury, the Bank of England and the regulators have not got anything right for decades. You would think they would get the odd forecast right occasionally just out of luck - but, sadly, they don't. A bunch of monkeys sitting at typewriters would have done better. You would think they might make a correct decision from time to time. But they don't. With unerring stupidity, and a very special brand of financial genius, they get everything wrong. Whatever they do makes things worse.

We are going to take a long, long time to recover from the coming deep depression. However gloomy you feel you probably do not feel glum enough. We cannot grow our way out of our financial problems because our banks are too bust and as a nation we owe too much. (Only once in history has an economy grown its way out of serious financial problems. That was America between 1938 and 1943. And the growth came as America charged England top prices for arms and armaments and made a fortune out of our misfortune.)

There are only two ways out of this financial crisis: inflation and austerity. The people aren't going to accept austerity. And so it's going to be inflation. Loads of it.

Our only defence is to recognise what is going to happen and to make our personal plans accordingly.

Our politicians aren't ever going to do that. Gordon Brown always used to blame the rest of the world for any problems the economy encountered when he was `in charge'. It was, he suggested, crazy foreigners who had pushed us back into a boom and bust economy. And the Coalition is now blaming the euro for our problems. (At least they are when they don't think anyone from Brussels is listening).

The truth (a rare commodity in political circles) is that the eurozone has very little effect on our economy. We hardly manufacture anything any more (the few things we do make are usually glued together, like IKEA furniture, on behalf of foreign companies) and our exports to the eurozone make up a fairly measly 13% of GDP. Looked at from the other direction that means that 87% of our economy has nothing whatsoever to do with Europe. And, just for the record, the 13% that we do sell to euro countries goes mostly to Germany and France - and not to Greece or Spain.

Cameron, Osborne, Clegg and company will never tell you this (even if they know it) but our economy is stuffed for entirely home-grown reasons. Our State is too big and far too expensive. No country can survive when the State spends 50 pence in the pound (which ours now does). The public sector has grown far too fat and much of what it does actually damages productivity in the relatively small part of the economy that actually makes things. And our debts are far too high. Only Japan owes more than we do and Japan has been in a mess for decades. If you add together sovereign, corporate and personal debt we owe more than 500% of GDP. That's bad. Actually, it's way past bad. Most of that debt was financed by borrowing that isn't available any more and companies and individuals are trying to pay back what they owe. For growth to increase, spending has to rise and spending isn't going to increase while people are busy paying their debts and worrying about their jobs. Besides, the banks are too much in debt to do any serious lending. Finally, the Bank of England's insane enthusiasm for destroying the strength of the currency by printing money is doing massive harm. And taking interest rates down to just about zero for savers isn't helping. These are the policies which have been popular in Japan since the 1980s and if you want to know how healthy Japan is just take a look at how their stock market has done in the last quarter of a century. (To save you the bother it's been going down with relentless enthusiasm.)

The Government isn't going to deal with any of our very real home-grown problems. And so the problems are going to get worse.

Chapter: 2

Benefits, Entitlements And The Nanny State

Introduction

We live in a world of rights, demands and expectations. The phrase `my rights' is as common as the phrase `my duty' is rare. We live in a world dedicated to the survival of the weakest. Millions of people are now brought up in homes where no one has ever worked and where no one intends to work. We have created a culture of expectation and a massive army of scroungers who feed from the State in the same utterly dependant, unquestioning way that a baby feeds from his mother's breast. The demands of the parasites are sucking the life out of our nation so rapidly that they will soon have run out of other people's money. Our society has broken down. All we have left is survival. Just about everyone we are in contact with makes us frightened, frustrated or angry. We distrust politicians, bankers, estate agents, doctors, business leaders, courts and the police. Behind everything lies the State. People are encouraged to have demands, rights and expectations but not to have any respect for others or any sense of service. Integrity is a word which appears only in dictionaries. Our society has encouraged people to mistake wants for needs. International corporations have grown rich by devising ways to encourage demands and to glorify instant gratification and short-term delights. People are encouraged to think short term; they eat too much, drink too much, take too many drugs (prescribed and otherwise), watch too much TV, use the Internet too much and gamble too much. People have become fat, like greedy pheasants gorging themselves so much that eventually they can hardly take off from the ground. Easy targets for foxes and weekend shooters. We are too harassed and too troubled by trivia, spewed forth by the mediocre-minded and those whose minds are closed, to be able to concentrate on, or dare to deal with, the really important stuff in our lives. As a result our State ruled society is rotten, intrinsically corrupt, bent, out of balance. Our society is organised to benefit the bad guys. Too many bad things happen to good people and too many good things happen to bad people.

The basic problem, of course, is that the State controls the way we think and the way we act. We need (but do not have) proper hierarchies with people responsible to someone above them and responsible for the actions of the individuals below them in the hierarchy. But we don't have hierarchical systems because that's not how fascist States operate.

We spend our formative years at school. We worry about, take and hopefully pass a seemingly endless series of virtually pointless examinations. The aim of each examination is to allow us to take another examination. After we have learned to read and write most of the education we acquire at school is a waste of time. We are taught a toxic mixture of lies, propaganda and useless information but we are never taught to think for ourselves. (In fact, in many educational establishments, thinking for yourself is punished.) Young people who might be expected to grow up wanting to change the wrongs they see around them are told what to read and when to read it. They are told what to think and when to think it. At school they are told which staircase to go up and which staircase to do down. They are told what they must eat and when they must eat it. They are told which games they are allowed to play, how to play them and when they are allowed to play them. They are told what to read and when to read it and what to think about it when they have read it. They are told when to talk and when not to talk (and what to say and how to say it). In order to fit neatly into their peer group they must have the right hairstyle, favour the right music and watch the right television programmes. They are prepared for corporate life (or bureaucratic life) right from the very start.

When they're older they will be told which receptacle to put their rubbish into, how fast they can drive their car, which forms they must fill in to do this and which forms they must fill in to do that. They will be treated like children at the age of 10, 20, 30, 40, 50 and beyond. It is no wonder that most adults still behave like obedient children. It is no wonder that although they may feel that much around them is wrong they do not fight, or revolt. (Occasionally, there will be mild protests but these are, generally speaking, inspired by mercenary motives. There was some dissent when the sensible Poll Tax was suggested. There are occasional protests about the price of petrol. There is little protest about the things that really matter: the big issues which do not have an immediate, obvious effect on our pockets.)

The people who might be expected to think about our country, and to think about the terrible things that are happening, have been trained not to think, not to rebel. They have been trained to do as they are told. Those who know what is wrong are often frightened to speak out. They know that if they stick their heads above the parapet then the police will film them and, if they keep still, they may well be shot. (If you wear a bomber jacket and carry a rucksack they will shoot you a lot.)

And, the State ensures that people take little interest in big questions such as liberty and democracy (and their absence) because they are overwhelmed by problems of daily existence. People are battling rules and regulations for so much of the time that they have no time to see, or fight for, the things that really matter. Our prejudices, beliefs and expectations are a result of very skilful, long-term indoctrination. The indoctrination has been managed by experts.

1

The Big State is constantly getting bigger. And many aspects of the State's interference are taken for granted. Why, for example, should we accept that the State should pay for all school education? Free education was introduced so that factory workers had somewhere to leave their children when they went off to work. Free schools weren't introduced because education is a right (as many people seem to think). There is no more fundamental human need than for food. But I haven't yet heard even the most ardent Statist argue that supermarkets should offer free food to everyone.

Why should women have a year's maternity leave when they have a baby? This rule has done more to damage industry than any other and has proved particularly damaging to entrepreneurs who, if they are daft enough to hire female employees of childbearing age, must risk losing key members of staff and being prevented by law from replacing them. If women want to have children then they should give up their jobs and stay at home. And why should men receive paternity leave?

2

We need to start asking some fundamental questions. If people want to have children why should the State pay for them? If people choose to have 19 children shouldn't they work hard and feed those children themselves? Should people on benefits be rich enough to have two cars, three digital television sets and a full sports and movie subscription to Sky TV? Many women seem to regard having babies as a career. And they expect taxpayers to pay their `wages'. Should anyone receiving benefits receive more than the minimum wage? Why should anyone who is a parent receive money simply because they have become a parent? Why is there no VAT on clothing for children? Why are the unemployed allowed free, or cut price, access to events and buildings where the employed have to pay full price? Why should people who are on benefits receive travel expenses if they need to go to hospital? Low paid workers (who may well have less money coming in) have to pay for themselves. Why are single mothers given a free flat? This encourages teenage girls to become pregnant. (Not surprisingly, England has one of the highest teenage pregnancy rates on the planet). Wouldn't girls be less enthusiastic about becoming pregnant if they were housed in a dormitory?

3

In 2012 it was revealed that one family was claiming £50,000 a year in benefits, and living in a five bedroom house - all at taxpayers' expense. The lady of the house explained `We're taking advantage of the system, but that's the system's fault. We'd be silly not to.' She added: `I feel this situation has been forced upon us by the Government. The minimum wage is too low and you lose your benefits if you work, but they're too easy to get if you don't work. If I have to get a job I want a good one. For now, I have to make the most of the system.' She admitted that she could work and said that she did voluntary work at a charity shop. `I'm better off volunteering than earning - we're well off and I'm not going to give that up until I have to.' She said that they didn't need a five bedroom house with a large garden but that it was in a nice area with good schools. `I know taxpayers are being punished,' she said. `I hate taking their money. But we're being allowed to get away with it.'

Her husband, a former factory worker, said that he would love to get a job but that `if I work more than an hour I feel ill and get stressed. I only get migraines every three weeks but I qualify for sick pay.'

A Department for Work and Pensions spokesman said that a handout of £50,000 a year is the equivalent of a salary of £72,000 a year before tax.

4

`If the maintenance of public credit, then, be truly so important, the next enquiry which suggests itself is, by what means is it to be effected? The ready answer to which question is, by good faith, by a punctual performance of contracts. States, like individuals, who observe their engagements, are respected and trusted: while the reverse is the fate of those who pursue an opposite conduct.' - Alexander Hamilton, first US Secretary of the Treasury 1790

5

The Statists always have an excuse for the latest bit of nonsense. They say that what they are doing is to protect us from money launderers, terrorists or ourselves. You can excuse anything with these three. Fans cannot take pasties and plastic bottles of water into sports grounds for 'security reasons' (although once you are safely inside they will happily sell you as much as you can eat and drink). Health and safety idiots chop down conker trees, bulldoze gravestones and stop clowns blowing bubbles (lest children get the soap in their eyes). In all these cases the spoiltsports are protecting us from our greatest threat: ourselves. These all seem rather silly things. But they aren't; they are part of a pattern of oppression and it is easy to believe that there is a purpose. Oppress and suppress at every possible opportunity and you will soon acquire a compliant and silent population.

6

Today, nothing remains the same for long. We live in times of deliberately unsettling instability. The State (and its ever-loyal servants) doesn't want us to feel at peace. The State wants us to feel nervous and unsettled because then the State can do with us what it will.

7

`A democracy will continue to exist up until the time that voters discover that they can vote themselves generous gifts from the public treasury. From that moment on, the majority always votes for the candidates who promise

the most benefits from the public treasury, with the result that every democracy will finally collapse due to loose fiscal policy, which is always followed by a dictatorship.' - Alexander Tyler, history professor at University of Edinburgh in 1787

8

People on benefits are given cheap transport, cheap stamps, free prescriptions and all sorts of other perks. This is a nonsense and seems further designed to make employment unpalatable and to encourage those who regard permanent unemployment as a viable and preferable career structure. Why should someone who is living on benefits, and receiving more money than someone with a job, receive special financial treatment?

Providing public service housing, free home care for people with disabled children, free transport to hospital for patients who are unemployed and so on and so on is just another form of taxation; charging the better off for the benefit of those who are more demanding, or more adept at understanding the system. The trouble is that these benefits are not free at all. They destroy real jobs because the better off families have less money to spend on cars, holidays, books and so on and so jobs are not created or are lost. Since public services are always inefficient and expensive, purchasing power is lost and wasted for ever on projects and staff and on people who frequently have wants rather than needs. And, because we spend so much money on these things, thousands of old people die of starvation and dehydration.

9

Employers used to pay people when they were off sick as a kindness. Today, employees regard it as a right that they will be paid when they are too ill to work. Indeed, many workers now insist that if they have not taken their `allotted' sick days then they must be allowed to take those days off as holiday. And Europe's highest court has ruled that workers who become sick while on holiday can take another paid vacation. This is utter madness.

10

`Mr Tucky's farm exhibited to me what I never saw before, four score oxen, all grazing upon one farm, and all nearly fat! They were some Devonshire and some Herefordshire. They were fatting on the grass only, and I should suppose that they are worth, or shortly will be, thirty pounds each. But the great pleasure with which the contemplation of this fine sight was naturally calculated to inspire me was more than counterbalanced by the

thought that these fine oxen, this primest of human food, was, aye, every mouthful of it, destined to be devoured in the Wen, and that too, for the greater part, by the Jews, loan-jobbers, tax-eaters, and their base and prostituted followers...literary as well as other wretches who, if suffered to live at all, ought to partake of nothing but the offal, and ought to come but one cut before the dogs and cats!' - William Cobbett, Rural Rides

11

The State provides far better protection for those for whom it has direct responsibility than for others. This is particularly true for those who work for the State (who have far more rights than anyone else) but, in addition, people who receive benefits from the State, or who are looked after by the State, have far more rights than people who work. For example, elderly people who pay for their own care do not have the same protections under the Human Rights Act as those whose care is provided by the State. The elderly who have saved their money, and who are, consequently, forced to pay for their care, are less able to sue unscrupulous or badly run care homes if they are poorly fed or left lying in soiled sheets. And so, although it may seem bizarre, it is perfectly true that the middle class elderly have far fewer rights, and far less dignity, than the elderly who have spent all their money and who are being looked after by the State. (The legal reason for this is that care homes can be treated as `public bodies' under the Human Rights Act, meaning that they could be sued for failing to treat elderly people with respect. But this law only applies to residents who are funded by the State - excluding those who have saved for their old age - and providing yet more evidence showing that the bureaucrats and legislators in Europe despise the prudent and the independent.)

12

We have created a society in which many people are born with unreasonable expectations. There has also been a dramatic, unaffordable and unsustainable increase in both the number and extent of the rights which are regarded as inalienable. An increasing proportion of the population now expect to be given a life free from work, and full of pleasure, at the State's expense. This is clearly unsustainable.

13

All attempts to cut Government spending are opposed by two groups: public sector workers and those on benefits. For selfish reasons these two groups want the rest of the country to continue to support them in the style to which they have become accustomed. And since the number of electors employed by the State, or being supported by the State, is now great enough to ensure a Parliamentary majority there is little or no chance that anything will change until the nation goes bankrupt or there is a revolution and those who are paying the bills say `enough'.

14

Our unwieldily benefits system penalises the genuinely needy who also happen to wish to remain dignified, while allowing those who are prepared to work the system, and who put their effort into manipulating and taking advantage, to get rich at the expense of the State. England's 120,000 problem families cost taxpayers an estimated £9 billion!

15

`Just because you do not take an interest in politics doesn't mean politics won't take an interest in you.' - Pericles 430 BC

16

Travel within England is now so expensive that employment is, for many people, not a realistic option. For example, someone who goes to work in central London will pay £30 to £35 a week to travel by bus or train. (Travelling into London by car, and then parking, would cost so much that even bankers might blanch.) In small market towns it costs £20 to £50 a week to park for a five day week. How can shop assistants and office staff afford that? The payment isn't even tax deductible.

17

The availability of generous benefits has made it difficult for employers to hold onto staff. Low paid employees know that they will almost certainly be better off if they are fired.

18

Millions of people who are officially regarded as unfit to work are nevertheless able to enjoy active lifestyles. Anyone who can visit a racecourse, sit in a pub or play a computer game is fit to work.

19

Folk who don't have at least one job by the age of 25 are likely to spend their entire lives on benefits. Many of them will supplement their money by turning to crime. This has the added advantage of giving them something to do in the evenings.

20

Our courts now pass greater sentences on those who have been found guilty of `hate crime' or `racially motivated crime'. This, of course, is politically correct nonsense and I suspect that every judge must see it as such. The cause of a crime is irrelevant and to suggest otherwise is clearly discriminatory because it implies that the woman mugged and maimed by a thug is less injured or less important than the woman mugged and maimed for reasons which can be described as `racial'. I doubt very much if the two women see their injuries as lesser or greater. In political terms the advantage of this sort of legislation is, I suppose, that it has taken us down a road which enables the courts to send people to prison for many years simply for saying something which can be judged politically incorrect. Or, indeed, for *listening* to someone else say something which can be judged to be politically incorrect.

21

Incompetence is now the norm among State employees. Money is wasted by the train load and incompetence is rewarded with yet more bonuses. In May 2012, I was sent a new red logbook for our truck. The Government department responsible for this unexpected act of generosity, the Driver and Vehicle Licensing Agency (DVLA), told me that I must destroy my old blue log book. They explained: `We are replacing all existing blue V5Cs (their name for a log book). The new certificate is being introduced following the theft of a number of blank blue V5Cs. The aim is to reduce the risks to motorists of buying a stolen or cloned vehicle.' Don't they lock up the damned certificates at night? Put them in a drawer? How much has this cost us all? Tens of millions? Hundreds of millions?

22

Everyone now wants to be bailed out by the State when things go wrong. Originally, the State took on responsibility for caring for people who were old, ill or unable to find work. Today, that responsibility has exploded. Even bankers and house owners expect to be bailed out by the State when things go wrong. The only people operating without a safety net are the self-employed and the small businessman.

23

Our politically correct society now actively encourages those with severe learning difficulties to form relationships with members of the opposite sex. The result is, inevitably, children who either have to be adopted (because the parents cannot possibly care for them) or, if the parents keep the children, a phenomenal cost to the nation in attendant social workers and services.

24

The rising cost of the National Health Service is due not so much to providing care for the elderly but because of the rise in the number of people demanding surgery and treatment for non-life threatening health problems: women who demand infertility treatment and breast enhancement surgery and would-be transsexuals who demand free treatment. These are all lifestyle choices which should not and cannot be paid for by the National Health Service. It is, indeed, arguable that the State-run NHS should not provide free maternity care. Women who choose to have babies aren't ill. They are pregnant because they want to have a baby. Why should the impoverished State fund these parental ambitions?

25

When it was suggested that benefits should be limited to £26,000 per family the plan was voted down by unelected Bishops in the House of Lords.

26

There are now millions of people for whom life on benefits has become a lifestyle choice. And many of those have been extremely adept at understanding how best they can manage the system to their advantage. The number of households in England where no one has ever, ever worked has doubled in the last decade and is now around 300,000. The children of those households will grow up accustomed to think of unemployment as normal. Some will be taught to think that getting a job is a mug's game. The modern welfare state discourages self-responsibility and encourages a sense of entitlement. It is immoral in principle to take money from a man who works in order to give it to someone who doesn't want to work. We have created a world in which it is the unfittest who are most likely to survive. And we cannot afford the world we've made. Supporting a welfare state is a rich country's game (rather like paying for a yacht big enough to have its own helipad is a rich man's game). And we're not rich enough for such luxuries.

The people who live on benefits remind me of the inhabitants of those remote Pacific islands who pray for gifts from their mythical deity. The English have, as a nation, virtually lost the idea of self-reliance and personal responsibility.

27

There are so many laws that we are all criminals now. England now struggles along under 21,000 different regulations. I bet you that within the last week (probably less) you have, probably unknowingly, broken at least one law. If you run a business then you doubtless break at least one law a day. (It will, of course, have been defined as a `regulation' or `rule' but in my world when the punishment for breaking a `regulation' or `rule' is arrest, charge, court appearance, fine and possible imprisonment then the `regulation' or the `rule' is a law.) We are all of us drowning in information about new laws. And yet if you don't act in accordance with the rules you are in trouble. We are all ignorant but ignorance is no excuse. A specialist lawyer admitted to me that he can no longer keep up with the new laws relating to his own very specialised area of the law. If he cannot keep up with his own speciality what chance do the rest of us have?

28

In England today, the State allows burglars to stay out of prison but puts old age pensioners into prison if they make protests about paying unjust taxes or refuse to pay the BBC's annual licence fee on the perfectly accurate and reasonable grounds that the BBC is outrageously biased (for example in favour of the European Union) and is not doing what it is supposed to do.

All this is practical fascism. The burglar is no threat to the State but the old aged pensioner is. And in our world today, the State always comes first.

Despite (or, perhaps, because of) these topsy-turvy interpretations of the law, there are now around nine million people in England with criminal records (common or garden motoring offences don't count as criminal offences). This means that one in six people is a criminal. Maybe Royal Mail should have thought of this when they decided to leave mail with neighbours. Their new policy means that one in six parcels will be handed to a criminal instead of to the rightful recipient.

Our oppressive, law-laden society has created a sense of lawlessness and contempt and disregard for the law.

29

I doubt if there is any legislation which has done more harm to the economy than the law which gives women who choose to leave work to have a baby the right to insist that their employer holds their job for them for a year. It is hardly surprising that no sensible employer will hire a woman of child bearing age unless there is no other suitable candidate available.

30

Social services do bugger all for real people in real need. Yesterday my wife saw a middle aged woman rummaging in a bin for food. This was on the main street in the Cathedral City of Wells. The Princess opened her handbag and gave the woman all the money she had. Social workers everywhere are too busy attending meetings to deal with the people who really need help.

31

In our State-run world there is no justice. Now, all we have left is knowing what is right and what is wrong and being able to differentiate in our hearts and minds between what is wrong and what is right and then living our lives accordingly.

32

In our courts today people of power and influence are rarely if ever to blame for anything. Politicians and public sector employees are hardly ever found guilty. The only people who are to blame are those who are regarded as being outside the system - e.g. the self-employed. And so we learn never to start a lawsuit unless the reason for the lawsuit is so dear to us that we are prepared to fight until we are bankrupt and destroyed. We do not start lawsuits expecting justice. We start them only because we want revenge so badly that we are prepared to destroy ourselves while nibbling at 'them'. And we learn not to start a lawsuit because we know we are right. If we do then we will probably lose and our sense of injustice will destroy us. (It is fairly well known among lawyers that in order to get an innocent person's conviction squashed the judges must be assured that no one in an official capacity was to blame, and certainly not the police.)

33

I have for some years been confused by the fact that while driving on speed restricted stretches of motorways I am invariably overtaken by lorries travelling at 10 mph to 20 mph faster than the ordained limit. The explanation is simple: lorry drivers simply don't care whether or not they lose their licences. Most are poorly paid and know that if they lose their licences (and, therefore, their jobs) they will receive just as much money in benefits and, instead of racing up and down motorways, they will be able to stay at home and watch daytime television.

34

The State has steadily destroyed the middle classes. Today, only the very rich, and people on benefits, can afford to have lots of children. In our new world you need to be very poor (and to allow the State to worry about everything) or very rich (and able to look after yourself). The middle classes are stuffed. And will be stuffed for some considerable time to come. This matters because the middle classes are always the backbone of any nation and any community.

35

If you give people free homes, free food, free satellite television, free Internet access, and free mobile phones then they soon begin to regard all these as their bread and butter rights. They resent the fact that other people, people who work hard, have more `things'. And so they too want more. They become resentful, angry and bitter. They demand more money, more gadgets, more rights. And if they aren't given them they steal them. In our nation today the people who demand the most receive the most. The ready availability of free money encourages a huge sense of expectations and entitlements. People regard free money as their right. Increasing numbers of young people believe the world owes them a living, an iPhone, a Play Station and a nice, late model BMW with tinted windows and wire wheels.

36

`Early-rising, sobriety, provident carefulness, attentive observation, a regard for reputation, reasoning on causes and effects, skill in the performance of labour, arts, sciences, even public-spirit and military valour and renown, will all be found, at last, to have had their foundation in a fear of poverty: and, therefore, it is manifest that the existence of poverty is indispensably necessary, whether a people be in a wild or a civilised state; because without its existence mankind would be unpossessed of this salutary fear.' - William Cobbett (Cobbett's Sermons: On the Rights of the Poor)

37

It seems obvious that the lowest paid worker should receive more than the highest non-worker paid on benefits. But this is not an accepted truth among those who make the decisions about how public money should be spent.

38

If being grown up means taking responsibility for your own actions (a definition which the law seems to suggest) then we have a nation dominated by scrounging layabouts who behave like children.

39

No one ever measures the value of projects the Government pays for. When a new building is commissioned, or a road is built, no one ever bothers to see whether the project has been financially sound. When a company opens a new factory or a new shop they will want to know whether their investment has paid off; they will want to know whether the money was spent wisely or not. Governments never bother to find out whether or not they are spending taxpayers' money wisely.

40

Our interfering State, speaking with the voice of health and safety experts, took down celebratory Jubilee bunting in Whitehall and stopped people putting it up elsewhere. In almost every imaginable way, the State now decides what we can and cannot do.

41

As the State gives more, so people demand more. A woman recently complained because a 700-year-old castle provided no access for her pram. As a result the building had to be closed to the public.

42

The State no longer approves of individuals (soldiers and boy scouts) being required to take an oath of loyalty to the Queen and to God. In future the oath of loyalty must be to the European Union.

43

The State has decided that same sex marriages must be allowed. And so, although the vast majority of electors are opposed to the idea, the State will get its way.

44

Over 1,000 different agencies can enter your home without a warrant.

45

The Government now spends very nearly half of the English economy. One in five people in England works for the Government, local authorities or public corporations of one sort or another. The vast majority of them are clerks and petty bureaucrats without whom the State would function more, not less, effectively. In other words nearly one in five people is holding their country back, doing more harm than good. We would all be better off if they went on permanent strike and stayed at home to watch television.

46

The Government should encourage job creation not through daft schemes but by cutting red tape and taxes for entrepreneurs. Politicians and commentators claim that the EU does not allow us to cut red tape. But Germany has done so (with great success) despite being a committed, leading member of the EU and being bound by the same rules as England.

47

The Government has produced a 200-page document telling people how to use ladders. I assume that someone will soon write a 20-page document explaining to citizens how they should lift and carry 200-page documents without hurting themselves.

48

`A nation can survive its fools, and even the ambitious. But it cannot survive treason from within. An enemy at the gates is less formidable, for he is known and he carries his banners openly. But the traitor moves among those within the gate freely, his sly whispers rustling through all the alleys, heard in the very halls of government itself. For the traitor appears no traitor; he speaks in the accents familiar to his victims, and he wears their face and their garments, and he appeals to the baseness that lies deep in the hearts of all men. He rots the soul of a nation; he works secretly and unknown in the night to undermine the pillars of a city; he infects the body politic so that it can no longer resist. A murderer is less to be feared.' - Marcus Tullius Cicero*

49

My insurance company tells me that in order to satisfy the regulations I must keep all my insurance documents for a minimum of 40 years.

50

Many of the new regulations which are introduced hit small firms badly. Big companies have whole departments filling in and filing forms but small businesses have to struggle. On the whole, big companies welcome complex new red tape because new regulations keep out new competitors. In fact big companies often encourage new regulations, and pay lobbyists to suggest them to European Union officials.

51

Despite our nation being wrapped in red tape, and bludgeoned by health and safety regulations, the evidence shows that the rules and regulations simply do not work. A recent study showed that 60% of the people who work in cafés preparing food have faecal matter on their hands. That really isn't surprising because the same survey showed that 30% of all people in cafés never wash their hands after going to lavatory. Staff who prepare food, or touch it at all, should wear plastic gloves.

52

Vince Cable (surely the most dangerous man in England now that no one with functioning cortical tissue takes Clegg seriously) is a dedicated advocate of State intervention. Like most people in Government he seems to have no affinity with, or sympathy for, people who try to run small businesses. As business secretary he has opposed sensible attempts to reduce the number of regulations affecting small businesses. He, like endless eurocrats, doesn't seem to understand that too many rules destroy common sense and make people intellectually, morally and spiritually flabby.

53

Small companies pay £6 billion a year to consultants for help in complying with State regulations. The total spent on complying with regulations is estimated to be £16.8 billion a year for small companies.

54

The cost of the red tape introduced by the State is, of course, passed on to the consumer. And the weight of all the purposeless and suffocating regulations pushes up the cost of products and services and pushes down the quality of what is made and what is done.

55

Computer aficionados like to claim that the Internet helped produce the on-going revolution in the Middle East. This is nonsense. The revolutions which produced such changes in Turkey and Libya were not sparked by the Internet. They happened after a young Tunisian fruit seller called Muhammad Bouazizi set himself on fire when municipal inspectors not only made it impossible for him to make a living but upended his cart (tipping his fruit and vegetables onto the road) and spat in his face when they found that he was trying to sell fruit and vegetables without a licence. All over the world governments have started to license and regulate jobs. They are doing this not because they want to protect people from incompetence but because they realise that it's a rather sneaky way to charge a good many annual fees. Within the EU and the Middle East armies of State-employed regulators strut around enforcing pointless rules and charging fees which few people can afford. It's real fascism in action.

England is now introducing licences and certificates for all trades and professions. These must, of course, be paid for. Some of these new rules come from the EU. Others seem to be modelled on American regulations. (In the USA, 40% of all workers need certification: including hairdressers, florists, second-hand booksellers and ballroom dancing teachers). Naturally, all the fees paid for these annual licences and certificates are paid to the Government (or to some Government run quango).

56

When Governments steal with force (or the threat of it) but then fail to do what they have promised, then they are behaving fraudulently. Today, politics in England is a cesspit of corruption, cynicism, greed and self-interest. Our State is too powerful, too invasive and far too expensive. But until there is some sort of genuine revolution nothing will change. The people who work for the State will never do anything to reduce its size, power or cost.

57

We live in a Christian country but we have been told that we have to suppress our Christianity. Employees are banned from wearing Christian crosses but no one dares stop Muslim women covering their heads. No one tells Jewish men that they cannot wear their skullcaps.

Christian adoption agencies, understandably opposed to the idea of homosexual couples adopting children, have had to close because their honestly held beliefs must take second place to the demands of the State. Under intense pressure from lobbyists the State is moving from enforcing tolerance of homosexuality to enforcing approval of it. The first gives freedom to homosexuals but the second is plain and simple censorship which takes freedom away from everyone else. The Government Equalities Office (yet another department straight out of Orwell) has begun what it calls a `consultation' with the public and is asking citizens whether they agree or disagree with the plan to open marriage to all. But, and this is the key, they also say that `this consultation is about how we best remove the ban on same-sex couples having a civil marriage, not on whether this should or should not happen'. That doesn't sound like much of a consultation to me. It's a prejudiced, bigoted fait-accompli. The State is now deciding how we think about things which have nothing to do with it and anyone who values their liberty should protest. (The problem, of course, is that when the State makes up its mind about something it uses all its power to enforce its view. Anyone who questions the new, politically correct attitude on same-sex marriage is likely to find him or herself sitting in an interrogation room at their local police station. That's pure fascism in practical action. 'You will think how we tell you to think.')

Citizens who want to celebrate Christmas are told that they cannot decorate their windows or their streets because to do so might upset people of other faiths. No one in authority ever seems to realise that this is our country, that we are a Christian country and that if visitors don't like what they see they can always move somewhere else. No one in authority seems to care that if we travel to a country where another God is worshipped, and where the laws and customs are different, we are, quite rightly, expected to behave respectfully and politely. No one in authority even seems to give a damn that the very people whom they claim they are protecting (the Muslims, for example) really don't give a damn whether or not we all wear crosses and hang Merry Christmas banners from every tree and every lamppost. The State (and those who promote it and those who serve it) has no time for Christianity because people who have a religion to comfort them will always be more difficult to oppress.

58

Even though common sense would suggest the opposite, I have no doubt that the financial crisis will result in more regulations and more Government. This will reduce the ability of private businesses to survive, let alone grow. The irony is that the crisis was largely caused by too many bad regulations and too much bad government.

59

Governments should concentrate on looking after their citizens, providing a decent infrastructure, sorting out disputes and providing protection from bad people (whether home-grown or foreign). But, increasingly, our Governments have taken our resources and used them to protect themselves and their pals and to promote their own agenda. They use the police to protect themselves and they use the State to enrich themselves. Hitler and Stalin are rightly regarded as bad leaders but even they didn't steal the citizen's money for themselves. They did their best to protect their nations. Our new breed of leaders have taken leadership to new depths of corruption and dishonesty. All around the world (including in England) prisons are stuffed with leading politicians who lied and deceived. But it is not those who are in prison who are my main worry: it is those who ought to be in prison but who are in still in power.

60

We now live in a world of 'targets'. (They came originally from the USSR). All State departments use targets. The problem is that the targets can be adjusted to fit reality. And too often the targets are never set very high at all. For example, I have just seen a 'How are the police performing?' leaflet from North Somerset. Their current performance for 'sanction detection rates for overall crime' is a woeful 30.5%. This makes them 19th out of 43 nationally, and since their target was to be 20th they have clearly achieved their target. Their detection rate for serious acquisitive crimes was an even more woeful 14.7%. They came 26th out of 43 and conveniently their target was 26th and so they achieved that too. I can imagine there was much celebrating and possibly even handing out of bonuses. There are targets in hospitals these days and, at long last, leading members of the medical establishment are complaining that the Government's target figures for hospitals are affecting the quality of care provided. (I think I wrote about this problem around seven or eight years ago.) The problem, as ever, is that doctors, and hospitals, are now judged by targets which are set by bureaucrats who know nothing about medicine, patients' needs or the basic principles of good health care, and who make sure that they, and their families, are well protected by private health subscriptions - usually paid for by taxpayers.

61

The tragedy is that people who think they have a relationship with any professional (doctor, banker, lawyer or whomsoever) are naive and doomed to disappointment because all professionals now belong to the system. Some (doctors) have been bought and turned into public sector workers. Others have been brought under control with legislation (lawyers). And others (bankers) are controlled by a State approved corporate culture which puts short-term profits above everything else. Everywhere we look the State comes first and people come a long way last. The sad result is that many doctors, lawyers and other professionals now aim only to make enough money from their jobs to enable them to retire and to do something else with the rest of their lives. Thanks to Statism, words such as `vocation' are now of purely historical interest.

62

On Monday 8th August 2011, London looked uncomfortably like a Middle East hotspot. The only big difference was that the looters and thugs in London were not politically motivated. They were mostly criminals and they were using the Internet to communicate with one another and to plan their thieving.

Do none of those in power understand that the hoodies who were having fun smashing up shops and stealing mobile phones don't care what anyone says (or does) to them?

Forty years ago I worked as a Community Service Volunteer in the toughest part of Liverpool and later, when I was a medical student in Birmingham, I ran a nightclub called `The Gallows' for kids who would otherwise have been on the streets.

Time and time again the kids I was working with got involved in fights which resulted in serious injuries. They simply didn't care because they didn't have anything to lose. Only when they felt they belonged, had responsibilities, and had a future to lose, did they behave responsibly.

When life is so bad that there is no downside, the bleatings of politicians and the threats from the police aren't going to make any difference to young people who have become feral.

And today things are far, far worse because today's young people have been brought up knowing that they have rights. For a new generation life is now all about rights. There are no responsibilities.

There are only two solutions. A short-term one and a long-term one.

The short-term solution is that street violence has to be subdued with violence. The looting and the destroying have to be stopped with truncheons and firm arrests in order to protect the innocent, the hard-working and the honest. Nothing else will work.

The long-term solution is that life must be made better so that the looters and destroyers have something to lose: homes, belongings, work, pride and hope. They have to learn respect and dignity. And none of that will happen until politicians and policemen start behaving honestly and honourably. And I can't see much danger of that happening.

Meanwhile, the police must be firmly told a few home truths.

i. Stop shooting people who aren't shooting. It tends to annoy and frighten people who don't have guns.

ii. Policemen who shoot citizens who aren't shooting must be suspended and arrested. No exceptions. The police shoot far too many people these days. And there never seems to be any justice.

iii. People who loot buildings and set fires must be arrested immediately. Even the ones who look frightening (because they are wearing balaclavas) must be arrested. The police are paid very well to take personal risks. That's the job. Any officers who don't want to be policemen, protecting life and property, should become librarians and take a massive pay cut. Too often the reaction of the police (standing around or running backwards and forwards) seems egregiously incompetent at best and cowardly at worst. It is the failure of the police to take action which leads to the exacerbation of looting and vandalism.

63

Too many of the people working for the State spend public money in a way that they would never dream of spending their own money. When spending ten million pounds, or a billion pounds, they do not think of that money as being made up of £50 taken from this person's wage packet and £20 from this driver's petrol bill. They think of it as Monopoly money and they treat it as such. They spend and waste public money in a way that they would never dream of spending and wasting their own money.

64

The English Government is the worst investor in the world. And Gordon Brown was the worst of the lot. It was, of course, Brown who sold our gold at the very bottom and lost the nation billions as a result. And now Cameron, Osbourne and Clegg (a trio which sounds suspiciously like an upmarket estate agency) are desperately trying to flog off RBS (the bankrupt and disgraced bank) at a 50% loss.

65

The State, or rather the people who make the decisions on its behalf, seem to have no idea at all how the real world operates. The big motorways near Bristol (the M4 and the M5) are currently undergoing some sort of repair or improvement. I have no idea what the workmen are supposed to be doing, although I do know that hardly any of them seem to be doing it whenever I pass by. There is no notice telling motorists what is being done but there is a large notice informing travellers that the road works and inconvenience will last two and a half years. Two and a half years! You could build a motorway in less time than that. The Chinese could put up a motorway in less time than our workmen spent erecting the speed cameras (which were, of course, the first things to go up). The cost to motorists, business and the nation will surely be measured in billions. These are busy roads and every journey involving these two motorways now takes at least half an hour longer than it should do. There is, in addition, a huge extra cost in terms of the petrol used up by cars and lorries idling or going too slowly. The damage to the economy will be vast.

66

The State now spends over half our money. That's a dangerously high figure. State spending in Russia is approaching 50% and outside observers regard that as a very dangerous sign. We're more of a statist State than Russia.

67

A writer in the *Guardian* recently suggested that we should all be able to examine any citizen's finances. 'Transparency underpins a culture of social justice and civic duty,' she claimed, suggesting that 'secrecy encourages inequality'. Apparently the citizens of Norway, Finland and Sweden can already study one another's earnings, savings and finances online. Wonderful. Pure Statism. Pure fascism.

68

The State now runs medical care in England and it is important to remember that all the doctors and nurses who work for the NHS are civil servants. As they have shown time and time again their primary professional allegiance is not to their patients but to the State. The doctors' strike in June 2012 (organised to protest about the Government's proposal that taxpayer funded pensions for doctors should be altered very slightly) was typical of the sort of unadulterated greed exhibited by public sector workers. It was notable that the striking doctors chose to withdraw their services to patients rather than do anything - such as failing to fill in forms - which might inconvenience bureaucrats or the Government. (The General Medical Council, which exists to maintain standards in the medical profession, was predictably silent when the strike took place.)

69

`If you give me six lines written by the hand of the most honest man, I would find something in them to have him hanged.' - Cardinal Richelieu

70

Official letters are always written in such a way as to make the recipient fearful, frustrated and powerless. Everything the State does is designed to threaten and terrify. Every official document comes with `urgent' printed on it and with threats and punishments defined or implied. We live in a new EU world which resembles the USSR more than it resembles the England whose history and culture we are now forbidden to remember and celebrate.

71

`A paranoid schizophrenic is a guy who just found out what is going on.' - William Burroughs

72

Back in 1988, in my book *The Health Scandal,* I forecast that by the year 2020 one third of the population in the developed world would be over the age of 65 and that in every home where there were two healthy parents and two healthy children there would be four disabled or dependent individuals needing constant care.

I predicted that unemployment would be common, that stress related diseases would be endemic and that developed countries around the world would face bankruptcy as they struggled to find the cash to pay pensions, sick pay and unemployment benefits.

I forecast that, tragically and unfairly, resentment, bitterness and anger would divide the young and the old, the able bodied and the dependent, the employed and the unemployed, that there would, within 20 years of the start of the 21st century, be anarchy, despair and civil war with ghettoes of elderly and disabled citizens abandoned to care for themselves.

For years those who have forecast the end of the human race have talked of nuclear war, starvation in the Third World and pollution as being the major threats to our survival. But, back in 1988, I argued that the decline I predicted for the year 2020 would be triggered not by any of these forces but by these much simpler and entirely predictable developments. And I was absolutely right. We are heading for a medical and social catastrophe. Every day that goes by makes that catastrophe increasingly inevitable. Everyone will suffer: today's elderly, tomorrow's elderly and tomorrow's young too.

When I first published this forecast, the medical and political establishments refused to take my warning seriously. I was dismissed as a scaremonger. No one would broadcast the TV series I wanted to make and my book was studiously ignored. Even though I personally bought around two thousand hardback copies of the book and sent them to every Member of Parliament, most leading journalists, many doctors and hundreds of public libraries the whole issue remained largely undiscussed.

In recent weeks some sections of the media have at long last begun to recognise that we are truly facing a colossal problem - and that the growing size of our elderly and disabled populations will pose enormous problems to our society. But neither politicians nor commentators have yet stumbled on the true background explanation for what is happening - and nor have they offered any practical advice on how we can best protect ourselves against the problems which are coming.

When I wrote *The Health Scandal* I estimated that by the year 2020 we would have reached the position whereby more than half the population would be `dependant' - either through age or disability. It now looks as if my calculations were accurate. If anything they were rather conservative. There seems to me to be little doubt that, in the next thirty years, age will have a far more divisive effect on our society than race, sex or class have ever had.

In developed countries total populations are increasing very slowly but ageing populations are increasing at a dramatic rate. For example, during one recent decade the total population of England increased by less than one per cent. But in the same period the pensionable population rose by ten per cent. In many westernised nations one person in five is already a pensioner. By the year 2020, a third of the population in most developed countries will be pensioners.

Several things make this explosion in the size of the elderly population particularly significant.

First, there is the fact that among older populations there is inevitably a higher proportion of disabled and dependent individuals. The incidence of chronic disease rises rapidly among older age groups. Half the beds in

National Health Service hospitals are occupied by patients suffering from some sort of stroke. Stroke patients generally need to stay in hospital for long periods of time and they need intensive nursing care. More and more of our hospital beds will be blocked and unavailable for emergencies. All this will inevitably mean that waiting lists for non-urgent surgery will get longer and longer and the number of people in our community suffering from disabling and untreated problems such as arthritic hips will grow even faster. The steady increase in our elderly population will mean that the quality of health care will steadily deteriorate. Our population is getting older and sicker. The general population was never as unhealthy as it is now. Millions are encouraged to be aware of every symptom and to insist that every sign of physical or mental illness be investigated. The Internet taught us to expect all information and entertainment to be free. But the NHS taught us to expect 'free everything' for every symptom; it taught us to abdicate all personal responsibility. The body is able to cure nine out of ten illnesses itself but this extraordinary self-healing ability is ignored and often suppressed. Inevitably, the incidence of iatrogenesis (doctor induced disease) has been rising rapidly for years. Today, doctors and nurses are, along with cancer and circulatory disease, one of the biggest killers in the country.

The second reason why the explosion in the size of the elderly population is dangerous is that the number of young people is falling. And the result is that in the future a smaller and smaller working population will have to support a larger and larger dependent population.

That takes us neatly into the third reason why the explosion in the size of our over 60 population is likely to produce real problems: money.

Most workers who are currently paying pension contributions still assume that the money they are paying will be invested and repaid to them when they reach pensionable age. But that is not the case. The pension contributions paid by today's workers are used to pay the pensions of yesterday's workers - today's pensioners. If pension programmes were being organised by private individuals they would be described as pyramid or Ponzi schemes and the organisers would be in prison.

The pensions that today's workers will receive when they retire will be paid by the regular contributions made by tomorrow's workers. But the working population is getting smaller and smaller. And the retired population is getting bigger and bigger. You don't have to be a genius to see the disaster we are heading for. Within a decade or so the size of our elderly population will have begun to concern politicians. By then it will be too late.

This is a problem that we should be worrying about now. It is, without a doubt, one of the biggest problems our society must face. It is something I've been writing about, in detail, for nearly 30 years but our politicians still don't seem to have noticed it and very few members of the public seem to understand it.

The inescapable overall conclusion is that the incidence of illness and disability is going to rise and rise and the availability of public resources is going to fall and fall. And if you are currently between the ages of 35 and 55 then the chances are that by the time you reach the sort of age at which you might hope to retire you will discover that any publicly funded pension you might receive will either be very small or non-existent and the availability of sheltered or nursing home accommodation will be extremely limited.

If you are currently under the age of 35 then you are going to have to pay a steadily increasing percentage of your earnings in income tax and national insurance deductions. You can safely ignore anything politicians say about cutting taxes. The fact is that taxes are probably never going to be lower than they are at the moment. The young are, I suppose, in the very worst position of all. Throughout their working lives they are going to have to struggle to pay towards the care of a relatively larger and larger elderly population. When they themselves reach retirement age they will be in even bigger trouble for they will probably not have been able to save anything to look after themselves. And State pensions will, if they exist at all, be minute.

73

Our ancestors lived in a world about which they understood very little and where they were constantly in danger. They had many things to be afraid of: death, pain, starvation and being eaten alive by wild animals to mention but four.

We, in contrast, should lead relatively fear free lives. But we don't. All the evidence firmly shows that fear plays a much bigger part in our lives than it ever played in the lives of our ancestors. Why? Because society needs us to be frightened so that we remain subservient.

Fear is a powerful driving force which helps to push us forwards. Fear encourages us to accept things we do not like, to do work we do not enjoy and to spend money on things we neither want nor need. Fear cripples us but keeps us compliant. It is not by accident that countless people - politicians, commentators, experts, industries and advertising agencies - all deliberately do what they can to keep us afraid. When did you last hear a politician, pundit or expert offering undiluted comfort and reassurance?

Fear is one of the most potent of all forces and it used to control us and to manipulate our emotions. Fear is everywhere and is constantly used by people who want to manipulate us. Politicians and police chiefs frighten us about street violence in order to encourage us to give them more power. Politicians make us frightened of our enemies abroad for the same reason. If they cannot find some useful enemies then they will create some. Television and radio mean that we can be frightened more speedily and more effectively than ever before. Fear helps our society to sustain itself and to increase its power.

Science fiction writers have, in the past, often written about a future in which man loses power over his world because computers and robots have take control.

That hasn't happened. But we have, unthinkingly, lost power in a quite different way. We have lost power and handed over control of our lives to an untouchable, nebulous, almost indefinable force. When we are feeling angry or upset with the world we often blame `them'. When we feel that we are being forced to do things against our will we blame `them'. When we feel frustrated or cheated we blame `them'. When we are hampered by injustice or wounded by unfairness we say that it is `their' fault.

But there is no `them', of course.

The man who seems to represent injustice - and who may seem one minute to be one of `them' - will, the next minute, be standing shoulder to shoulder with us sharing our complaints. The man in a suit who, when sitting behind his desk, seems to be cruel, uncaring and utterly devoid of understanding, will, when he finds himself in a different situation become nervous and uncertain. The woman who works in a government office and treats supplicants with more contempt than compassion (and who seems to her victims to be one of `them') will find herself becoming a victim if she needs to visit a hospital as a patient. The customs officer who greets passengers with a sneer and a scowl (and therefore seems to be one of `them') will lose all his authority and power when he has to queue in his local post office to buy stamps.

The men and women who seem to be `them' aren't really `them' at all. They are each of them given their temporary `them' quality by the institutions for which they work. It is the institutions which have the real power.

The man who sits behind the desk is merely borrowing or representing that power. When he steps out from behind his desk (either temporarily, to go home at night, or permanently, to retire) he loses all his 'themness' and once again becomes an innocent in a cruel and distant world.

If you carefully examine the way the world is being run at the moment you could reasonably come to the conclusion that most multinational corporations and most governments are more or less exclusively controlled by ruthless, James Bond villain style psychopathic megalomaniacs.

What other explanation could there be for the fact that drug companies make and sell drugs which they know are both dangerous and ineffective? What other explanation could there be for the fact that food companies make and sell food which they must know causes cancer and contains very little of nutritional value? What other explanation could there be for the fact that arms companies sell products deliberately designed to blow the legs off small children? What other explanation could there be for the fact that tobacco companies continue to make, promote and sell products which they know kill a high proportion of their customers?

And what other explanation could there possibly be for the fact that bureaucrats, civil servants and politicians allow all this to happen?

There is another explanation for all these things.

For the very first time in history the main opponents of justice and fair play, the proponents of abuse and tyranny, have no human form. We have created new monsters: new monsters which we cannot see or touch (we cannot see or touch them for the excellent reason that they do not exist in reality). Over twenty years ago (in a book entitled *Animal Rights Human Wrongs*) I put forward the idea that modern corporate structures have acquired lives of their own; that these inanimate creations have ambitions, aims, purposes and needs of their own. Companies need to keep making regular profits in order to satisfy the shareholders, the directors and the employees. And they need to keep making profits in order to survive. In the end the company's needs overrule the needs and consciences of the people working for it. The employees, particularly the directors and executives, become slaves to the needs of this all-devouring entity. (Clearly, what is true of companies is also true of countries.)

74

Much unhappiness and frustration is caused by the fact that in our society the law is commonly confused with justice, liberty, freedom and equality.

In truth the law has very little to do with these fundamental moral principles. The law exists to help society defend itself; it is used by those who represent society as a weapon with which to dominate and discriminate against individual powers and freedoms. The law is man's inadequate attempt to turn justice - an abstract theoretically concept - into practical reality. Sadly, it is invariably inspired more by the prejudices and self-interest of the lawmakers than by respect or concern for the rights of innocent individuals.

These misconceptions about the purpose of our law lead to much disappointment. And these misconceptions help to create a considerable amount of underlying stress.

No society has ever had as many laws as we have and yet few societies can have ever had less justice.

Many of the laws which exist today were created not to protect individuals or communities but to protect the system. It is because such crimes threaten the security and sanctity of the system that theft and fraud often attract harsher sentences than crimes such as rape and murder which affect individuals, whose rights are seen as less significant.

The irony is that although the law was originally introduced to protect individuals and to reduce their stresses the law has itself become a tyrant and a major cause of stress. Today few individuals can afford to take advantage of the protection offered by the law. The law oppresses the weak, the poor and the powerless and sustains itself and the powers which preserve it. The enormous costs of litigation mean that there is one law for the rich and no law at all for the poor. The result is that the law threatens and reduces the rights of the weak and strengthens and augments the rights of the powerful.

Things are made worse by the fact that the people employed by society to uphold and administer the law on behalf of the ordinary people too often take advantage of their positions to abuse their powers. The interpretation of the law is so often at the discretion of those who are paid to uphold it that those who have been hired by society become the law itself. Neatly and effectively, society protects itself against threat and bypasses the rights of individual citizens.

Too often society allows officers of the courts to abuse their power to satisfy their own personal ambitions, grievances and prejudices. In return, society in its broadest and most undemocratic and domineering sense is protected by the people who benefit from its patronage. It is the worst sort of symbiotic relationship.

The final irony is that as respect for the law (and those hired to uphold it) diminishes so the divide between the law and justice grows ever wider.

When people who are given the power to protect society disapprove of something which threatens their status they introduce a new law. As political parties come and go so we accumulate layer after layer of new laws. To the lawmakers it doesn't matter if the new laws conflict with the old laws as long as all the laws help to strengthen the status of the State.

Meanwhile, as the oppression of individuals continues, lawlessness (and disrespect for the law) grows among officials and those in power. Brutality, arrogance, corruption and hypocrisy have all damaged public faith in the law but the only response from society has been to create new laws to outlaw disapproval. Society's primary interest is to protect itself, and society is not concerned with justice, freedom or equality since those are values which are appreciated only by individuals. Those who have power are concerned only with their own survival and with perpetuating their power. The simple truth is that we live in a corrupt society which creates countless stresses for ordinary people.

When we complain about 'them' we are really complaining about the world we have created for ourselves; we are complaining about unseen forces which structure and rule our society; we are complaining about forces which are now utterly out of our control.

For the first time in history we have succeeded in creating a world, a society, which now exists solely to defend, protect and develop itself. We have created a society whose institutions have acquired power of their own. These institutions - governments, multinational corporations, multinational bureaucracies and so on - now exist solely to maintain, improve and strengthen themselves. These institutions have their own hidden agendas and the human beings who work for them may think that they are in control - but they aren't.

The biggest threat to the survival of the human race (and the planet upon which we live) comes not from the atomic bomb, or the fact that we are steadily destroying the very fabric of our world by polluting our seas, our rivers, the air we breathe and even the space which separates us from other planets, but from the fact that we have created a social structure in which we, as human beings, now exist as mere drones. It is this new social structure which is pushing us along at a great speed and `forcing' us not only to destroy our environment but also to abandon all those moral and ethical values which it is reasonable to expect to be fundamental in a `civilised' society.

It may be a little difficult to accept the concept of institutions having agendas of their own but the reality is that this is exactly what has happened.

The people who appear to run large institutions, and who themselves undoubtedly believe that they are in charge, are simply institutional servants.

Consider, for example, the chairman and directors of a large multinational pharmaceutical company. These well-paid men and women will regard themselves as being responsible for the tactics and strategy followed by the company for which they work. But in reality it is the company itself - an institution which only really exists on paper - which is in real control.

Every multinational company has a constant thirst for cash. In order to satisfy bankers, brokers and shareholders companies need to produce quarterly figures which show a nice big, fat profit on the bottom line.

The people who work for a company may think that they are in control but in reality they aren't. The directors have to do what is in their company's best interests. If they don't then their company will falter and that can't be allowed to happen. The company, the unimaginably powerful corporate demon, must come first.

So, for example, if the directors of a drug company find that one of their products causes lethal side effects they may, as human beings, feel ashamed about this. Individually the directors may want to withdraw the drug immediately and to apologise to the people who have been injured by their product. But this course of action would not be in the company's best short-term interests. Withdrawing the drug would doubtless cost the company money. Research and development costs would have to be written off. And apologising would expose the company to lawsuits. So the directors, acting in the company's best interests, must keep the drug on the market and deny that there are any problems. In these circumstances the company (a non-human entity which only exists on paper) is in control. The decisions are made not in the interests of people (whether they be customers or directors) but in the interests of the corporate `being'.

The problem is compounded by the fact that, big as they are, multinational companies have no souls and no sense of responsibility. Moreover they never think beyond the next set of profit figures; they are ultimately ruthless and (since they are inanimate and bloodless) utterly 'cold blooded', but they are also ultimately short-sighted. Big institutions, like computers, are inherently, irretrievably, stupid. They do not realise that their behaviour will, in the long run, lead to their total destruction - partly because it will annoy and alienate their customers and partly because it will eventually result in the deaths of many of their customers!

By and large, the men and women who run large drug companies, arms companies, food companies and genetic engineering companies don't really want to destroy the world in which we all live. They know that their families have to breathe the same air as everyone else. They know that they too need good food, clean drinking water and a healthy environment.

However, despite the evidence being to the contrary the people who run these companies probably think that they are doing good and useful work. They have denied the truth to themselves in order to avoid coming face to face with a reality which would probably drive them insane if they accepted it. It is only through denial and self-deceit that most of the men and women who work for tobacco companies can continue to sell a product which causes so much misery and so much death. Adolf Hitler killed fewer people than the big tobacco companies have killed. But I doubt if many of the people running big tobacco companies think of themselves as evil.

I have met men and women who run large organisations (such as drug companies). Some recognise that what they are doing is immoral and they excuse themselves with such trite and shallow phrases as 'If I didn't do it someone else would' and 'I've got to pay the mortgage'. These are, of course, variations on the same excuses favoured by the men and women who operated the gas chambers during the Second World War. The brighter and more sensitive individuals usually see through these excuses in the end; they often become depressed and accept treatment with their own products. But many men and women who work for such companies quite honestly and sincerely believe that they are doing useful and indeed valuable work. They have become so deeply institutionalised, and are driven so completely by the needs of the corporate beast, that they genuinely feel no shame about what they do. They have rationalised their actions and denied to themselves the truths which are apparent to outside observers.

Occasionally, this constant denial and self-deceit breaks down and absurdities appear. For example, England's Members of Parliament have, as members of an institution, consistently voted to allow multinational

90

corporations to pollute our drinking water and to tamper with and pollute our food. And yet MPs themselves, as individuals, are so conscious of the value of the pure food and clean drinking water that in the House of Commons they have arranged to be given spring water to drink and to be fed on organic food which has not been genetically modified. The men and women who vote to allow our water to be polluted and our food to be genetically modified are voting as representatives of institutions rather than as representatives of people. They know that they are creating a world in which the food is unfit to eat and the water unfit to drink. But they can't stop it happening because they are operating for the benefit of institutions rather than people.

The huge organisations which now run the world have developed identities, strengths, purposes and needs of their own. And in order to continue to grow in size and in strength those organisations need to ignore or suppress as much of the truth as they can - and to ignore the truths which they cannot suppress. The world is now full of evil companies (Goldman Sachs, Google, Monsanto and virtually every drug company on the planet to name but just a few) which exist for no other reason than to make profits and to grow. Obviously, the people who work for those institutions must also ignore and suppress the unpalatable truths (and they must find ways to hide from the reality of what they are doing).

How else can anyone explain the fact that the American Government has decided to continue to damage the ozone layer - despite knowing the consequences? How else can anyone explain the fact that because antibiotics are being consistently and deliberately and knowingly used irresponsibly infectious diseases are once again a major cause of death? How else can anyone explain the fact that genetic engineers are creating foods which may or may not be safe to eat? How else can anyone explain the fact that drug companies keep on producing - and selling - products which do more harm than good?

The industrialists, the politicians and the administrators who allow these things to happen are just as vulnerable to the consequences of their actions as you and I. They - and their families - cannot buy immunity to the problems which they are creating. And yet nothing changes.

The same self-centred, amoral materialism which has characterised political life for the last few decades, and which has simultaneously accompanied a downfall in morality, can no longer be seen as just another unfortunate blip in human development. The horrors of today will not be easily conquered, and will not be conquered at all unless we acknowledge the breadth and depth of the exceptional problem we now face.

Some years ago, Dr Albert Schweizer saw the first signs of what has happened. `Another hindrance to civilisation today,' he wrote, `is the over-organisation of our public life. While it is certain that a properly ordered environment is the condition and, at the same time, the result of civilisation, it is also undeniable that, after a certain point has been reached, external organisation is developed at the expense of spiritual life. Personality and ideas are often subordinated to institutions, when it is really these which ought to influence the latter and keep them inwardly alive.'

We cannot trust our existing politicians, or the systems which they wrongly believe they control, and so what is the point of trying to persuade them to do what we want them to do - and what is right?

We have only one option: to take back the political power which is rightfully ours. We have to take back power from the institutions which now rule our lives. And we have to take back power from the weak, spineless and unthinking politicians who serve these many political and commercial institutions with such uncritical faithfulness.

Conclusion

England has, for some years now, been run by the elected representatives of people who don't work, have no intention of ever working, and don't pay tax. The organisation of the electoral system, and the importance of the three party system, means that this is unlikely to change until there is a revolution and the people who work, and pay tax, demand some serious changes and announce that they *will*, in future, be treated with dignity and respect by those who represent the State. It is difficult to avoid the feeling that the country is now being run for the greedy, the selfish and the lazy. Our young folk need to tie their shoelaces, pull up their trousers to hide their hideous underpants, grit their teeth and contemplate the awfulness and the rigours of going to work. And while they are being encouraged to recognise that authority comes with responsibility and that scented candles and bed cushions are a choice not a right, we must also take action to restrict the power of the numerous organisations and institutions which have grown in power, stature, wealth, status and authority and which would treat us all as slaves.

Chapter 3

Bankers: Greed, Fraud and Hubris

Introduction

Just why no bankers have been arrested, humiliated and jailed is a mystery. They should, by now, be learning to bend over and grab their ankles whenever they see large men with cauliflower ears and a fundamental yearning approaching down the corridor. The bankers who oversaw the disastrous fall of Northern Rock, RBS, HBOS, etc., have mostly found highly-paid employment. They helped cause the economic mess which will now dominate our lives for decades but they are largely immune to the consequences. Even the appalling Fred Goodwin ('the world's worst banker'), who would, in a decently run society, now be prisoner 628362 serving a long sentence in Wormwood Scrubs, has found new employment. (It is worth remembering that his bank, RBS, reported pretax losses of almost £41 billion in 2008.) Goodwin should have been put into the stocks for a week, dragged through the high street of every town in England, pelted with household rubbish and sewage and then taken to court and sentenced to a lifetime in a small, bare cell. All Goodwin's chums in the banking world should have received the same treatment. But the difference between what should have happened and what really happened is vast. In 2012, the banks in England were paying out still increasing amounts of money on salaries and bonuses, leaving next to nothing (and in many cases nothing) for the owners (and bosses) of the banks. There are, literally, thousands of bankers in London who are paid over £1,000,000 a year. But I wouldn't trust any one of these idiots to go to the post office and buy me a stamp. If I had a stamp and asked one of their absurdly overpaid idiots to stick it on they would, I have no doubt, somehow manage to stick it on upside down. These, remember, are idiots who can borrow money at 1%, lend it out 30 times at 20% and still make a loss. That's quite a skill. Rioters in London were (rightly) sentenced to two years imprisonment for stealing a pair of pumps. But Goodwin receives £700,000 a year for life for helping to bankrupt the nation. He is not alone. Matt Ridley, of Northern Rock shame, still seems to think his institution failed through 'bad luck'. None of the guilty bankers seems to have exchanged their expensive suits for sackcloth and ashes.

American born London mayor Boris Johnson has said that it is time to stop abusing the bankers. He is, as he usually is, quite wrong. If our economy ever recovers it will be despite the banks rather than because of them. They are still sucking the life blood out of the system. Their staff, like bloated leeches, are never satisfied.

1

During the banking meltdown of 2007 and 2008, top bankers argued that if pay and bonuses were cut for their staff, and if the traditional `heads we win, tails you lose' philosophy were ended, the banks would have difficulty in keeping their good people. It did not occur to them that companies which go bankrupt are not, by definition, run by competent people. It was, perhaps, not entirely surprising that bankers failed to see the flaw in their pathetic argument. I did, however, find it alarming that regulators and politicians also failed to see the flaw. No banker explained precisely what their staff members would do for a living if they were dumped from jobs carrying multi million pound a year salaries. (I think it is fair to assume that none of them was likely to be in line for the only other overpaid employment - as professional footballers.) I cannot think of any easier job than being a banker. Even being a catwalk model or a newsreader probably requires more talent.

2

Bankers, chief executives and EU staff members seem to enjoy flaunting their wealth. They are, on the whole, enjoying the delights of conspicuous waste at someone else's expense. I read this morning about someone who had used a private jet to fly her dog to the doggie stylist for a trim. And I hear that £50,000 birthday parties for children are, in banking circles, now considered rather commonplace.

3

It is not only bankers who are enjoying a ride on an overloaded gravy train. The staff of organisations such as the International Monetary Fund do pretty well too. For example, the boss of the IMF receives a salary of $467,940 plus additional allowances of $83,760. And, like all staff at the IMF she pays no tax whatsoever. (This makes it rather difficult for the IMF to complain about people, such as the citizens of Greece, who also prefer not to pay any taxes.)

4

`It's Goldman Sach's world - we just live in it.' - Barry Ritholtz of Fusion IQ

5

Long after RBS had been rescued by English taxpayers the Scottish bank was still sponsoring the Scottish rugby team. Was I the only Englishman to be more than slightly peeved by this? If you are ever looking for a definition of irony or barefaced cheek try this: when Scotland played England in the Six Nations Cup, the Scottish team was sponsored by RBS. Remember, RBS, surely the world's worst bank, was rescued at enormous cost by English taxpayers and is now owned by English taxpayers. And it was rescued to save Scotland from a mess, to save Scottish politicians from embarrassment and so that Gordon Brown could prove that he was sticking to The Scottish Claim of Rights. Sitting in the stands there were, I suspect, more than a few RBS employees enjoying English taxpayers' hospitality while they cheered on Scotland.

6

RBS has turned into a catastrophe. The £49 billion spent by Brown to buy the loyalty of Scottish voters has gone down the drain. So has the additional £40 billion taxpayers have forked out to keep alive a worthless, overleveraged institution built on the vanity of the world's worst banker and a bunch of clowns which made poorly designed acquisitions. Executives at the bank are still encouraged to back trucks up the vault door and fill them with packets of brand new fifties. A bunch of illiterate hoodies high on cheap lager could have run the bank more efficiently and probably even made a profit. And yet the idiots who are working there are still being rewarded like heroes. Moreover, bankers at RBS are constantly whingeing about the fact that the Government (which damned near owns the bank on behalf of taxpayers) wants to interfere with the running of the bank and the distribution of bonuses. I don't understand this. The bank went bust. The people running it screwed up. And now RBS complains because the owners want the right to say how the bank is managed. Isn't that what company owners are supposed to do? The truth is that the long-serving executives working at RBS don't deserve a salary let alone a bonus.

7

Thanks to morons like Gordon Brown the booms and busts are getting worse. As Karl Marx predicted it is the booms and busts that will cause our ruin. Sadly, our current bust is not going to be followed by a boom.

8

Bankers got away with their absurdly incompetent behaviour because over-lobbied politicians have for years been far too banker friendly. The Labour Party of Blair and Brown was desperately close to the bankers. And the Coalition Government is owned by the finance industry too. (Clegg's daddy? You have three guesses: fishmonger, male model or banker. If you chose anything other than banker I am very disappointed in you.) More than half of the Tory Party's funding comes from bankers. It has been hardly surprising that our recent governments have bent over forwards to accommodate the needs of the people who have cost us untold billions. Not one banker, let me remind you, has been fined or sent to prison. Our so-called leaders have, on the contrary, stayed on good terms with most of them. The bankers must be blinking with astonishment at the fact that they have got away with the biggest heist in history. Moreover, bankers still don't understand the meaning of the word responsibility. In June 2012, the Royal Bank of Scotland managed to create chaos for 17 million customers. For six days those customers could not access their own money. It turned out that someone at RBS had decided to change the bank's software system while it was operating. (This was later described as being akin to an airline trying to service an engine with the plane flying at 30,000 feet.) Afterwards, in what I assume he intended to be a sign of contrition, the boss, the man responsible for this fiasco, offered to forgo his annual bonus. The humungous error, which left people hungry and unable to pay their bills, was described by the bank as a `glitch'. I bet they wouldn't have described it as a `glitch' if everyone earning more than £50,000 a year had been sacked. The basic problem, of course, is that the Royal Bank of Scotland is now a State-owned institution. And this creates three problems. First, the people who work for RBS are civil servants and, like civil servants working for the NHS or the Royal Mail, they don't give a damn about members of the public. Second, all State-run businesses turn into a shambles in the end. Third, the Government seems unable to operate any sort of computer system without producing huge problems. The NHS paid around £12 billion for a computer system that didn't work and wasn't ever likely to work. (Simply putting everyone's medical records onto Facebook would have been quicker, free and just as private.) The Inland Revenue makes endless errors with its computerised records and when it isn't making mistakes it simply loses millions of confidential tax records at a time. Now that RBS has become a State-run enterprise it is, perhaps, hardly surprising that it is an even greater shambles.

9

The banking disaster proves (if there was ever any doubt) that we live in a kleptocracy. There are more democratic banana republics around. Everything is run for the politicians and the bankers whose interests must be protected. We are even importing more highly-paid bankers because they are, apparently, essential immigrants. Maybe our home-grown bankers can't screw up the economy adequately without outside help. If you or I made the sort of egregious errors bankers and politicians have made we would be limbering up our fingers for some long-term mailbag sewing. But bankers and politicians simply demand bonuses and forgiveness. `Whoops, sorry pardon,' they mutter. `Simple human mistake.' And that, it seems, makes everything fine. I must try that next time I'm in trouble for doing 61 mph on a dual carriageway.

Taxpayers are having to bail out banks so that the people who work there don't suffer. Taxes are being used to cover the private losses of investment banks. It seems to me that capitalism has collapsed and has been replaced by a particularly nasty version of statism or socialism.

10

When I was young, people called me a gambler. As the scale of my operations increased I was known as a speculator. Now I'm called a banker. But I have been doing the same thing all the time.' - Sir Ernest Cassel, private banker to King Edward VII

11

During the last half a dozen years, when the world's banks stuffed the rest of us, only the American bank Lehman Brothers was allowed to go bust. (In the years during which he 'destroyed' the firm, the boss, Fuld, received $484 million in salary and other payments. This was by no means an abnormal level of compensation.) A zillion other banks shared lorry loads of free taxpayers' money so that they could stay in business and keep paying salaries and bonuses. (Goldman Sachs boasted that it required no government bailout. The truth is, however, that the world's worst company did receive $69 billion from the Federal Reserve. Maybe $69 billion wasn't a big enough sum to appear in the Goldman Sachs accounts. Or maybe they've got into the habit of lying so much that they just couldn't help themselves.)

If you or I take a gamble and we lose money then we lose money. If it's a big gamble we go bust. If we listen to the advice of our investment adviser and lose money then we lose money. If we invest in a badly regulated pension fund we get stuffed and lose our pension. But the bankers can't lose. If they make money they win and they keep it. If they lose money the taxpayers cough up and the bankers use the bail out money to give themselves bonuses.

It is unbelievable but true that in the weeks after the start of the financial crash in 2007, bankers in London received around £12 billion in bonuses. More than 4,200 individual bankers received bonuses of at least £1.5 million each, on top of their multi million pound salaries. This, remember, was immediately after the banks had to be bailed out because some of them had gone bankrupt. This was in London alone. And much of this money was handed over to bankers working at Scottish banks that had gone bankrupt; people who should have been receiving writs and jail sentences, not bonuses. A teenage hoodie who smashes a car window and steals a radio will be punished. A driver who causes an accident while talking on his mobile telephone should expect to go to prison. A businessman who doesn't realise that the tax laws have changed and pays too little tax can expect to have the full wrath of the courts wrapped around his neck. But none of the bankers who caused financial mayhem in England has been punished. These selfish, shameless idiots wrecked businesses and destroyed savings. Today's bankers and investment advisers will always act exclusively in their own interests and never in the interests of their customers or clients. They always think short-term and are always incurably greedy. (The question remains: `Why does a man or woman who has £100 million in the bank still feel so greedy that they must steal another £100 million?')

Millions of innocent people have been deeply affected by the greed and stupidity of the bankers. I have no doubt that some people were killed by the stress the bankers caused. There were probably banker-induced suicides. But the bankers have been protected from the law by their political friends, their lobbyists and their wealth. Savers, pensioners and those on fixed incomes have seen their savings disappear so that those with financial incontinence could be saved from the consequences of their actions.

Why aren't hard-working people rioting in the streets, hanging bankers from lampposts and burning down the damned banks? (I'm not recommending that people should do any of these things, you understand. Just curious as to why they aren't.)

12

The number of individuals who say they trust Government institutions has, in recent years, fallen to around a third. (Given that a large number of people earn their living from the Government this figure is extraordinarily high.) Similarly only about a third of the population regard business bosses as credible, or worth their money. But for banks the figure is even lower and studies show that it is now almost impossible to discover anyone in the country who trusts, or has respect for, bank executives and directors. The fact that bankers are forever protesting that they are misunderstood makes not one jot of difference. Most people now trust bank staff less than they trust second-hand care salesmen and estate agents. And rightly so.

13

The structure of our once stable economy was destroyed by Gordon Brown. (I explained why and how in terrifying detail in my book *Gordon is a Moron,* which is now out of print but which should be available in well-run charity shops and in the car boots of discerning Sunday salespersons.)

Brown has been responsible for destroying the lives of millions of honest, hard-working citizens. He deserves to be hung for his crimes. Or at the very least drawn and quartered. No, that's too light. He, together with his banker pals, should be put in the stocks, whipped, stoned, burned, buried, dug up and subjected to the whole damned process until hell freezes over or a politician tells the truth whichever is the sooner.

14

In my book *What Happens Next?* I suggested that high street banks and investment banks should be kept separate, so that depositors' money wasn't at risk. The Government has accepted the suggestion but isn't likely to act on it until 2019 at the earliest because investment bankers have protested that if the new rule is introduced they'll have to gamble with their *own* money.

15

Today, nothing has changed. The banks are still poorly regulated. The accounting rules are still weak. The bankers are still allowed to lie, cheat, steal and be unbearably stupid. Modern bankers think up amazing ways to cheat their customers. They will, it seems, do anything and everything to gouge more money out of the trusting, the susceptible and the honest. For example, banks and building societies offer special deposit accounts for the over 50s. You might imagine that since these accounts are described as 'special' and are limited to a particular age group, the bankers would be offering some sort of incentive, a bonus attraction. Not a bit of it. The average interest rate on the most popular 20 accounts for the over 50s is, as I write, around two thirds of the average overall interest rate on offer. In the early summer of 2012, an investor who put money into a top paying deposit account could expect, on average, to earn (a miserly) 3.17% interest. But an investor who put money into a special deposit account designed for the over 50s would receive, on average, an interest rate of 2.23%.

Our banks have huge debts and poor assets and they're getting weaker and less solvent by the week. Most banks have overstated their assets. They have lied, lied and lied again and are in a far worse mess than we can imagine. The banks aren't going to want to lend money to strangers for a long, long time.

16

In 2012, as England sank deeper into economic chaos caused largely by daft bankers, it was estimated that 200 staff at Barclays would receive bonuses of at least £1,000,000 each. One bank. Two hundred employees. All receiving a million pound bonus. What did they do for that money? Hand out paying in books? Fill up the ATMs? Three Barclay's employees shared £100 million in bonuses. If they shared it equally they received £33 million each.

Barclays' boss, an American called Diamond, moaned about the use of words such as `casino banking' and `rogue trading' to describe what goes on in our banks. He boasted that `we have some fantastically strong financial institutions in this country' but he didn't explain how strong financial institutions had cost England the best part of £1,000,000,000 and nor did he name the strong institutions. He certainly could not have been talking about Barclays because although the bank had paid him £50 million in salary, bonuses and sweet allowances its share price had slumped by 80% in five years. I wonder if the shareholders think Diamond was worth all that loot. In March 2012, Diamond finally described the bank's performance as unacceptable. Nevertheless, he was given a pay package of £17.7 million, including a multi million bonus. He happily accepted all this loot. The bank also paid a tax bill of £5.75 million for him so that he didn't have to pay it himself out of his miserly pay packet. No one mentioned it but they presumably paid for someone to chew his food for him too.

17

The world is awash with wasteful, crooked governments, insolvent, badly run banks (fraudulently giving illusions of solvency), overleveraged companies struggling to compete with companies in emerging economies, rising millions who are unemployed, millions who have huge credit card debts which they cannot possibly pay back and millions whose homes are worth far less than the debt owed to the mortgage company. The future is bleak. It is going to be difficult (a euphemism for damned near impossible) for investors to make any money in these circumstances. And people need to take care with their savings, to invest cautiously and to do whatever they can to preserve what is left of their wealth in order to help them survive the harder times which lie ahead. It was, therefore, with some horror that I spotted a Barclays Bank advertisement in February 2012 which screamed: 'Why wait? Have it now.' How very irresponsible. How very Barclays.

18

Meanwhile, and rather frighteningly, Barclays is building up its debts. The bank, once regarded as safe and even dull, has leverage of 33 times, and institutions with that sort of leverage can get into real trouble very quickly. Barclays currently has £1.6 trillion on its balance sheet, more than our country's entire annual output of goods and services.

Credit given to bankers or investors is like steroids or amphetamines when given to an athlete. A bit of it helps performance and, although extremely dangerous, seems harmless enough. Since everyone is doing it no one thinks anything much of it. And so usage increases. And is eventually deadly.

19

No one can argue that bankers are highly-paid because they are clever or good at what they do. They aren't either. And bankers today are as arrogant, cruel, self-serving and deluded as they ever were. Most of all they are still greedy and stupid.

20

Here's the way the EU is operating at the moment. Commercial banks (many of which are either bankrupt or knocking on the door of bankruptcy) lend money to the European Central Bank so that it can use the money to bail out bankrupt countries such as Greece and Ireland. These bankrupt countries need the money so that they can bail out their own bankrupt banks. So our banks (some of which are owned by taxpayers) are bailing out the bankrupt banks in bankrupt countries. And it seems that there are an endless number of bankrupt banks hanging around outside the ECB with their begging bowls, waiting for a few billion euros. I sincerely wish I was making this up but, sadly, I'm not. The ECB is lending this money to European banks at 1%. In February 2012, Scotland's great bank, RBS, borrowed five billion euros of this virtually free European money and still can't make a profit. I don't know about you but if I could borrow endless money at 1% interest I would buy Tesco bonds at 5% or gilts at 3%. Oh, silly me, that's what they do. It's no wonder they don't want to bother making loans to small businesses which might need help, guidance and money. (But how do they make a loss, you ask? Surely they can't possibly not make a profit. Look at the salaries and bonuses they pay out, I reply.)

21

The number of clients at the State owned bank RBS went down from 26,000 to 5,000 after Goodwin and his pals destroyed the company, so the bank reduced its staff from 24,000 incompetent buffoons to 19,000 incompetent buffoons. Look at the figures and you may feel you need to scratch your head. There are still over 1,000 individuals at RBS earning (or, rather, being paid) over £1,000,000 each a year. Plus huge bonuses. In 2010, RBS (84% owned by taxpayers, which makes its employees civil servants) handed out bonuses of £1 billion, despite making a £1 billion loss.

22

RBS lost money, jobs, reputation and everything else a group of bankers can possibly lose and yet it is still constantly offering investment advice to the world at large. Who the hell takes any notice of anything anyone working for RBS has to say?

23

At the end of May 2012, the chairman of the Royal Bank of Scotland (Sir Philip Hampton - and what the blazes did he do to deserve a knighthood?) told the bank's investors that they may never recoup the losses they had suffered. `I don't think shareholders' wealth is likely to be restored any time in my lifetime or some lifetimes beyond,' he said. A few days later it was leaked that the Government was planning to give RBS a few more billion of taxpayers' money. As my Princess pointed out it is extremely unlikely that if the bank had been called the Royal Bank of England it would have received a penny in support. RBS was saved solely for political reasons. And it was saved by Gordon Brown, a Scotsman who had signed a document in which he promised that he would always put Scotland first. And, yet again, it was English taxpayers who paid the price.

24

While cautious, prudent, hard-working savers and taxpayers suffer in order to help pay back the debts incurred while their governments were running things, Blair and Brown are earning vast sums for advising and lecturing the world on financial matters. Brown receives £60,000 for lecturing on finance (which must surely be the new definition of chutzpa) while Blair's cheques usually have more noughts. Any sensible person who is not now tempted to become an anarchist should receive medical attention.

25

Banks have become so accustomed to gambling with other people's money that they are now encouraging people to gamble with their own money. In February 2012, I saw an advert for spread trading (a form of betting) from the Halifax. `Now there's a way to make the most of markets that fall as well as rise' promised the advert. The Halifax is, of course, a part of one of the bankrupt Scottish banks, so at least they know a lot about market falls.

What I find astonishing is that our Government, which effectively owns this sorry organisation, is encouraging people to gamble with whatever savings they have left.

26

Iceland didn't support its banks when they went bust in 2008. They didn't bail them out because they couldn't afford to. Iceland is now relatively healthy again. Creative destruction is a vital form of therapy for mouldy capitalism.

27

In early 2012, the difference between bank rate (0.5%) and the ordinary overdraft rate (19.5) was higher than ever before. Not surprisingly, two thirds of Britons admitted that they were worried about their levels of debt. It was surprising, however, to discover that the banks could still not make a profit - even with a guaranteed 19% gross profit on every loan.

Bankers constantly claim that they need to pay huge salaries for staff in order to attract the brains they need.

I would have thought that recruiting a bunch of cretins and morons would prove more efficacious. Even they would surely be able to make a profit under such advantageous circumstances.

28

In late June 2012, it was revealed that thieves working at Barclays Bank (surely one of the most irresponsible institutions on the planet) had deliberately altered LIBOR (the rate at which banks lend money to one another and, therefore, to businesses and individuals) to benefit themselves. Other banks were almost certainly involved in this blatantly fraudulent activity (possibly including two banks largely owned by English taxpayers) and there have even been suggestions that someone at the Bank of England might have been in some way involved in the decision to make money out of cheating taxpayers, savers, pensioners, mortgage holders and just about every other English citizen. The result was that shareholders in Barclays Bank were fined £290 million. That's a perfect example of moral hazard. The bankers steal and, when they get caught, the shareholders pay the price. The thieving villains who had deceived, cheated and stolen have not been imprisoned or even fined and I doubt if they will be. How much did they steal? How much did they try to steal? Billions. It was one of the most fundamental betrayals in banking history. (As an aside, the responsible thieves must be among the most stupid people on the planet. They conducted their thieving by e-mail.) In one of the most empty gestures of all time, the American boss of Barclays, Bob Diamond, originally said that he would waive some or part of his bonus for the year. Well, yippee. That was rather like an 18-year-old burglar, who had stolen money from a thousand elderly widows, offering to give up sweets for a day in recompense. Diamond, after some inappropriate resistance, eventually resigned but the entire contents of the executive suite at Barclays should have been arrested, tried and sent to prison for life. And every penny they'd earned from banking should have been confiscated before they were tried so that they couldn't afford fancy lawyers. The failure of the bank to understand just how banking has to change was illustrated by the fact that when he resigned in disgrace the hubristic Diamond was rumoured to have taken with him a £2 million pay off. Was he party to major league crookery or an incompetent buffoon who didn't know what was going on at his bank? I have no idea but any severance payment was entirely inappropriate and undeserved and simply served to further damage the already flimsy level of trust in our banks.

29

Lloyds Bank, once a decent and profitable enterprise, was wrecked by the merger with HBOS because of absurdly reckless lending by Bank of Scotland bankers. (It seems that both RBS and HBOS bankers had been contaminated by something in the Scottish air and had gone quite mad. Traditional Scottish meanness had somehow been transformed into egregious greed.) When it was decided that the combined bank needed to lose a lot of lower paid staff, thousands of employees at Lloyds Bank branches were sacked. To add insult to injury the EU then forced Lloyds to sell hundreds of branches against the wishes of three million long-standing, long-suffering customers.

30

Speaking in Glasgow in November 2011, Scotsman Alistair Darling, the former Chancellor of the Exchequer who authorised the multi-billion bail outs of Scottish banks RBS and HBOS, said that the banking crisis didn't happen because of subprime market problems but because of bad decisions taken by Scottish bankers - bankers who are now enjoying huge billionaire lifestyles on their payoffs, pensions and bonuses.

If the Scots truly want independence (and I sincerely hope they do) then they will owe England about a trillion pounds for saving their damned banks. (In reality, of course, an organisation called SNP, representing the meanest and nastiest of Scots and the main proponents of independence, want to keep England's oil and dump the toxic Scottish banks on England. (Much of the North Sea oil is in English water and the wells were developed by English companies and by English taxpayers.) To be fair, I don't blame the Scots for trying to grab what they can. If I could declare independence and keep all my money while donating my debts to some dumb Scotsman I would do so in a flash. The reality is that the current Scottish nation is built on health and social work, education, administration and defence and social security. All public sector work. There is very little industry remaining north of Carlisle. There is a little bit of tartan kilt manufacture and a few whisky distilleries but that's about it.

31

People who work in fish shops probably take home a lot of fish. People who work in bookshops are undoubtedly rarely short of a good book to read. And people who work in investment banks take home samples too. They've rigged the rules so that it doesn't seem like stealing: but by any sensible interpretation of the rules that's exactly what it is. Today, the bank robbers are the people working inside the bank.

32

Central banks such as the Bank of England seem to be working for and on behalf of the big banks and hedge funds. They are destroying the lives of hard-working taxpayers (their employers) in order to preserve the financial system.

33

'I believe that banking institutions are more dangerous to our liberties than standing armies. If the American people ever allow private banks to control the issue of their currency, first by inflation, then by deflation, the banks and corporations that will grow up around the banks will deprive the people of all property until their children wake up homeless on the continent their fathers conquered.' - Thomas Jefferson

34

In March 2012, when Cameron went to the USA to meet Obama he also met the boss of Goldman Sachs, the world's most reviled financial institution. (He may, for all I know, have gone to the USA to meet the guy from Goldman Sachs and just bumped into Obama as an afterthought.) Whenever there is news of financial malpractice there is, it seems, always an alumni of Goldman Sachs in there somewhere. Goldman Sachs might have died if the Federal Reserve (stuffed to the gills with Goldman alumni) hadn't allowed the firm to convert itself into a bank so that it could borrow emergency funds from taxpayers (the villains at Goldman Sachs afterwards claimed that they hadn't borrowed anything). Goldman Sachs alumni are all over the world in positions of great power. Italy is being run by an ex Goldman Sachs employee. The head of Greece's debt management agency began there. The president of the ECB was employed by Goldman until 2006. Henry M. Paulson, who was George W. Bush's Secretary of the Treasury from July 2006 until January 2009 had spent the previous 32 years working at Goldman Sachs. And, of course, it was Goldman Sachs who helped Greece cook the books and deceive the rest of the world about its economy. Goldman Sachs has done as much as any other organisation to create the world's economic problem. And now they're 'helping' to put things right. The current CEO of Goldman is 'worth' around $450 million. If we must be at war with someone we should be at war with Goldman Sachs. We would have all been a lot better off (financially and spiritually) if, instead of waging war in Iraq, Afghanistan and Libya our spineless leaders had declared war on the loathsome Goldman Sachs and the bosses of RBS, HBOS and a couple of dozen other similarly obscene financial outfits.

35

When Matt Ridley, the vastly overpaid former chairman of the failed bank Northern Rock, was questioned by MPs after his bank had collapsed (the first bank run for 150 years) Ridley moaned: `The idea that all markets would close simultaneously was unforeseen by any major authority. We were hit by an unexpected and unpredictable concatenation of events.'

With people like Ridley at the helm it is hardly surprising that our banks collapsed. If people didn't expect the unexpected (and make plans accordingly) they would never buy insurance. Every imaginative and cautious investor knows that you have to expect the unexpected. It's what investing is all about. It's what life is about, for heaven's sake.

The collapse of Northern Rock added around £100 billion to our debts.

36

Here's yet more proof that the people who work in investment banking are, at best, half-wits. These people operate by making trades. One of the half-wits sells something and another half-wit buys it. It's hardly brain surgery. It's like shopping except that you don't have to go anywhere to do it. You just sit there and peck away at a computer keyboard or hold a telephone to your ear. And yet they get these simple trades wrong with ruthless efficiency. Every day, on Wall Street, the traders make over $500 billion worth of failed trades. They get it wrong to the tune of half a trillion dollars a day. An old lady who made that many mistakes when out shopping would be quietly taken into care for her own protection.

37

Even the banks that haven't gone bankrupt have still managed to make huge errors. It seems commonplace now for banks to admit that an employee has lost a few billion pounds in error. These are big, big banks with risk management systems and backroom people paid to keep an eye on things. And yet they manage to lose billions of pounds before anyone notices. These days a mistake involving only a couple of billion doesn't really attract much attention. You have to lose £5 billion or so to make anyone take notice. Only idiots operating in chaos could consistently screw up as much as the bankers screw up.

38

One half-witted bank employee was offered a special $50 million bonus because one of his bets had paid off. He was so insulted by this derisory offer that he walked out.

39

Bankers like you to think that the money they lend out is the money that has been deposited with them for safe keeping. Mrs A takes her savings of £1,000 to the bank and puts it into a deposit account. This is real money which she has earned by scrubbing floors. The bank then lends that £1,000 to Mrs B so that she can buy a new house, a new car and a new coat. But the bank also lends the £1,000 to Mrs C, Mrs D, Mrs E, Mrs F, Mrs G, Mrs H, Mrs I, Mrs J and so on down the alphabet. The same £1,000 is lent out many, many times.

The money which is deposited is real. But the money the banks lend out is created money and so the banks lend out vastly more money than has been deposited with them. The argument is that all the depositors are unlikely to want their money back at once and so the real money which they have can be lent out many, many times. (When there is a panic, à la Northern Rock, the Government steps in and bails out the bank with taxpayers' money.)

The bottom line is that the bankers are being paid interest, fees and penalties on far more money than actually exists because the money they lent was simply created out of thin air.

In return for the loan of its imaginary money the bank receives real money from Mrs B (and the rest of the alphabet). Moreover, if Mrs B cannot pay the interest on what she has borrowed the bank will take the house, the car and the coat from her. And if she has had to provide other security they will keep that too.

On the face of it, it is difficult to see why the banks aren't making a fortune for their shareholders. As I write this the big clearing banks are paying many of their depositors interest of less than 1% on the real money which has been deposited. And they are routinely charging 20% on the money they lend out. So the bank has £1,000 on deposit from Mrs A and pays 1% a year interest. And it lends out that £1,000 to Mrs B, Mrs C, Mrs D and so on. And charges 20% a year interest from each of them.

How, you might think, can banks possibly not make a profit?

The answer is as simple as it is shocking.

Over the last six years seven of the world's largest banks have generated pre tax profits of $124 billion but during the same period they paid their staff $362 billion. In other words the banks paid their staff almost three times as much as their entire profits leaving huge debts and nothing left for improving the business or paying shareholders.

Incidentally, the profits should have been much, much higher. All those interest payments from Mrs A and millions like her add up to quite a chunk of change. But the bankers used the money they were taking in for their own `investments'. The bankers could do this because the banks have special departments which make investments in complex financial instruments which no one much understands. Mrs A's money isn't put into a vault and protected. It is the basis for all those loans to Mrs B, Mrs C and the rest of them. Plus the bankers use Mrs A's money as seed money for the gambling and they leverage up the money they have by taking huge gambles. The bankers are keen to do this because if the bank makes a profit with Mrs A's money they are paid huge additional bonuses. And if the bank loses some or all of Mrs A's hard earned money the bankers still get their salaries and are still paid bonuses for trying. It's a no risk gamble. Unfortunately, in recent years the bankers have proved to be extraordinarily inept at making investment gambles. They have lost billions. The men and women who threaten to go elsewhere if they are not paid millions of pounds in bonuses for losing money are stupid and incompetent beyond belief. Where did the money go to, you may ask. Well, much of it went to the people running hedge funds who turned out to be much smarter than the people working for the banks.) So, that's exactly why the banks went bust.

And that is why the Government had to use taxpayers' money to bail out the banks so that Mrs A didn't realise that her money had disappeared.

You might think that the Government would have insisted that the banks change their ways and stop paying out more than they were making. You might have imagined that the politicians would say to the bankers: `Hey, you morons, stop using Mrs A's money for your gambling. If you want to gamble use your own damned money. And no more million pound bonuses for losing money.'

Not a bit of it.

40

In the simple old days a bank would make a loan and manage it. Employees at the bank (ones who wore smart dark suits made in Savile Row, rather than flashy Italian silk rubbish) were responsible for approving the loans and for making sure that the customers were sound. If something went wrong action could be taken quickly. Today, the derivatives market means that no one checks, no one cares and no one knows who has lent what to whom. But the bank bosses, like robber barons, take money from everywhere, impoverishing their shareholders and the lesser workers. And the banks have created a bizarre parallel world for themselves in order to delay the embarrassing consequences of their actions. So, for example, if an official for a large, international company or a country somewhere goes to a bank and says: 'Sorry, lads, but we can no longer pay the interest on our debt, let alone pay back any of the loan' the bank's response will be to say: 'Don't worry. We will lend you some more money so that you can pay back the interest on the first loan, the interest on the new loan and also pay back some of the first loan.' And that is exactly what has been happening for the last few years. The banks benefit because they can say to the world that they have good assets, good loans and good borrowers who are paying back what they have been lent. The problem will come in the future, of course.

41

In a healthy society there is a gradual transfer of wealth from those who borrow to those who do not borrow. In our society low interest rates and high inflation have produced the opposite effect. That's not healthy. It discourages thrift and prudence and encourages waste and Brownian economics.

42

Toyota's long established financial rule No 1 is: 'Other people's money, borrowed money, quickly turns into an enemy. Money is a trustworthy ally only when you earn it yourself.' I think it's safe to assume that Fred Goodwin never worked at Toyota.

43

Economists, politicians and bankers all sneer at the idea of a gold standard. Of course they do. They hate gold because it is something they cannot control. But if countries were forced to link their currencies to gold then everyone would benefit. Oh, everyone except economists, politicians and bankers. You don't think that could be why they object to the idea do you?

If countries had to link their currency to the amount of gold in their national vaults then central banks would be forced to control their printing of money and their lending. Debt bubbles would not develop, inflation would be controlled and solid investment would be encouraged.

Politicians hate the idea of being constrained by their nation's gold stocks because being free to print as much money as they like enables them to take control of every aspect of their country's economy. By printing money they can devalue the currency (this upsets people who have saved their money but it helps exporters) and they can eradicate the nation's debts by increasing inflation.

Bankers hate gold because if they can't create money out of nothing their profits will be severely limited.

And economists hate gold because if currencies have to be fixed to gold and the amount of a currency available is linked directly to the amount of gold stored then there will be very little opportunity for chaos. And without chaos there will be nothing for economists to do. (For decades many of them have made their living out of commenting on and making forecasts about national finances. They are invariably wrong but that doesn't seem to stop people hiring them.)

44

As recently as the 1980s, banking was a dull business. Banks were solid, trustworthy businesses suitable, as investments, for little old ladies, widows and orphans. Men in striped trousers and frock coats looked after their customers' savings and lent money to solid, respectable businessmen and home buyers. In those good old days bankers followed the 3.6.3. system. They borrowed at 3 %, they lent at 6% and they were on the golf course at 3 p.m. But the customers weren't cheated. And taxpayers didn't have to bail out the banks.

But, almost overnight, banking went from dull to a credit fuelled spending spree. Bankers were suddenly teenagers enjoying a bank holiday weekend at the fair. Everyone leaving university wanted to become a banker and become very rich.

In 1980 the big four banks (Barclays, HSBC (including Midland), Lloyds and Royal Bank of Scotland (including National Westminster) were stable, boring and reliable. Customers and shareholders felt that they were `safe'. By 2012 those same banks had become anything but stable and definitely weren't reliable. Neither customers nor shareholders felt that they were `safe'. In 1980 all the directors of those banks were English. By 2012 a third of them were foreign (many, heaven forbid, American.)

45

In the old world people got rich through building up businesses, discovering oil or buying and improving old properties. It was easy to argue that those people deserved to get rich. And easy to argue, too, that what they did helped the world around them. Today, talentless people get rich through luck and leverage and through gambling with other people's money (heads we win, tails you lose). There is little hard work, little inspiration and no social worth. Today there is, it seems, no part of the banking system that is not corrupt, fraudulent and working against the interests of private investors and pensioners.

46

Most of the banks in London are American owned. The staff and the banks pay little or no tax to our Government.

47

In most companies it is traditional for the owners, the people who take the risks, to take the biggest share of the profits. In the film world it is the producer who makes the big money. In the shipping industry it is the ship owners who get very rich. But in banking it is the gambling traders and the bosses who make all the money. The owners (the shareholders) just take the risks. That's not a fair or sustainable form of business.

48

Between the years 2005 and 2010 HSBC deliberately missold unsuitable financial products to nearly 2,500 customers (average age 83), selling them bonds designed to fund long-term care. In reality the customers were too old and too ill to benefit from the bonds because there was a high penalty if the five year bond was redeemed early. (Not surprisingly a number of the 83-year-olds found that they needed the money for care before the five year period was up.) The bank was fined £10.5 million for this fraud. The shareholders paid the fine. The bankers who did the selling were not punished. They kept their salaries and bonuses. Why was this fraud not investigated by the police? Why were the perpetrators not arrested, charged, convicted and imprisoned? When is a fraud not a fraud? When it's conducted by a bank. When banks and insurance companies commit heinous crimes against innocent, trusting members of the public, it is always the shareholders who pay the fines. The bankers who committed the frauds, and who benefitted by receiving huge bonuses, suffer not at all. Other banks sold unemployment insurance to the self-employed knowing that self-employed customers couldn't claim on the policies. Why aren't these bankers in prison? The bottom line is simple: don't ever believe anything anyone at a bank tells you. Modern bankers are commission driven crooks.

49

When Lloyds Bank had the bright idea of buying HBOS (one of the Scottish banks which had gone bust as a result of a mixture of greed and incompetence) I wonder if they realised exactly what a crock they were buying. Did they realise that HBOS had managed to lose £10 billion in one year? If they knew this then the bosses of Lloyds should have been arrested for going ahead with the deal. If they didn't know this then they should have been arrested for failing to protect their shareholders.

50

An executive director at the Bank of England has described the banking industry as a pollutant.

51

When Goldman Sachs was accused by a former employee of ripping off clients, a columnist in the *Financial Times* wrote: `surely there isn't a commercial enterprise in the world that doesn't set out to do this' (rip off clients).

If that is the world that *Financial Times* staff inhabit then I find that quite depressing. It's not a world I want to inhabit.

52

American finance organisations are now targeting the English poor. They are lending money to people who cannot get loans from traditional banks and charging 5,000% interest. One company currently advertising loans on television proudly announces that it has an APR of 4,214%. These usurious practices are, apparently, perfectly legal.

53

When Napoleon returned from Austria, where he had been launching his campaign against the Austro-Russian alliance (and probably promoting his new book, film and CD) there was a run on the Banque de France which was almost forced into liquidation as a result. Napoleon immediately summoned his council of ministers and fired his Minister of Finance. He then offered the three man management committee a choice between prison or a fine of 87 million francs. (They chose the fine).

54

Lloyds bank was recently named Bank of the Year. This was presumably because it won the competition for getting most complaints, cheating the most customers and being almost bankrupt. But I don't understand. RBS has lost even more money and cost taxpayers more. So, why didn't RBS get the award?

55

Anyone could run a bank. It's not as if it's as hard as being a paediatric cardiologist, opening the batting for England or even cleaning public lavatories (not that that is something anyone does any more). It is quite true that modern banks have some very complicated products. But the staff don't understand them. History has clearly shown that the intricacies and problems of collateral swaps, security lending and counterparty risks are underestimated and poorly understood - even by the people who created them and sold them.

56

If I am paid to look after a neighbour's £100 but I put the money on a horse and the horse loses I am responsible. Morally and legally the loss of the money is my responsibility. This doesn't work for bankers. They can put your money on a horse, lose it and walk away with no penalty.

57

In 2009, the *Financial Times* named Lloyd Blankfein, the CEO of Goldman Sachs, as its person of the year. This probably tells us more about the *Financial Times* than Blankfein who would, in a decent world, be on America's Most Wanted List.

58

It hasn't only been commercial bankers who have betrayed our trust. Central bankers have, if anything, done even more damage. The Bank of England has for three years either been run by highly-paid rolls of carpet or its taxpayer-funded employees have been deliberately using inflation to get rid of the nation's debts. The Bank has consistently missed its own inflation targets so badly that there are only two possible conclusions: either the people running the Bank are half-witted morons of the Gordon Brown variety or else they have been deliberately misleading the nation about inflation and then allowing inflation rates to rise.

Inflating away the nation's debts may be a slick, sleazy and efficient way to get rid of Gordon Brown's reckless, imprudent extravagances but it has had a massive effect on the citizens.

The individuals who helped create the financial crisis by greedily borrowing far more money than they could pay back have benefitted enormously. Over-ambitious house buyers who took on mortgages they couldn't afford have seen their interest rates fall and house prices remain absurdly high. They, like the greedy bankers, have made money out of the crisis they helped create. The people who are too lazy to work, earn or save have not been badly affected at all. Government employees have done very nicely. They still have their absurdly over-generous pensions. And the cuts to the public sector have, so far, been insignificant. But savers, people who have worked hard and carefully spent within their means, have been hammered by the Bank of England's policies. And non civil servant pensioners, relying on private pensions, have also been beaten up, battered, mugged and left to beg for scraps.

All this happened without any debate and without any public approval. The Bank of England has simply imposed their policies on the nation without discussion. When you really need it democracy is hiding in the cupboard under the stairs. It is my considered opinion that the biggest threat to the prudent comes not from crooks like Madoff and Stanford but from governments, the European Union, regulators and central banks. They are the thieves who are stealing the value from hard-won savings and pensions.

59

It has recently become clear that financial services groups such as brokers and banks (even large, well-known ones) no longer keep client money ringfenced from their own cash.

Banks are supposed to keep the customers' money separate from their own in order to protect customers in the event of insolvency. But the money isn't separated. American banks and brokers seem to be the most likely offenders, and auditors can no longer be relied upon to spot any such problem.

PwC, the nation's biggest accountant by sales, was recently fined £1.4 million for failing to discover that billions of dollars of client money had not been properly ringfenced at JPMorgan Chase, the American bank. The same accountant was auditor to MF Global, the broker-dealer which collapsed in 2011 leaving $1.2 billion of customers' funds missing.

60

There are two main reasons why investment bank traders are so reckless. The first is that they are playing with other people's money. They don't care if they lose money because they themselves cannot lose: they can only win.

If their gambles produce profits then they receive huge bonuses. If their gambles result in huge losses they still receive their vast salaries and, believe it or not, they also receive bonuses. The bonuses they receive when they lose money aren't as big. But they are still bonuses. That's the first reason why investment bank traders are reckless. The second is that these days traders are young and aggressive. Studies have suggested that financial traders have relatively high levels of testosterone relative to the general population. These high levels of testosterone rise when a young trader starts work. The shouting and cheering and general pressure encourages a high testosterone environment: a mixture of dangerous over-confidence and aggression.

So, the people who are looking after investment funds and pension funds are inveterate gamblers (who cannot lose) and they are also aggressive and highly fuelled with testosterone. Is it any wonder that investment managers and hedge fund managers do so badly? The only surprise is that they have not yet caused a global melt down and lost the savings of every investor on the planet.

61

Robot trading (computers trading with other computers) now accounts for 70% of all equity trades. A new computer chip designed and built solely to trade can now do deals in 0.000000074 seconds. Investment banks have spent $300 million on new transatlantic cabling so that they can cut 0.006 seconds off equity orders between London and New York. The traders who use all these facilities are not investing because they think something is a sound business proposition. They aren't interested in capital growth or dividends. They are investing to make a few billion in the next half a second. And that's gambling not investing though for the people who do it it isn't gambling because they can't lose. If they lose money they get fat fees and small bonuses. If they win money they get fat fees and big bonuses.

62

Virtually all the growth of the last 50 years has gone into the pockets of the very rich. The middle classes and the poor are no better off in real terms. Countless billions have been stolen by bankers, investment fund managers and company directors, very few of whom have done anything to earn it.

The sad truth about modern banks is that they frequently play customers for marks. They keep the best investments for themselves. They put their clients' money in stuff they themselves want to sell. They use their knowledge of how people are trading to make money themselves. They advise companies to merge or make acquisitions not because it is good for the shareholders or employees of those companies (except the ones at the top) but because it is good for the bank.

63

Bankers and investment company managers are cheating customers out of billions. An investor who puts £50,000 into an active fund that provides typical returns over 25 years will pay out more than £100,000 in charges (most of which are unnecessary and unjustifiable). The bottom line is that private investors pay at least £3 billion a year more in annual fees than they should be paying. And things are getting worse. Many managers are now charging performance fees on top of the usual variety of management fees. Performance fees encourage managers to gamble with their clients' money. Churning (constantly buying and selling) also helps to increase the costs which can be added to the bill. Modern financial services are all flim flam, Ponzi schemes and much gambling on obscure and complex securities which no one (certainly not the people using them) understand. There are endless hidden charges and commissions and enormous moral hazards. The average active fund charges twelve times as much as a passive index fund and yet produces a worse performance.

64

A survey in the *Boston Review* in USA showed that 25% of non-Jewish Americans blamed Jews for the financial crisis. This news was greeted with much talk about ethnic hatred and the invariably inaccurate accusation of anti-semitism. But one observer commented that it is difficult to see why it was only 25% and wondered if, perhaps, the other 75% were simply afraid to say what they felt because they suspected that they would be accused of anti-semitism.

65

Money managers didn't see the financial crisis coming because they weren't looking for it. They don't 'do' macroeconomics and they have no time for geopolitical risk assessment. It is here that the private investor can beat the bankers and fund managers. I always find it a good idea to look ahead when driving.

66

There's a myth that hedge fund operators, venture capitalists and private equity specialists are clever people who are worth the billions they take home. Wrong. These people aren't bright. They're just people who have no sense of right or wrong and a burning desire to make money at any cost. Here's how they work.

Imagine a man who makes his living as a freelance gardener. He earns £5 an hour. A private equity specialist sees him and is impressed. The private equity specialist offers to manage the gardener. He negotiates with the garden owners and charges them £6 an hour. He pays the gardener his £5 an hour and keeps £1. He sells shares to the public at a P/E ratio of 100 because it's a brilliant new company that is better than anything involving mobile telephones or the Internet.

So the gardener now has a capital value of £125,000. (That's 100 x £5 x 250 days a year.)

The private equity manager now goes to a hedge fund and borrows £100,000 against the value of the gardener. He keeps the £100,000 as his fee for structuring the whole deal. He now has £100,000 to spend on champagne. The hedge fund has a bond which is worth £100,000 and the shareholders in the company owning the gardener have stock worth £125,000.

Everyone is getting rich. But they want to get richer and so the gardener is under pressure to work harder and longer hours. Next, the private equity specialist brings together a group of gardeners to create a Multinational Garden Tidying Conglomerate. Soon pension funds, insurance companies and hedge funds have investments (either bonds or shares) in this new business.

The final move is that the private equity specialist sells the business to a new investor who borrows money to finance the purchase. Everything then collapses because there is too much debt and the money earned by the gardeners doesn't cover all the costs.

The postscript to the story is that the gardeners get fired and the weeds grow unhindered.

That's how the modern finance industry works.

In the old days a company would go to a bank or investors for capital and there would be a relationship between the various parties concerned. There would be trust. Today, finance is all about speed and leverage and dumping the business on to the next guy before the music stops.

67

Never in the field of finance has so much money been charged by so many for so little as is now being charged by hedge funds.

Investors in hedge funds would have done twice as well between 1998 and 2010 if they had invested in US treasury bills (which paid 2.3% a year in that period). When inflation is considered the average hedge fund investor lost money. But the average hedge fund manager became very rich indeed.

In that twelve year period, investors received a grand total of £6 billion while the managers charged £275 billion in fees. This is not surprising since hedge fund managers charge massively more than conventional managers. But over the years since 1998, hedge funds have been beaten dramatically by corporate bonds and tracker funds.

Another set of research showed that hedge funds delivered returns of zero between 2004 and 2009 (actually they managed a return of 0.05% but that was before inflation). The real figures are even lower than this because they don't include the figures for hedge funds which went bust (which is quite a lot of them) and simply stopped reporting their results.

And who was investing money in hedge funds? Pension funds - themselves run by overpaid professionals. And so the real losers were small investors and pensioners.

The truth is that very few, if any, clients have got rich by investing in hedge funds. But there are quite a number of hedge fund managers who are now billionaires.

68

It isn't only hedge fund managers who have failed their customers. Private equity managers and venture capitalists have also done very badly for their investors (though they too have mostly done very well for themselves).

69

One of the great, enduring mysteries of life is how banks manage to make a loss. Just think about it. Fred and Freda lend their savings of £1,000 to the bank. They put it in a deposit account and receive a gross, before tax, interest payment of 2%. The bank pays them £20 a year. The bank then lends out that £1,000 to 30 individuals or companies. That's leverage. The bank takes the £1,000 and pretends it is £30,000. The other £29,000 doesn't actually exist. The bank just pretends that it exists and lends it out. The people borrowing the money pay an average of 20% for the privilege. So, from that £1,000, the bank receives a total of £6,000 a year in interest (30 x

£200). The bank's gross profit is £6,000 less the £20 they pay out in interest to Fred and Freda. I know that the bank has to pay wages, heat and lighting and so on. But how on earth do they manage to make a loss? The answer, of course, is devastatingly simple. They manage to make a loss partly because they pay out absurd amounts out in salaries and bonuses to senior employees. Last year, for example, well over 4,000 bankers in London received an annual bonus of £2,000,000 or more each. And those huge, undeserved bonuses were awarded on top of equally huge and undeserved salaries. And the other reason for the losses is that they also gamble with the £1,000 lent to the bank by Fred and Freda. They use the money lent to them to gamble on buying bizarre financial derivatives. If these high-risk investments are profitable the bankers give themselves more money in bonuses. If these risky investments go bad, and the money is lost, then it is the bank which takes the losses. The bankers just give themselves slightly smaller bonuses. It's not surprising they don't make any profits for the shareholders. The only mystery is why these people aren't all in prison. Why are they allowed to get away with what is, in reality, nothing more than fraud and theft?

70

When we buy investment products we rely on ratings agencies. These are highly-paid companies which make a fortune out of giving little stars to countries and companies and products. They decide how safe something is financially and then give it a rating. Sounds good. But there are two problems. The first problem is that the people who pay the ratings agencies are the people who are being rated. This is, of course, utterly absurd. The second problem is that the ratings are so often just plain wrong that they really aren't worth the electricity needed to pull them up on your computer screen. I have a crazy thought: could the first problem and the second problem possibly be related in some way?

71

Hedge funds rely on bullshit and luck. Most funds lose money. A few funds make a lot of money (largely through luck) and they receive all the publicity. Hedge fund managers make their money by charging outrageous fees. The usual fee structure is a 2% basic fee, expenses and 20% of any profits. There are funds of funds as well. These invest in a number of hedge funds and charge a 1% fee, plus expenses and expenses. They take a 10% performance fee for investing in the hedge funds. No one investing in a fund of funds stands a chance of making any money.

72

When hedge funds and other investment ventures fail it is never their fault, it is always the result of an unexpected, unprecedented event. They even have a name for these rare events: they call them black swans.

But rare events aren't all that rare and should never be unexpected by wise investors. Anyone who fails to plan for disaster when preparing an investment portfolio is behaving recklessly. And, for the record, black swans are not uncommon. The town of Dawlish in Devon is awash with them. I even have a photograph, which I took, of a black swan sitting on her nest.

What do I know? How dare I criticise these billionaire fund managers? Well, I've run five investment portfolios for many years now. With no leverage whatsoever I've averaged nearly 20% a year gain for the last decade.

73

In May 2012, it was revealed that a huge American bank called JP Morgan had lost billions of dollars in a financial gamble (bankers called it a trade) which, it seemed, no one on the planet really understood. The boss of the bank, Jamie Dimon, had been a firm opponent of the idea that banks with government guaranteed deposits should not be allowed to speculate on their own behalf with depositors' money.

74

Also in May 2012, it was revealed that an RBS banker was being investigated for lying.

They caught just one?

75

Bankers receive huge taxpayer subsidies that aren't even counted by governments when they are working out how much banks cost the taxpayers. For example, the value of the Government guarantee of £85,000 per depositor is said to be worth £200 billion a year to the banks. Without that guarantee, banks would have to pay depositors a far higher rate of interest.

76

Bankers have proved themselves incapable of coping satisfactorily with the fractional reserve banking system which enables them to borrow £1 and lend it out many, many times to other customers. And so we need to abandon the damned silly system. Bankers should be allowed to lend out a maximum of 80% of what they can borrow from real life customers.

77

The fact is that investment managers are not as clever as they tell people they are, nor as clever as they are paid to be. Irrational human behaviour influences everything including investments. It is laughable to claim that the financial markets are efficient. Only someone brought up to believe that computers are clever could possibly believe that.

Conclusion

We should attack and vilify the investment bankers far more than we have done. We've been far too lenient with them. Our bankers have no standards, no dignity and no respect for their customers. They are semi-literate, half-witted, duplicitous, shameless, greedy and dishonest. They exhibit a level of ruthless selfishness which is staggering. I find it impossible to think of `bad' adjectives which do not apply to bankers. These are people who have no real reason to exist. They do not have any social purpose. Their simpler brethren, the bank employees who hand out cheque books and fill up the hole-in-the-wall cash machines, have a reason to exist. The men and women who gamble with other people's money, the investment bankers, the Goldman Sachs operatives, exist only to steal money from the rest of us; they are absurdly overpaid confidence tricksters who operate above the law because they have bought the law and the politicians who make it. Nothing will improve until the banks are forced to start behaving responsibly. And that won't happen until we have politicians in power who regard bankers as a menace instead of as an endless source of party funding, fine wine and expensive meals.

Chapter 4

Inflation: Up, Up And Away

Introduction

By printing more money the Bank of England has pushed down the value of sterling. If you expand the money supply you must inevitably reduce the value of the money. That is the definition of inflation. Prices go up as a result of inflation because suppliers, manufacturers, importers and so on must still meet their costs. When the value of a currency falls the price of all imports (including such basic essentials as food and oil) must rise. When a country imports much or most of its food and oil then the inflation rate will be particularly high. And yet spokesidiots for the Bank of England constantly express surprise that their printing of more money always seems followed by a rise in the inflation figure. They are either very, very stupid or else they are lying to us. The Governor of the Bank of England has recently written nine successive letters explaining why inflation was higher than allowed or expected. (I assume he just simply told a secretary `Send the inflation letter'.)

1

The Government should encourage job creation not through daft schemes (which largely seem to involve shovelling millions into the outstretched hands of their pals) but by cutting red tape and taxes for entrepreneurs. Despite its membership of the EU (the source of most of the daft and destructive regulations which make life so impossible for entrepreneurs and which seem designed to discourage any sort of investment) Germany did this some years ago. For example, they repealed much of the legislation controlling small companies with less than ten employees and allowed entrepreneurs to make staff redundant if things weren't going well. When the Conservatives wanted to introduce similar legislation to that existing in Germany the Liberal Democrats immediately stomped on it. Because they are Statist organisations committed to creating a Statist society both the Labour Party and the Liberal Democrats do everything they can to discourage new non-public sector jobs.

So everything is stuffed.

Companies won't spend. Companies won't invest or hire. And the Government can't raise enough in taxes to pay its current liabilities, let alone pay off its debts.

We cannot increase our exports because we don't make anything much to export and no one would want to buy anything from us anyway (because it would be too expensive and too shoddily made) even if they could afford to buy it.

We could reduce our imports but that would mean doing without food, oil and high definition 3D television sets.

Moreover, the Government, which doesn't know what else to do about the stuffed economy, keeps destroying the currency. The buffoons who run the Bank of England give the appearance of having not yet worked out that this makes imports more expensive and therefore guarantees a high inflation rate. Their constant bleating about inflation coming down might suggest that they are either drunkenly optimistic or as stupid as Gordon Brown. But the truth is worse than either of these possibilities: the men in expensive suits know that printing more money pushes up inflation because that's why they are doing it. They are deliberately impoverishing the elderly and the prudent in order to try to protect the stupid, the reckless, the feckless and their chums working for the penniless banks.

Of course, all other governments are doing exactly the same thing for exactly the same reasons. And so, in order to compete in this bizarre downward spiral, the Bank of England will carry on printing more money. (They say they aren't printing money but that's a weaselly way with words. They may not be actually printing money but pushing a button and doubling the amount of currency in existence isn't not printing money just because you haven't actually gone to the trouble of producing the notes.)

And the end result is that inflation is eventually going to soar. Everything will be alright for a while and then the inflation will come with a rush and neither the Bank of England nor anyone else will be able to stop it and if they think they can then they should all be locked up and sedated.

I'm not an officially accredited financial adviser and I can't even make suggestions about how to beat this lunacy without ending up sharing a cell with a former MP or a bloke with cauliflower ears, a broken nose and a penchant for throwing bricks through jewellery shop windows but I have a suspicion that wise folk have been buying real stuff that will still have a value when a £50 note won't be worth picking up off the pavement. I bet there are quite a few wise old owls who have stocked up on precious metals such as gold, silver and platinum and on things like rare stamps, rare coins and rare books. The wise know that all fiat currencies are vulnerable. There are no exceptions. There is only one really reliable currency: gold. The economists may scoff. But the economists are invariably both wrong and poor.

2

The Government always likes to keep the inflation figure as low as possible. There is a political reason for this in that it looks good if the Chancellor can tell Parliament and the country that the nation's inflation rate is under control. But there is also a (more important) economic reason: many of the payments the Government makes are related to one of the official inflation rates. (There are two: the Consumer Price Index and the Retail Price Index. Having two gives the Government more room for manoeuvre.) The amount of money that pensioners will receive depends upon these official rates and so it is in the interests of the Government (and those running private sector occupational pension schemes) to keep the rates low. Even more important, however, is the fact that the Retail Price Index decides the money the Government has to pay out on index-linked gilts. Adjusting the RPI downwards (in commercial terms this is more commonly known as fiddling the figures) enables the Government to make a dramatic reduction (probably as much as 40%) in the sums which will be paid out to private pensioners, for whom politicians and civil servants, who have enormously advantageous pension schemes paid by taxpayers, have absolutely no sympathy whatsoever.

(Those who bought index-linked gilts to try to protect their savings or pension fund might take some comfort from the fact that the Bank of England has around 80% of its own pension fund in index-linked bonds - which rather suggests to me that despite their apparent surprise at rising inflation rates the bozos at the Bank of England were, despite appearances, bright enough to know very well that inflation was likely to go up, up and away. And the Bank of England has the right to object to any changes which it considers might damage the wealth of the holders of these bonds. Since the Bank of England's employees have shown that they don't give a damn about other people's pensions we will have to rely on them caring about their own. I'm confident that they will.)

3

I have explained how the Government fiddles the inflation figures in several previous books (including *Moneypower*) but the best of their little tricks must surely be this one: if something which is normally measured as part of the inflation figure goes up in price then it is removed from the basket of items used to measure inflation! If that isn't fiddling the results then I don't know what is. This (and numerous other examples of egregious dishonesty) ensure that the official inflation rate bears absolutely no resemblance to the real one which will usually be two, three or four times as high as the official one. My estimate is that the real inflation rate in England has rarely (if ever) been below 10% for the last couple of decades. This means that if you have £100 on deposit in the bank and you are receiving 1% interest (after tax) then the real value of your £100 will, at the end of the year, be reduced to £91. If this continues for a few more years your wealth will, literally, disappear. Deliberately induced inflation is nothing more or less than officially sanctioned, officially organised theft.

4

Even without the money printing efforts of the Bank of England, inflation is bound to rise because in China the Communist Party is keen to create an additional 45 million jobs. You can't create that many jobs merely by taking in more laundry. This huge need for jobs will inevitably drive the demand for commodities of all kinds (including copper, which will probably be in deficit by the end of 2012). The 45 million people who get those nice, sparkly new jobs will all want to spend their money buying goodies made with the aid of stuff (such as oil or wheat) that we need too. And so the price of everything will rise. And as the value of our currency is driven lower and lower so that will mean more inflation at home.

Plus, I hate to mention this, but there is another problem.

There aren't another 45 million people in China still looking for jobs.

Most of the people who wanted to move into cities and towns have already done so. And there simply aren't many people left to be sucked up by growing factories.

Why is this a problem?

Because when there are more jobs than applicants there is only one possible result: wages will rise.

And when wages in China go up the result is higher prices.

And that means more inflation in England.

5

In the last ten years China has grown to be the biggest car market in the world. And the Chinese don't want cheap Chinese rubbish. Last year Rolls Royce sold more cars in China than it sold in England, Wales and Scotland. Within another decade one third of all the world's new cars will be sold in China. (Why else do you think the car companies are keen to hold a Formula One Grand Prix in a country where they have to paint the seats in such a way as to make it look as though real people are actually watching the race?)

6

I read recently that workers at Unilever in Nepal want a 50% pay rise. They've just had a 69% pay rise. I don't blame them. They've been working for beads and blankets for far too long. Their wage increases will affect the prices of everything we buy because those workers will have more money to spend. We will be competing for the raw materials used to make things and so the prices of things will go up.

7

Those who regard globalisation as something new and shiny should know that in the early 19th century around 60% of the world's GDP was in Asia. The Industrial Revolution, which started in England and eventually spread to the rest of Europe and to America, left Asia behind and by the 1950s the Asian economies constituted less than 18% of global GDP.

8

In February 2012, Apple gave its Chinese workers a 25% pay rise. This will increase inflation in two ways. First, it means that the cost of the stuff they make will inevitably go up. Second, those workers will have more money to spend on shoes, burgers and cars and so the cost of the ingredients used to make shoes, burgers and cars must also rise. Apple is not, of course, the only foreign owned company to be increasing the wages it pays its employees in China. The Chinese Government is encouraging Chinese unions to demand that foreign owned companies pay higher wages. Why? Because this brings more money into China.

9

The Chinese Government is also encouraging the local citizens to buy gold with their savings. They don't want their people putting too much of their money into dollars, euros or English pounds - all of which will soon be pretty worthless.

10

The Bank of England's policies have hit pensioners and savers particularly hard. By bringing interest rates down to an all time low the Bank's public employees have wrecked annuity rates. Those reliant on private pensions have suffered most.

11

The Government and the Bank of England constantly predict a fall in the rate of inflation. How can they possibly say this when they must know that their policies are pushing inflation up? The only conclusion is that people whom we are paying to regulate our economy are lying. When inflation rises, rises and rises still more they will claim it is because the price of food and oil has gone up. This is as bad as a kid blaming the ball when he kicks it through a window. The Bank of England, the Office of Budget Responsibility (did they get the name of that quango out of a George Orwell novel?) and the Government constantly blames our problems on unexpected increases in world energy and commodity prices. Unexpected?

12

The Bank of England is also using inflation to bring house prices down. During the Gordon Brown inspired spending boom, the price of houses rose to absurd and unprecedented levels. Most sensible observers suggested that house prices had to fall by around 50% to be affordable. The Bank and the Government knew that this would be disastrous. Millions of people had borrowed money to buy overpriced homes that they couldn't afford. If house prices crashed, the lending banks would lose billions more and millions of greedy people would be thrown out of their homes and would have to live more modest lives. And so the Bank, and the Government, deliberately created policies designed to protect those who had borrowed too much to buy houses they couldn't possibly afford. Instead of allowing the price of houses to fall to a sensible level the Government is destroying the prudent and the elderly by reducing the value of the money that was used to buy those houses. And the beauty of inflation is that it can help bring house prices down to a more sensible level without anyone really noticing what is happening. The house that costs £300,000 today may well be wildly overpriced in today's money. But when a bag of chips costs £10 and a motorist has to pay £200 to fill up his tank the £300,000 house will seem far more reasonable. The house will probably still cost £300,000 in a few years time (because the seemingly inexorable rise in house prices has slowed) but the £300,000 will be worth less. In England, the real rate of inflation is now higher than it has been for decades and rising inflation means that house prices can fall without obviously falling. The cost of a house in 2012 wasn't much below the cost of the same house in 2008 in real terms. But when inflation is taken into account house prices have fallen fairly dramatically in value.

13

'The global system of fiat currencies will eventually end up in a devaluation race.' - Ludwig von Mises.

14

In 2009 in North Korea, Kim Jong II announced that the country's old won bills, worth 10,000 won each, would be replaced with new 10 won notes. To make things worse he announced that only amounts of up to 150,000 won could be changed. Any more than that would be lost for ever. Two and a half thousand years earlier Dionysius of Syracuse restamped one drachma coins as being worth two drachma, thereby halving the value of the coins. In the past, governments shaved the edges off coins, or diluted the quality of the gold or silver used in making coins. Today, they just print money or add another zero onto the computer balance sheet. Governments deliberately use inflation as a weapon because they know that even quite modest rates of inflation can halve a nation's debts in less than a decade. Our caring Government (the one we elected to look after our interests) will keep interest rates low and encourage high levels of inflation both to reduce its own debts and to help greedy house owners get out of the debts they incurred when they bought houses they couldn't afford. Since equities always suffer when interest rates are low, and since the Government's policies have resulted in poor returns from gilts and bonds, investors are doomed to become even poorer. It is important to understand that this is not an accident. It is Government policy. And the Government will continue to take money from those who have saved and to give it (in large quantities) to those who have been imprudent and who have spent more than they should have.

15

With inflation officially at 5.2% (it is of course far higher than this in reality) those on benefits will receive a 5.2% increase while workers have a pay freeze and investors receive 0.5% gross return on their money

Conclusion

Politicians talk about inflation as though it were something out of their control. They discuss it as though it were some supernatural force, like a tornado or a heat wave. Ignore this bleating nonsense. Inflation is man-made. Governments like it because inflation helps eradicate past debts. The problem is that once you've set it in motion, inflation is impossible to control. I have written in previous books about inflation in Germany and Zimbabwe. Just for a change, consider what happened in Brazil in the 1990s. Inflation then peaked at an annual rate of 2,100% and prices rose so fast that cheques lost 30% of their value while being cleared.

Chapter 5

A Disenfranchised Nation

Introduction

We have been disenfranchised by the party system and by the rise, rise and rise of corrupt, immoral politicians - many of whom could accurately be described as psychopaths. Most people in England want to leave the EU, want a halt to immigration and want all illegal wars to stop. But no leading party, or politicians, ever talk about offering these options to the electorate. There is no sense of public service and the concept of `duty' remains a mystery to politicians and their regiments of advisers. We have been disenfranchised and we now live in the sort of kleptocracy which has, for decades, given Africa a bad name. It is hardly surprising that disillusionment with politicians is widespread. We have been ill-served by a new breed of professional politicians who largely began their careers in student politics and who now regard politics as a career, a business. Most are, at best, inept. Modern politicians, who would be best advised to just stand there, always feel the need to do something. Invariably the something they choose to do is self-serving and damaging. Until the electors are better served little is likely to change for the better but much is likely to change for the worse.

For the time being, there is much fatalism; people have lost their will as well as their independence. Many electors assume that there is now no alternative to deceit and corruption. Those who know that they are being lied to don't know what to do. And those who know what to do are fearful of the consequences.

1

We describe ourselves as free people living in a free country. But we have little or no control over our destiny and our votes are of little consequence. We live in a country where the police kill innocent citizens and go unpunished and where the Government spends billions of pounds of our money to protect the absurd salaries and bonuses of a few well placed bankers. We live in a country where people like Blair, Brown, Cameron and Clegg acquire all the power and treat the rest of us like serfs. The only voters who count now are the zombies (the state employed and the scroungers). There are enough of them to vote to defend the generous State.

Voting is now a pointless exercise because there is little discernible difference between the three main parties. Millions who are on benefits will simply vote for the Government which gives them the most money. And since the majority of citizens are dependent upon the Government for their daily bread it is easy for politicians to buy votes and ignore taxpayers. There are tens of thousands of lobbyists who will bribe politicians to do what their masters want them to do and the result is that our politicians (for whom dignity, honour and respect appear to be alien) have allowed government by lobbyist rather than government by voters. I'd rather have whatever the electorate choose to throw at me than a world designed exclusively by a mixture of Murdochs, arms dealers and drug companies.

And, of course, if you are a desperate politician you can always just fiddle the results. This isn't just something that happens in the scruffier parts of the world. Stealing elections happens in America. And there is no reason at all why it cannot, and does not, happen in England. The use of postal votes and voting machines has made it extraordinarily easy to fiddle the results. (Not everyone is quite as stupid as Bernadette Chirac, the 78-year-old widow of the former French president. Her election as a local councillor in her husband's old constituency area was annulled after a tribunal in the town of Limoges decided that the election had to be rerun. Tellers found that Mrs Chirac had done exceptionally well in the election. Indeed, she had done rather too well. She had acquired two more votes than the number of registered voters in the area.)

2

In the 16th and 17th centuries every man who entered public life did so knowing that there was an excellent chance that he would end his career in the tower or on the scaffold. Those of us not in public life went wrong somewhere

131

and allowed the politicians too much freedom. Perhaps the problem is that we treated them too damned decently.

3

Our politicians loudly instruct other nations to become more democratic but it sometimes seems as though modern English democracy is just a way for insiders to give themselves and their cronies huge sums of money gouged out of trusting taxpayers. How many English voters wanted their Government to build up huge debts, to give billions to the European Union, to fight illegal wars so that the Americans could grab other people's oil or to take money from the prudent and give it to Fred Goodwin, scroungers, and bankrupt Scottish banks?

Voters don't get the chance to vote on issues which affect them, they simply end up voting for parties with hidden agendas and deals.

When democracy started, the idea was that electors would be invited to vote on specific issues. For example: 'Shall we go to war?' Even Italy, one of the countries now run by an EU appointed ex Goldman Sachs dictator, once practised proper democracy. Back in the 15th century, voters in Florence were invited to decide whether or not their money should be used to build a cathedral and if so how big the cathedral should be, how it should be designed and how much should be spent. That's democracy in action.

In Paris, the Princess and I were recently asked by the mayor of our arrondissement for our views on whether our street should be pedestrian only and where the buses should run. That's proper democracy.

In England (and, indeed, the USA) democracy (like capitalism) is now so far removed from the original meaning of the word that those who talk about it should be arrested for fraudulent trading. Our democracy is a corrupt and degenerate version which has nothing to do with real democracy, just as the form of capitalism now practised has nothing to do with real capitalism. ('Ah diddums has the poor little banker lost all the other people's money and got nothing left to play with? Have some more and let mama know when it's all gone.')

Once they are elected and in power our governments categorically ignore the public view on everything. Petitions are shredded or burnt without even being read. They go into the front door of Number 10 and straight out of the back into the shredding van.

4

One of our problems is that too many of the people who have grabbed power in England in recent years are devout worshippers at the twin shrines of political correctness and multiculturalism.

What ill-defined, dangerous and bizarre social nuisances these are.

What exactly are they? What are the rules? No one really knows except that they are aspects of a levelling process, conducted with menacing thoroughness by the enthusiastic followers of an errant branch of McCarthyism for whom the enemy is western culture in general and English culture in particular.

The irony, of course, is that most of the proponents of these twin evils (and certainly the most vociferous and powerful of them) speak only one language (English) and earn their living as paid servants of the English State. Their aim is merely to destroy for they have no other culture to offer, other than the general principle that anything which can be branded `ethnic' trumps everything else.

What do they mean by `multiculturalism'? Wearing a sari occasionally? Listening to native Indian music from time to time? Eating a curry every Thursday evening?

For what are we throwing away our traditions, our history and culture?

When these people (who seem embarrassed and ashamed by the success of their cultural ancestors) call for the end of western culture (or English culture) they are calling for the demise of the only culture they have. With what do they intend to replace it?

The odd thing is that the English are the only proponents of multiculturalism. I haven't noticed the Chinese, the Arabs, the Israelis, the Scots or the Indians promoting multiculturalism. I haven't seen the French get too excited about erasing Napoleon from their culture or removing Charlemagne from the history books. For heaven's sake the French still get excited about Joan of Arc.

In the cold light of day the proponents of multiculturalism and political correctness are truly stupid, soulless people. But we laugh at them at our peril for they have aided in the destruction of our national identity and they have done enormous damage to our democracy. They, more than any other group, have damaged our lives and disenfranchised us. Toxic multiculturalism and political correctness are elitist (in that they are favoured by academics, civil servants and BBC journalists - all of whom are public sector workers, paid by the State) and destructive.

5

I believe that England would be best served by a sovereign independent English parliament, packed with passionate, independent voices representing every shade of opinion. We need dignity and respect back in politics. Instead, we have just over six hundred clipped and shampooed poodles representing the three parties and obeying every instruction from Brussels. The poodles are isolated and protected from reality and they have little or no idea what the voters really want. England is now run by a toxic mixture of Scottish nationalists and politically correct, cryptorchid incompetents who think there is nothing wrong with armies of Romanians coming into the country, claiming a small fortune in benefits and then selling the *Big Issue* for extra money to pay for their holiday home in Greece. Our future is controlled by undistinguished self-serving poseurs and buffoons.

6

What we really need are politicians who have achieved enough in real life to be able to go into politics without bowing to pressure from lobbyists and bureaucrats. Arnold Schwarzenegger uniquely ran California for the benefit of the people - because he could. Sadly, we get politicians who have no experience of life and no achievements outside politics. Our politicians know so little that they think they know what is good for us. They want a world full of rules and regulations, rather than leaving us to make our own decisions, and they desperately want to decide how we spend our time and our money. Politics is now a profession that attracts hustlers, tricksters, grasping power-hungry psychopaths, men and women who don't have the brains or application for proper jobs but who fancy the idea of making a good few bob (and becoming famous) out of politics. They are opportunistic psychopaths.

A few decades ago Tory sleaze was largely sexual in nature. Much of it was of little real consequence and simply provided entertainment for the readers of the sort of tabloids produced by the Murdoch empire. Only Labour politicians stooped to taking bribes, cheating on their expenses or selling out their country, their Government and their electors for a fistful of fivers. Today, nearly all political sleaze is financial. This is a result of the fact that most modern politicians are in politics solely for the money. They have had no other career, they have no other source of income, they have no skills, no knowledge and no personally acquired wealth. All this is bad for the country because men who are independently wealthy (either in hard cash or in terms of marketable skills) are far less likely to give in to financial temptation than men who are struggling to maintain three homes, several cars and a mistress on a Parliamentary salary.

7

When the Beatles were cheered at JFK airport as they arrived in the USA for the first time, the 5,000 teenagers doing the wild cheering were there because they had been paid a dollar each and given a free T-shirt. Politicians learn from entertainers. When Tony Blair entered Downing Street the cheering hordes, waving flags and wearing their Party T-shirts, were Labour Party workers and supporters planted there to make Blair look popular.

8

Our politicians are constantly discovering new and complicated solutions to some very simple problems. Invariably and inevitably these so-called solutions make things worse.

9

In 1944, when our last Coalition Government was fighting Hitler, a poll of Britons showed that 57% thought that the politicians were acting in the their own interests, or the interests of their party, rather than in the interests of the country.

10

The chances are high that the disgraced Labour Party (the one that destroyed our country) will be back in power at the next election. The necessary but controversial austerity programme will make the Tories so unpopular that, almost unbelievably, the deeply uncharismatic Miliband will win power. The only good news is that Clegg's party (destructive, fascist, dangerous and the most utterly nannyish, repressive party ever invented) will secure fewer votes than UKIP, the BNP, the Green Party and whatever remains of the Monster Raving Loony Party. Clegg, the inhuman face of the EU, is surely finished as a politician in England but doubtless has a great future as an EU Something Well-Paid, working at an institution where incompetence and unpopularity are not regarded as a disadvantage. When he loses his party, his seat and his ministerial car at the next general election the country's most unpopular politician will doubtless want to start with a nice well-paid job as an EU Commissioner. (The people who voted for Clegg have such poor judgement and such low intelligence that they should be banned from driving, owning scissors, having responsible jobs or going shopping unless under adult supervision.)

11

According to acting guru Stanislavski one quality is more important than any other for an actor: charm. The party political spin doctors realised some time ago that the same thing is also true for politicians. It is why Blair (who has plenty) got away with mass murder and why Brown (who has none) didn't get away with gross incompetence. The great weakness of the party system (and its way of forming up behind a telegenic leader) is that these days our leaders are people who win popularity contests not because they say wise things but because they look good on the television. The party system gives us unoriginal, unimaginative, smug and pointless drones. It gives us Cameron and Clegg - a pair of upper class, privileged twits with little experience of business or the real world (though Clegg did once, thanks to his banker father, have a work experience post in a bank). My first thought is that it is perhaps hardly surprising that we are in a mess. My second thought is that the unelected (and unelectable) professional Scotsman Gordon Brown was not telegenic but did succeed in destroying our economy. My third thought is that our party political structure is irreparably corrupt and there is an easily sustainable argument that all wise and sensitive individuals should become anarchists, with the avowed hope that the whole damned, dishonest edifice will collapse so that we can rebuild something better in its place.

12

'Why do you want a political career? Have you ever been in the House of Commons and taken a good look at the inmates? As weird a gaggle of freaks and sub-humans as was ever collected in one spot.' - P. G. Wodehouse, Cocktail Time

13

Politicians who fail are routinely kicked upstairs to the House of Lords. The ones with better contacts become President of the World Bank, President of the IMF, one of the many Presidents of the European Union and, indeed, President of anything which carries a huge salary, a huge pension, a huge staff, a huge expense account and a huge office.

14

If 600 MPs are corrupt enough to fiddle their expenses, how many are corrupt enough to sell out their constituents or their country? And how surprising is it that public sector workers take advantage of their status and power to steal and cheat and lie, when MPs do it?

15

In our increasing complex world it is absurd that anyone should become an MP under the age of 50.

16

Is Clegg an alien? He is certainly not of this world. How did anyone come to vote for him? Were they drugged? If someone asked me to sign the forms to have him locked up as a danger to himself and the community I'd have my pen out in a shot. The man is barking, but dangerously barking. He doesn't think he's a tree or Napoleon or a rice pudding. He thinks the EU is a good thing. And that is infinitely more dangerous than thinking you're a tree.

17

Lobbying is legalised bribery which no one objects to because the people being bribed are the people making the laws and the people doing the bribing have money, sports tickets and crates of champagne in their armoury. It is because of lobbyists that it is impossible for those who oppose vaccination, vivisection, genetic engineering and other dangerous activities to get any sort of hearing from politicians.

18

Every few years electors get to overthrow the Government as long as they immediately reelect them (or another one which is quite indistinguishable). The basic problems remain uncorrected. Our political system needs fundamental reform. But, without a revolution, that is not something for which our politicians are ever going to vote.

19

In our bizarre society there are no penalties for lying or gross incompetence. Gordon Brown, Tony Blair and Fred Goodwin all got rich and are getting richer. None has been to prison. Journalists still ask Brown and Blair for views on world affairs and the economy when they should in reality ask them only about prison conditions and the likelihood of their acquiring first hand experience of our legal system. Have there ever been former Prime Ministers more regarded with contempt than Tony Blair and Gordon Brown? No one person in history has done more harm to England than Gordon Brown and yet Brown, who has now apologised for everything he didn't do (such as the sending of orphans to Australia a zillion years ago) steadfastly refuses to apologise for destroying the country and helping to take us into two illegal wars. Who will apologise for Brown's bad actions? Certainly not Miliband who was a member of a cabinet which took us into an illegal war and is, in my opinion, just as much a war criminal as his predecessors.

20

Politicians have made it clear to journalists that the publication of unpleasant, scary truths is not welcomed. And so much of our media (including that most compliant of media organisations, the BBC) obediently reinforces the EU's propaganda, protects the political establishment, steadfastly refuses to question the official line on anything and does its determined best to destroy any opposition and to keep original thinkers well away from its publicly-funded studios.

But politicians really don't have to worry too much for even when `bad news' is published it will likely be ignored or, at least, quickly forgotten. If it cannot be suppressed it will be glossed over and overwhelmed by the constant influx of new irrelevant nonsense.

In his book *Fog Facts*, Larry Beinhart (the author of the novel which became the magnificent film *Wag the Dog*) explains that although the important facts are there, available to anyone who has the time to find them, we tend not to see them because they are lost in a confusing fog of information. And so, explains Beinhart, George W. Bush got away with stealing an American election partly because the media covered up the truth and partly because the American people didn't want to see the truth. Sometimes it takes more courage than most people can find to face up to the truth when doing so is likely to make you feel you have to do something about it.

21

Appeasement encourages aggression and abasement encourages oppression.

22

Around the world there is a far higher proportion of crooks among senior politicians than among any other group of citizens. A surprising number move straight to prison when they leave office. Most have done far better for themselves than charging taxpayers for packets of biscuits or moat cleaning operations. (It is no exaggeration to say that most corporate chief executives and senior civil servants are also crooks - and most abuse their positions of power.)

23

`Egotism is an infirmity that perpetually grows upon a man, till at last he cannot bear to think of anything but *himself, or even to suppose that others do.' - Hazlitt, writing about politicians*

24

Archaeologists found the 10,000-year-old skeleton of a politician. How could they tell it was a politician? By the way it was lying.

25

Our world has been ruined by overachievers, people who have risen further than their talent merited. Brown, Clegg and Goodwin are three obvious examples.

26

I have decided to award the first Bono Award for Sanctimonious Hypocrisy to our deputy Prime Minister, Clegg, who makes the nauseating Bono (for whom, in my opinion, the word 'hypocrisy' was invented) look modest and decent and Prince Edward look brainy and charismatic.

The Bono Award, which consists of a large mirror, will be given to individuals, countries and companies who have shown exceptionally high levels of self-glorification, self-importance, hypocrisy and nauseating general sliminess.

Clegg won the first award against determined competition from David Cameron and Vince Cable. He won because, in my view, he manages to be weedy, loathsome, patronising, supercilious, hypocritical, stupid and arrogant all at the same time. After John Prescott I didn't think we'd ever have a worse deputy Prime Minister. But Clegg has succeeded in out-Prescotting Prescott and must now surely be the most unpopular politician in England since Blunkett.

Despite Clegg's success, I suspect that Vince Cable is now the most dangerous man in the country (no one takes Clegg seriously). Cable, who makes Prescott and Brown look like intellectual giants and stalwarts of integrity, will be personally responsible for keeping us in depression for years. He is officially in the Government as Business Secretary but he won't hear of getting rid of red tape and actually wants more of the damned stuff. It seems to me that he doesn't know anything about how small businesses are run or much care about the travails of the people who try to run them. If he thinks small businesses are beneath him he should remember how big businesses start.

27

Our 'leaders' have no strategic plan for the country. We are, at the same time, America's poodle, a half-hearted member of the European Union and leader of the Commonwealth. We fail in everything we do.

28

Gordon Brown should be put into the stocks. The entire country should then be entitled to file past and make him aware of their feelings. (Women could take theirs prepared in a bottle).

29

Politicians always mess things up. They are constitutionally dysfunctional.

30

The Liberal Democrats act as though they are a department of the European Union commission. They seem opposed to anything which might improve the chances of small businesses surviving let alone growing. I suspect that Liberal Democrats hate entrepreneurs because they aren't part of the State.

31

Scottish politicians are helping to run (and ruin) English life. I have never seen it mentioned anywhere (other than in my own books) that Gordon Brown (and many other leading Westminster politicians) have signed The Scottish Claim of Rights. This document states: 'We...do hereby declare and pledge that in all our actions and deliberations (the) interests (of the Scottish people) shall be paramount.'

The Scottish Claim of Rights has also been signed and approved by (among others) the former Chancellor Alistair Darling, the former speaker of the House of Commons, Michael Martin and all rabid, rancid, tartan-wearing Scottish nationalists.

32

Stupid people and intelligent people all get one vote each. Since there are more stupid people than intelligent people in the world it is obviously the case that stupid people run the world. England is run by people who have been elected by morons, cretins and village idiots. In a world dominated by stupid people it is perhaps hardly surprising that the people who become most successful are increasingly stupid. I offer Tony Blair, John Prescott, David Blunkett and Nick Clegg as evidence. Gordon Brown had a brain put together by unskilled labourers using bits and pieces which they had picked up from a pathology department car boot sale.

Remember, you only have to fool 40% of the 60% who vote in order to control a country.

33

Myrmidons are unscrupulous followers or subordinates who do stuff unquestioningly. Our modern politicians are surrounded by myrmidons.

34

Ministers are appointed to their posts because they are particularly well suited to the work they are expected to do. So, for example, our Foreign Secretaries know lots of foreigners and our Home Secretaries are expected to have lots of homes.

35

It is rational for individuals to fill up their petrol tanks whenever the nation is threatened with a petrol strike. But when lots of people behave in this rational way the result is chaos. How could the Coalition Government not understand that when they recommended that we should all fill up our petrol tanks and, for good measure, fill up spare cans with petrol, the result would be a petrol shortage and *total* chaos?

36

Cameron, public relations man and lounge lizard, made a huge mistake in accepting a Coalition with Clegg. The problem was that the Tories were so desperate to get hold of the perks of power (the chauffeur-driven limousines and so on) that they were prepared to do anything - even form an alliance with Clegg's boys. If, after Gordon Brown had been booted out Cameron had had the balls to hold another election, and to ask for a clear majority, he would have won. No one with functioning cortical tissue wanted Labour in charge of anything. But Cameron clung to Clegg and landed the country with an appalling portfolio of promises and policies which have continued to damage England. In my opinion, neither Clegg nor his pathetic pal Cable has any understanding of, or enthusiasm for, enterprising businesses, and the libraries full of rules and regulations which they have enthusiastically imported from their very best pals in Brussels have finished off what small chance we might have had of getting through the next few decades without sliding into a lengthy economic depression.

37

The world has changed in recent years. Today, whatever the politicians can do which will screw up the country they will do. They will always find a way to make things bad and then to make things worse. They are selfish and incompetent. Actually, they are, almost to a man or woman, psychopaths. Instead of being led by clear-minded, passionate professionals we get interchangeable, egocentric megalomaniacs.

38

Enoch Powell was probably the last thinking politician, the last one who had the intelligence to understand that politicians need a strategy for leadership. Naturally, politicians also need the intelligence to create a strategy and to follow it through with the appropriate tactics.

39

You can tell a politician is lying by the fact that his mouth is open and words are coming out.

40

Too many people mind their own business these days. That's why there is so much violence and it's why our streets aren't safe and our politicians can't be trusted.

41

According to England's official sleaze watchdog, the chairman of the committee on standards in public life, Tony Blair is personally responsible for a collapse in public trust. His seven sins were:

1. The cash for peerages scandal. ('Lend us money secretly and we will give you a peerage.')

2. The illegal Iraq war.

3. Overriding Cabinet and Parliament.

4. Political interference in a fraud investigation. (Blair ended an enquiry into alleged corruption over BAE's arms deal with Saudi Arabia.)

5. A failure to properly investigate alleged breaches of ministerial code. (Those involved included John Prescott, David Blunkett and Tessa Jowell.)

6. Leaving the postal voting system open to fraud.

7. A reliance on spin doctors and special advisers.

Not surprisingly, the chairman was not reappointed when his three year term expired.

42

Both Labour and Conservative Governments have recently supported 'crony capitalism' - by which I mean supporting, and representing the interests of, their rich friends rather than the interests of business in general and entrepreneurs in particular. The result is that the poor suffer and get poorer (because prices keep rising through a lack of competition, incompetence and too much regulation) while the rich pals of the politicians get ever richer.

43

Politics and campaigning are now no longer about policy or information or promises. They are about image and perception.

44

The political parties have ensured that only existing political parties are allowed publicity. Broadcasters are only allowed to give airtime to candidates representing one of the parties that has already screwed up the country.

45

England is the only country without nationalistic leaders. It is politically incorrect for any politician in any of the major parties to defend England or the English in the way that politicians overtly promote Scotland and the Scots and Wales and the Welsh.

46

Blair and Brown led us into a bad, bad, bad, bad world. Blair, claiming his reward for taking us into an illegal war, has gone on to better paid things. Brown, however, is still working as an MP. He is still drawing an MP's salary. He is still building up a massive pension. And the man who wrecked our economy and destroyed the future for generations to come is still allowed to vote on our future.

47

Our country is being run by self-styled experts (e.g. management consultants and 'advisors') who have no experience and not much learning, who know little and have no common sense. Gordon Brown was a great believer in experts (possibly because just about everyone in the world knew more than him about everything and, therefore, appeared to be an expert).

48

A country needs governmental organisations which are managed well and serve some useful purpose. But our government departments would fail any `fit for purpose' test.

49

Successive governments, and councils everywhere, have got into the habit of wasting other people's money with considerable abandon. Politicians don't seem to understand the value of real money (money that has been earned, saved and taxed). National and local politicians who might worry about spending £100 of their own money will willingly spend £1,000,000,000 of other people's money on a small war or an administrative whim, without a second thought or, indeed, a first thought.

50

The people who created the world's problems are the same people who are trying to solve them and they are using the same policies to try to solve the problems that they used to create them. Brilliant.

51

In an attempt to save money (or, rather, to show that they are trying to save money and to manufacture public dissatisfaction with the idea of austerity) councils everywhere are turning off the street lights at night (when it's dark). Councils which do this save, on average, the cost of one medium sized and entirely pointless bureaucratic functionary. There are now hundreds of council bosses receiving pay of over £250,000. These are, of course, accompanied by the appropriate pension arrangements, more than adequate holidays and large expense accounts.

Councils are concreting over their remaining grass and flower beds and closing the few remaining public lavatories in order to cut costs. They ignore the fact that public gardens with flowers make life much better for us all (isn't that what progress is?) and provide real employment and training for gardeners and they ignore the fact that when public lavatories are shut people stop visiting town centres. Curiously, councils which are turning off the street lights still allow their staff to leave office lights on all through the night. Is any of this what the local taxpayers really want? I don't think so. But they're paying the bills. And if they're not getting what they want then they've been disenfranchised.

52

Plans from the Liberal Democrats for the reform of the House of Lords were attacked on the grounds that proportional representation would result in the two political parties UKIP and the BNP having seats in the new House. It never seems to occur to people who say these things that when they try to suppress political parties whose views they do not agree with they are suppressing the very essence of democracy.

53

The BBC, and other media, do not give any coverage to politicians who are not members of the three major parties, unless they are members or supporters of the Scottish National Party in which case they will be given as much coverage as they can cope with.

54

As Lenin pointed out, the purpose of terrorism is to terrorise. What he didn't point out (probably because he didn't spot it coming) was that today the biggest terrorists we have to face are our own Government. They are the real threat. Government officials tell us we have to behave normally in the face of terrorist attacks, but whenever there is a bomb scare they immediately close down vast amounts of surrounding area for hours or even days. Two days after an attempted (and failed) bombing of Glasgow Airport, flights were still being cancelled. This is behaving normally? It is, of course, all done quite deliberately. When a former Home Secretary sent tanks to Heathrow to deal with a `suspected' terrorist threat he didn't really imagine (at least I hope he didn't) that tanks were a good way to combat terrorists with bombs in their underwear. He sent tanks to the airport because it was a highly visible way to scare everyone travelling and everyone watching television and to persuade us to let them (the politicians) do whatever they like to keep us `safe'. It was a typical propaganda move for a bunch of politicians who will do anything - anything - to cement their hold on power. (The alternative explanation, of course, is that the Home Secretary concerned was a blithering idiot. And since the Home Secretary concerned was Blunkett that option cannot be entirely discounted.)

55

During a discussion about House of Lords reform, the sanctimonious Clegg rejected suggestions that the issue should be subjected to a referendum on the grounds that all three parties supported reform. It clearly did not occur to him, the arrogant little liberal, that all three parties could be wrong. And it is this same arrogance which prevents our paid for political servants allowing the electorate the chance to vote to leave the European Union.

56

European politicians in general, and English politicians in particular, know that the greatest threat they and the EU

face is nationalism (aka patriotism). They are aware that as anger with the EU, and its vast army of overpaid

eurocrats, continues to rise, so voters will turn back to small political groups which talk about sovereignty, national

respect, culture and history and which offer a return to old-fashioned values. These are serious times. Our country

is facing the greatest threat it has ever faced (including Hitler and Napoleon). Our future is as bleak as it has ever

been. Our economy has never been as bad. And yet in 2012 the Queen's Speech ignored everything happening in

Europe, ignored immigration (possibly the problem most people would put top of their list of worries), ignored fuel

prices and ignored the economy in general and the problems facing businesses in particular. Instead, the Coalition

promised to create six new quangos, reform the House of Lords, introduce a gold plated charter for snoopers and

force businesses to give yet more rights (and between six and twelve months paid leave) to the fathers of unborn

babies.

57

We have been told that we must tighten our belts because we are responsible for the mess the country is in. That

isn't true. Gordon Brown, a few other politicians and the bankers are responsible for the mess we are in. But we,

not they, are expected to pay the price. The bailout money has gone to the people who caused the problems. Many

of the people who caused the problems are now claiming that they can solve them. We're being punished for their

stupidity. And when it comes to elections we are offered a choice of idiots all offering the same policies and a bent

voting system that protects the party system and oppresses intelligent, independent, honest politicians.

58

'If the right to have a share in making the laws were merely a feather; if it were a fanciful thing; if it were only

a speculative theory; if it were but an abstract principle: on any of these suppositions, it might be considered as

of little importance. But it is none of these; it is a practical matter; the want of it not only is, but must of

necessity be, felt by every man who lives under that want. The natural and inevitable consequences of a want of

this right in the people have, in all countries, been pressing the industrious and laborious to the earth; severe

laws and standing armies to compel the people to submit to those taxes; wealth, luxury and splendour, among those who make the laws and receive the taxes; poverty, misery, immorality and crime, among those who bear

the burdens; and at last commotion, revolt, revenge and rivers of blood.' - William Cobbett, Advice to Young

Men

Conclusion

Since the days of the most treacherous of the treacherous, Ted Heath, we have been betrayed, not led, by a series of traitors and war criminals. (Some were both. For example, anyone who served in Blair's governments should be tried as a war criminal and traitor.) Politicians no longer listen to voters, but do things to them not for them. The Government will always screw things up. You can rely on it. And since lobbyists now control scientists, media and politicians you and I will learn no truths about important issues unless we ourselves have the courage to dig deep.

Our current breed of politicians cannot solve our problems because they caused them and they don't understand what they did wrong. Moreover, as long as they can wriggle out of taking the blame they don't care.

Most people want fairly simple things from their Government. They want stability. They want a halt to unlimited immigration. They want England to leave the EU. They want a halt in globalisation because it clearly doesn't work. They want an end to multiculturalism. They want more freedom and less Government interference. They want an end to health and safety nonsenses (which haven't made us healthier or safer). They want an end to political correctness. And they want an end to waste and greed in public life. None of this is likely to happen until the party system is broken. And, since the three parties control our electoral system that won't happen without some sort of revolution. So, sadly, it will be a long time before voters get the chance to change things. The lawyers, the lobbyists, the propagandists, the contractors, the cheats, the confidence tricksters, the scroungers, the bureaucrats have taken control and will not readily release their fingers from the levels of power. We cannot do anything about the problems we face because we no longer live in a democracy. Elections (even those of the landslide variety) are won by less than 25% of the vote and Governments are now kept in power in England by non-taxpayers and civil servants. Until there is a revolution we can only learn to adapt and survive.

Chapter 6

The Rise And Rise Of Psychopaths

Introduction

Research has shown that top jobs in politics, as indeed in many other walks of life, are frequently successfully held by people with psychopathic traits. Throughout history the possession of psychopathic traits has proved a useful passport to high office and today the party system actually makes it easy for psychopaths to rise to the top.

1

I doubt if I am the only doctor to have noticed this. But I'm probably the only doctor who will tell you. Our world is now being run by psychopaths. Most of the people we describe as `leaders' are psychopaths. They have taken over the world. (Incidentally, the terms psychopath and sociopath are effectively interchangeable - though academics do argue about them in ways which are of no practical relevance.) It should be no surprise that criminality is common among the world's leaders. A remarkably high proportion of Presidents and Prime Ministers end up in prison (and many of those who escape confinement only do so because they change their country's laws in their favour or because they bribe, bully or kill their opponents). If the percentage of convicted criminals among solicitors or doctors was a tiny fraction of the percentage of convicted criminals among former State leaders serious questions would be asked about the way in which solicitors and doctors were selected.

Psychopaths are selected for success because of their superficial charm, their ruthlessness, their overriding sense of ambition, their vanity and their selfishness. Psychopaths can kill (literally and figuratively) and we can't. It is their strength and, in their world, it is our weakness. They are insensitive overachievers. They suffer very little, if at all, from stress related disorders and are, therefore, at an enormous advantage in our stressful society. Look around you at modern television celebrities and sports stars and you will, I believe, see that many of them behave as they would if they were psychopaths. Is this because those who want to be really successful in sport or television learn to be ruthless, ungrateful, uncaring, dishonest and graceless? Or is it because the people who become most successful are psychopaths to start with? (Does it matter?)

When ordinary folk make mistakes they apologise, try to put things right and, quite probably, resign. When psychopaths make mistakes they lie and lie and lie again. When psychopaths lie they do so convincingly and without a blush; they don't apologise. They don't put things right. And, unless they are forced to do so, they don't resign. (Actually, psychopaths do occasionally apologise if they think that an apology can prove beneficial to their cause. And in those circumstances their apologies can be breathtakingly convincing.) The psychopath's default position is to lie, and their fallback default position is to blame someone else. Psychopaths are well suited to our world; they are the fittest and so they survive. And so the world becomes nastier and nastier and the sensitive and the meek and the mild are trodden on and crushed.

Men or women who are unfettered by moral scruples, who are prepared to lie or cheat their way to the top and who will make promises they know they cannot keep have a huge advantage over those held back by notions of decency and fair play. These days you almost have to be a psychopath in order to rise to the top without worrying about the lies you have to tell and the bad things you end up doing to stay in power. In our world, the acquisition of power depends on what you are prepared to do to get it. And psychopaths will do what it takes.

The top jobs in almost every walk of life are held by people who are psychopaths. These people aren't just a little bit psychopathic. They're full-blooded, dangerous, lock the doors and bolt the windows psychopaths. This is why everything is going wrong. Our world is now controlled by bad people whose actions are directed purely by their own purely selfish desires. It's why bankers and politicians do incredibly selfish and stupid things and keep doing them. Psychopaths are self-centered, callous and remorseless. They may appear to have many friends and associates but they don't ever form close relationships with people. They function without conscience and are, therefore, at an enormous advantage in our society. Our leaders are bad men and women and most of us do not understand just how evil they are and how uncontrolled and endless their wickedness really is.

It is important that we understand and acknowledge that psychopaths don't all become serial killers, rapists, swindlers, confidence tricksters and boiler room operators. They aren't all child abusers, gang leaders, cult organisers, mercenaries, drug barons or unscrupulous crooks. It is no secret among psychiatrists that many psychopaths become lawyers, doctors (including psychiatrists) and politicians. Psychopaths are ruthless, manipulative and permanently dishonest; they show significant personality traits and socially deviant behaviour; they show no lack of restraint and are remorseless in their dealings with others; they never learn from experience and will do things which you and I would regard as terrible to satisfy quite insignificant yearnings: actions and motives don't necessarily match in significance. Psychopaths lie far more than any normal person could believe possible and, partly as a result of that, have significant social skills. Psychopaths lie far more than most people can believe anyone would lie. And they do it so well. They are uninterested in anyone else's tragedy or joy and are indifferent to literature or art. They are unmoved, except in a very superficial way, by beauty, love, evil or horror. They have little or no genuine sense of humour (though they can fake a sense of humour just as well as they can fake other emotions). Most, of course, don't think that they are `different' and certainly do not regard themselves as in any way `ill' (unless they can use the idea of illness to their advantage). Psychopaths can use the truth (as they see it) to their advantage, they will create their own personal profiles to satisfy the needs of a professional questioner. (In prison, psychopaths are incredibly good at convincing parole boards and others that they feel sorry for any crimes they have committed, that they have changed and that all they need is a good hug and they will be fine. Myra Hindley, for example, was exceedingly skilful at persuading prison visitors such as Lord Longford that she was a changed woman.)

Just think of some of the lies politicians have told in recent years. Blair's infamous deception about weapons of mass destruction springs to mind. These days it isn't the small lies that trick us - it's the big ones, the Blair sized lies, the ones that take us into entirely unnecessary wars and make criminals of us all.

`It would never come into (average people's) heads to fabricate colossal untruths,' wrote Adolf Hitler. `And they would not believe that others could have the impudence to distort the truth so infamously.'

But politicians do tell big, deliberate, determined, self-serving lies. They lie and we believe them because, as Hitler pointed out, we cannot truly believe that they would tell lies that big. And they know that if they just keep lying they will manage to fool most of the people most of the time. Especially if they do it with a smile and a few disarming words. `I am a trustworthy sort of guy,' always works well when murmured softly with a smile and an air of surprise and disappointment that anyone could even contemplate thinking otherwise. (Of course, not all modern politicians are psychopaths. Some are just morons; far too stupid and far too emotional to be high level, well-functioning psychopaths.)

Psychopaths are not mad in the same way that the average serial killer is mad. They aren't driven by God to kill fallen women, like the Yorkshire Ripper. When psychopaths kill it is not because they are deranged but partly because they do not treat other human beings as thinking, feeling beings and partly because they themselves are cold, calculating and selfishly rational. Psychopaths understand when they are behaving badly, they know when they are breaking the rules and they are quite capable of stopping themselves. They continue to behave badly not because they can't stop themselves but because they don't see why they should change and they don't want to change because their behaviour is of enormous benefit to them.

Their behaviour leaves normal people feeling helpless, betrayed and bewildered; their behaviour is morally incomprehensible to the rest of us. Stupid psychopaths kill passers-by to steal their wallets. They do this without a second thought, and without remorse because the deed seems to them to be logical and justified. But most psychopaths aren't stupid and don't behave in this way. The most intelligent psychopaths manipulate and lie and use people in order to further their own ends. It's easier and more productive than banging people on the head with a brick. They deceive with a directness and a smoothness that can disarm and convince even the most experienced and cynical prison staff. They often seem witty and charming. They have difficulty understanding why other people become emotional and they tend to use their hands a good deal when they talk - even though this may be unnecessary and inappropriate. Their eyes may seem `dead' and their stare intense. They look people in the eye because they know it is a good way to obtain power over others. They can be captivating and skilful at finding out how to make other people do their bidding. They are quick to take advantage of the vulnerable, the lonely (and, when working as confidence tricksters or bankers, the greedy or larcenous) and skilled at making themselves look like victims. They smile and take your pride and your money and your innocence and your love and your hopes and your dreams; they casually and flagrantly violate all the social norms without being bothered by a twinge of conscience. Obligations and commitments mean nothing to them and they feel no need to honour promises or principles unless there is some obvious benefit to themselves in doing so. They are unmoved by the knowledge that their actions may cause hardship or create risk for others They leave everyone they meet sad but not much wiser. Most of their victims end up feeling that *they* have done something wrong. Onlookers and observers often sympathise with the psychopath because they too have been taken in by the smiles and the undoubted presence.

Men or women who are unfettered by moral scruples, who are prepared to lie or cheat their way to the top, and who will make promises they know they cannot keep, have a huge advantage over those held back by notions of decency and fair play. Individuals prepared to tell the `big lie' (in the belief that no one will suspect that it's a lie because it's simply too outrageous) have always had a tremendous advantage over sensitive, caring, honest folk. Most of us aren't used to dealing with people who lie consistently and shamelessly, we don't believe that anyone lies consistently and shamelessly, and so we are easily conned. Most of us have an unshakeable confidence in the goodness of man and so we are extremely gullible.

There is no doubt that leaders who possess psychopathic traits are at an enormous advantage. They have more freedom in their dealings with the public, with those with whom they work and with their potential enemies. They are good at self-promotion, they have enormous self-belief and they are able to control and manipulate people calmly, confidently, coolly and without any qualms. Psychopaths fake their emotions (which they learn by studying other people) and so suffer very little in circumstances which healthy people would find emotionally difficult. It is not surprising, perhaps, that many people in positions of power and many people who seem especially pushy are psychopaths. We should not be too surprised at this; after all psychopaths are surprisingly numerous and the incidence of psychopathic traits in our society is increasing rapidly. A few years ago it was estimated that just one in every 100 people was a psychopath. Today that figure is known to be much higher and it is believed that around 3% of people are psychopaths. The number of psychopaths living in fragmented families, or slum areas of inner cities, is likely to be considerably higher than this. This means that in every decent sized city or town there will probably be 100,000 psychopaths. A city of 5 million citizens is likely to contain 150,000 psychopaths. The average school or college or business will have several psychopaths in the building. And the psychopaths will not be cleaning the lavatories or filing bits of paper. They will be sitting in the best offices, planning how to take over their boss's job. How else can we possibly explain the number of bankers and chief executives who leave their companies in disarray and take with them huge bonuses and pensions but show absolutely no regret or remorse?

If you doubt my assertion that most countries and large companies are now run by people who are criminally insane just make a list of the leaders you can think of and then look at the following list of the signs, symptoms and traits commonly associated with psychopaths. If you go through the list (which was, incidentally, compiled using the data psychiatrists and psychologists use) while you are thinking of political figures you will, I suspect, be surprised to see how many people you can identify as psychopaths. Once you've completed this simple exercise you will realise why it is hardly surprising that there is no morality and no respect in our society.

Think your way through our leadership and compare their individual, personal qualities with the qualities of a rip roaring, cold-blooded officially diagnosed standard psychopath. You will notice, by the way, that I have not included violent behaviour on this list. That's because most psychopaths aren't violent. Why resort to violence when you can achieve your ambitions by other methods?

Psychopaths are often some of the following:

1. Exceptionally selfish.

2. Compulsive liars but skilful enough to `salt the mine' with an occasional nugget of truth or some small apparent revelation.

3. Deceitful and manipulative and prepared to con friends and enemies alike.

4. Egocentric.

5. Callous and indifferent to suffering; they don't experience fear themselves in the same way and so don't show compassion when others are fearful.

6. Grandiose and prone to dramatic, shallow and meaningless displays of feeling.

7. Filled with a sense of entitlement.

8. Lacking in personal insight.

9. Parasitic - they are accustomed to living off others or the State.

10. Bullying and abusive.

11. Able to trick and con people successfully and, if they have been caught lying or cheating, likely to claim that they made a mistake, that they've learned their lesson and that it was all a big misunderstanding. `Trust me,' they will say. `I'm really a trustworthy fellow.'

12. Superficially charming and glib.

13. Apparently strong, calm and confident.

14. Unable to experience love or compassion and, as a result, are insensitive and callous.

15. Not anxious and never irrational.

16. Filled with anger, rage and frustration.

17. Apparently sincere but invariably insincere.

18. Apparently likeable and sane.

19. Without shame or remorse; uncaring about the feelings of others; without any sense of guilt.

20. Unable to learn from experience.

21. Impulsive and unable to control their behaviour.

22. Constantly searching for excitement. They may, for example, engage in an unending series of casual sexual relationships.

23. Without any sense of responsibility (when things go wrong it is always someone else's fault).

24. Likely to neglect their family in every conceivable way.

Now try applying those criteria to the politicians, bankers and other leaders of whom you can think.

You will, I suspect, be surprised at the number of people whom you can identify as satisfying some of the basic criteria as psychopaths. But, then, how else could you possibly explain what has been going on?

Things aren't going to get better without a revolution. And that's not going to happen for a while (until more people see the light) because the psychopaths now control everything and, not surprisingly, they don't want anything to change. We can't vote our way out of trouble. So, until there is a revolution, all we can do is survive.

2

`It would be nice to have a world devoid of psychopathic leaders. For two reasons this is unlikely ever to come about. First, throughout history the possession of psychopathic traits has proved a useful passport to high office.

Men or women who are unfettered by moral scruples, who are prepared to lie or cheat their way to the top, who will make promises they know they cannot keep and may, in extreme cases, think nothing of assassinating their rivals, have a huge advantage over those held back by notions of fair play. A second reason for finding that top jobs in politics, as indeed in many other walks of life, are successfully held on to by people with psychopathic traits is that such characters are (though they may not know it) fulfilling Ashby's Law of Requisitive Variety. According to this law the successful control of any system depends upon the latter's complexity being matched by that of its controller. The possession of psychopathic traits is advantageous to a leader. They give him more degrees of freedom in his control and manipulation of those under him and most particularly in his dealings with potential enemies.' - Norman F.Dixon, Our Own Worst Enemy.

Conclusion

Bad things break the sensitive (Nietzche was wrong when he said that things that don't kill you make you stronger) but psychopaths ignore or brush aside genuine worries that would destroy ordinary people. It is the mental strength of psychopaths that enables them to rise to the top and it is that strength, that unswerving, uncaring, committed determination to achieve their own ambitions, whatever the cost, that is such a danger to society.

Chapter 7

Out Of Control Companies And Overpaid Bosses

Introduction

When company bosses (who are among the least talented and least hard-working of all employees) earn 300 to 400 times as much as the lowest paid worker it does not take long for the mass of people to see the injustice. When times are hard, and the average family is struggling to survive, the greed and excesses of company bosses arouse more than envy. But until there is rioting in the streets there will be little chance of much progress. The bosses enjoy their absurdly decadent lifestyles and will be reluctant to give up the chauffeurs, yachts and third homes.

1

The rich have become much richer. And everyone else has become poorer. This growing inequality is one of the causes of the economic crisis. When wages fall the wage earners have less money to spend. English workers now have £100 billion a year less to spend than they would have had if the bosses and investment bankers hadn't nicked all the money. That's a huge amount of money and it would have doubtless helped many manufacturers and retailers stay in business. The very rich spend their money in different ways to ordinary folk. There's another problem too: as wages have fallen in real terms so the incentive to work has disappeared. Giving too much money to the very rich and too little to everyone else has encouraged people to choose benefits over work.

This isn't a new phenomenon. The Great Depression of the 1930's was preceded by a sharp rise in inequality. History tells us that when wages lag behind output the result is a prolonged slump. High levels of inequality result in slowing growth and a leveraging down of demand which feeds on itself. The greedy bankers and corporate bosses have led us into a spiralling depression. We're on the road to self-destruction.

2

England is one of the most unequal countries in the world. Bosses earn massively more than other employees (and it is vital to remember that bosses are employees too). And things are getting worse. The salaries of England's top bosses, rose 187% in 2011 while the average pay rise for their employees was 3.2%. The people who own the companies (the shareholders) did worst of all. Dividends have been frozen or have fallen, while individual capital values are, in many cases, lower than they were ten, fifteen or twenty years ago. Between 2000 and 2010 the pay of chief executives went up by 108% despite the fact that shares as a whole are today worth less than they were worth in 1999. Bosses (for which read `barely competent managers and administrators') made millions while the actual owners of the businesses lost money and received little or nothing in dividends. The massive escalation in executive pay has impoverished everyone except the lucky executives themselves.

Why aren't shareholders screaming about this? Well, they are, of course. But no one listens. Shareholders can vote against directors' pay and bonuses but even though the company legally belongs to the shareholders the directors can ignore the vote. There's a real example of anti-democracy in action. The lunatics really have taken over the asylum. Moreover, institutional fund managers (who do the voting for shareholders who use nominee accounts, for unit trust investors, for pension fund investors and for investment trust shareholders, all of whom they are paid to represent) don't say anything about the obscene and undeserved salaries paid to company bosses because their own salaries are obscene and undeserved.

3

English companies are loaded up with debt, intangible assets and acquisition related goodwill. This is something that happens to English companies far more than to companies in Germany for example. It happens partly because the interest on all debt is deductible from taxes and partly because the boss who `grows' his company rapidly (by buying other companies) will have a grand excuse to demand a bigger pay cheque, bigger perks, more pension contributions, a more glorious office, more secretaries and a bigger jet.

4

Many of the bosses who have become enormously, obscenely, rich in recent years have done so not through talent or even luck but through knowing the right people. Capitalism has become crony capitalism. Those in power appoint their friends to positions of authority and wealth and the money then flows sideways in pay offs and kickbacks. Favours beget favours and the same group of corrupt individuals wallow in undeserved wealth. Chief executives use weak corporate governance (supplied by corrupt politicians) to steal from workers, shareholders, pensioners and taxpayers. Bankers in particular use political connections to cheat, cheat and cheat again. There are real problems with this brand of indecent behaviour. First, incompetent bosses hire incompetent subordinates (since they don't want to be threatened or shown up) and so talented individuals remain overlooked, oppressed and resentful. The consequences for the department, company or quango are disastrous. When the mediocre hold all the power then the results are, at best, mediocre. As the resentment and corruption grow so do the favours. Tax laws are changed. Regulatory exemptions are introduced to suit particular individuals and companies. And failure is rewarded richly.

5

It has been shown time and time again that all those absurdly highly-paid, pompous megalomaniacs running big companies play very little part in the success or failure of their companies. It is the external economy, credit bubbles and so on that result in company profits soaring or plunging. The bosses of financial firms are, in particular, linked to the national and global economy. In any company there are huge numbers of people who could do the top job just as well as the person in power. The boss just happens to be the person who is there. It has repeatedly been shown that if bosses make expensive changes to the companies they run then they will cost their shareholders money. The unchanged company, left to run passively, would have made more money. Interfering bosses destroy vast amounts of value. They make huge changes and organise takeovers in order to justify bigger staff numbers and, therefore, bigger salaries. These ambitious bosses take huge bonuses and, at the end of their tenure, leave shareholders with small dividends and a lower share price. Company bosses are just cheerleaders. Most don't create anything or do anything very much except have long lunches and give away shareholders' money to political parties and charities. They are smoochers. While underlings do the actual work (deciding what to make, making it, selling it, collecting the money and so on) the absurdly overpaid executives spend their days working out new ways to be paid: bonuses, share handouts, pensions, and allowances. It may be legal but by any decent standards you don't need to be a socialist to regard it as a sort of fraud.

6

Percy Shelley and Karl Marx didn't have much in common but while it was the poet Shelley who wrote that 'the rich have become richer and the poor have become poorer' it was Karl Marx who observed that the gap was widening. Both have been shown right. Shelley should, perhaps, not be regarded just as a great poet but also as a predictive economist.

7

If the regulators made directors personally, and legally, liable when companies did bad things there would be very little need for regulators.

8

It used to be true that you could never get really rich on a salary. That was right and proper, it meant that only the creative and innovative got really rich. It was called incentive. Today, you can become obscenely rich just by being a chairman or chief executive; a gormless company man; an empty suit; scowling at the staff and enjoying the perks. Most large organisation bosses are overpaid self-important morons and their work could be done by anyone. It would make good sense to make their jobs a lottery prize. `Pay £1 for a ticket and you could be boss of BT/BP/Tesco for a year.'

9

The best-paid boss in America took home $378 million last year. That was someone called Tim Cook, the CEO of Apple. Now Apple is the biggest company in the world (a fact which, in itself, rather draws attention to the madness of our time) but Cook didn't create the company or its slightly absurd products. The man who did create Apple, Steve Jobs, took a salary of $1 a year for each of the last four years he ran the company.

Apple, let us remember, is constantly being accused of taking advantage of workers in China. The company's slick and shiny iPads and iPhones are allegedly stuck together for a tenner and then sold for £500. That's the sort of mark up that is usually enjoyed by couturiers in the fanciest parts of the 8th arrondissement in Paris. There are bizarre stories about Apple employees in the Far East being paid $2 for a 14 hour day on a production line. If any of those allegations are even partly true then Apple's shiny products don't look quite so shiny. But it would be possible to see how Mr Cook can make so much money.

10

In the long-term, companies run by underpaid bosses generate much better profits for shareholders than companies run by overpaid bosses. Given the size of the goody bags some bosses take home that really isn't that surprising. Too many, it seems, forget who owns the company and who is entitled to some return on their money. They also forget two other truths: without shareholders there would be no bosses and most of the bosses employed today are interchangeable and replaceable.

11

A bunch of unelected, eurocrats working for the European Union have decided that companies must put more women on their boards - whether the women are competent or not. (Much the same thing happened in medicine when, several decades ago medical schools were forced to increase their intake of female students. The results have been disastrous.)

The tough targets, introduced by anonymous EU employees, will lead to mandatory quotas for female directors. The EU intends to introduce legislation across all 27 member nations of the EU stipulating the minium number of women that every company board must have. (Incidentally, the enthusiasm for `targets' which is now ruining every aspect of life in England and which comes largely from the European Union originated with Russia and the USSR. Targets were introduced to give the workers something to aim at, something to strive for. In practice, targets don't work, of course. The big problem is that the authorities tend to lighten targets so that they are always met. And so, for example, train companies will lower their punctuality targets to fit reality.)

Our world is falling apart and this is what the EU is doing to sort things out: introducing more blatantly sexist legislation.

And the legislation won't mean that *lots* of women will become company directors. It will almost certainly mean that a few women acquire a lot of directorships. Quota filling women will queue up to be put on company boards. In Norway (where it has been the law that company boards must include 40% women since 2003) there are a few `golden skirts' who sit on numerous boards and take home huge amounts of money. It is also a fact that as more regulations are introduced so more companies de-list from stock exchanges - leaving shareholders unable to sell (or buy) shares.

The big problem is that quotas distract from real issues. The real owners of companies (the shareholders) are the ones who need more powers. But the EU, being a fascist organisation, will not do anything to move power back from the boardroom to the shareholders. Nor will the EU do anything to persuade companies to put more effort into introducing medium and long-term strategies, rather than satisfying short-term targets.

12

An increasing number of companies now insist that their customers conduct all their business via the Internet. (In this they are following the bad example set by Government departments such as HMRC.) Personally, I believe that one should, whenever possible, avoid using either the telephone or the Internet when communicating with big businesses. You will waste hours and afterwards they will, if it is convenient to them, deny everything they said.

Send a letter through the post. I know that many large organisations don't give street addresses (try obtaining one for that arch baddy the Royal Mail, for example) but it is usually possible to find one in the end. Send your mail by recorded delivery so that there is evidence of it having been sent (because if you don't they will claim that they never received your letter). When dealing with large Governmental or quasi Governmental organisations you must recognise that you are fighting a war. These people are not, and never will be, your friends. They are not on your side.

13

If you want evidence illustrating the level of corruption in the business section of our society consider tobacco companies. Vast numbers of highly-paid individuals are dedicated to opening up new markets for a product proven to cause an early death among its consumers.

14

Whatever else you do with your life you will always be a consumer. To the people who make items as varied as motorcars, refrigerators, underwear, indigestion remedies, biscuits, coat hangers and kitchen sinks you are a consumer. To lawyers, accountants, surveyors, estate agents and even doctors you are a consumer.

In order to persuade you to become a customer the people who provide these products and services spend considerable amounts of money on trying to convince you that *their* products or services are better than anyone else's.

Every day your custom is solicited in a thousand different ways - some crude and some subtle. Every day you are bombarded with advertisements telling you to buy one of these and begging you to buy some of those and explaining why your life will be incomplete if you do not spend your money on a little of this and a little of that.

The professionals who prepare the advertisements with which you are confronted each day are only too aware of the fact that it is no longer enough for them to tell you the value of the product they are selling. These days the competition is so great that advertising agencies are no longer content to tell you how to satisfy your basic needs. Advertising agencies know very well that in order to succeed in the modern market place they must create new needs; they know that their advertising must, through a mixture of exaggeration and deceit, and through exploiting your fears and your weaknesses, create wants and desires, hopes and aspirations and then turn those wants, desires, hopes and aspirations into needs. Modern advertising is a scientifically based creative art which is designed to raise the intensity of our desires and build our dissatisfaction and our fears. The advertising copywriter is hired to create unhappiness. Advertising is, in short, an industry which only works when it puts us under unnecessary stress.

Modern advertising agencies know (because they have done the necessary research) that it is impossible to sell anything to a satisfied man. But, in order, to keep the money coming in, the advertising agencies must constantly encourage us to buy and so they constantly need to find better ways to sell us stuff and services that we do not really need.

Any fool can sell a product or a service that people need. If your shoes wear out then you will buy new ones or have the old ones repaired. If you are hungry and there is only one restaurant for miles then that restaurant will get your service. If your car is about to run out of petrol then a garage doesn't need to offer you free offers to get your custom.

As far as the advertising agencies are concerned the trick is to get you to buy shoes when you don't need to, and to buy shoes that are more expensive than they need be. In order to do this, advertising agencies use all their professional skills to make you dissatisfied with what you already have. They need you to be constantly dissatisfied and frustrated. Advertising copywriters want to take away your appreciation of the simple things in life because they know that there is more profit in making things more complicated, more expensive and more unreliable. They want you to be in so much of a hurry that you eat instant foods rather than growing and preparing your own vegetables. They want you to ride in a car rather than walk or ride a bicycle. They want to make you feel guilty if you don't smell right or don't buy the right breakfast cereal for your children. They want you to feel a failure if you don't have the latest clothes on your back and the latest gadgets in your home. Advertising is most successful when it persuades you to forget your real needs and to replace them with wants.

There is no doubt that the advertising industry is responsible for much of the sickness and much of the unhappiness in our society. Even if you do buy the products they want to sell you, you will still not find the satisfaction that they promise you for the advertisements are shallow and the promises hollow. Whatever exaggerated claims they make, you will be disappointed. Your sex life will not suddenly improve just because you change your perfume or deodorant. Your social life will not change because you buy the latest clothes. You will not be immune to traffic jams just because you buy a new car with metallic paint and electric windows.

The advertising professionals make many promises which they know they cannot keep and whatever claims they make the chances are that you will remain frustrated and even more dissatisfied than you were before you spent your money. Your hopes and expectations will be aroused and then disappointed.

To the spiritual and mental frustration created by all this disappointment you must add physical frustration too for the chances are high that the product you buy will soon fail. Obsolescence is built in and is essential to all new products. Built in mechanical or fashionable obsolescence enables the car companies to keep making and selling us new cars even though most of us already have perfectly functional vehicles parked outside our homes. You might think you change your car because you want something more reliable or more comfortable but you probably don't: the chances are that you change your car because the advertising copywriters have succeeded in persuading you that your present vehicle is out-of-date and unfashionable.

Even if you don't have the money to spend on new cars, kitchen furniture, clothes and other goods you will not escape. Advertising, designed to inflame your desires, will show you services you cannot buy and things you cannot have. It will create wants and then turn those wants into needs. Advertising creates frustration and disappointment, envy and dissatisfaction. If you are too poor to buy the things which are advertised you will simply never discover that the products on offer do not to satisfy the promises made for them.

Advertising is, without a doubt, one of the greatest causes of stress and is one of the greatest of modern threats to physical and mental health. Advertising agencies kill far more people than industries which pollute the atmosphere. Advertising is the symbol of modern society; it represents false temptations, hollow hopes and unhappiness and disenchantment; it inspires values which are based on fear and greed. Advertising succeeds by making people dissatisfied, restless and, ultimately, unhappy.

15

I received a text today to tell me that calls to one of the popular directory enquiries numbers will now cost £2.50 a minute. So, if I use this basic service to enquire about a number, and allow them to put the call through (taking two minutes) and I then speak for a modest 10 minutes the call will cost me £30.00. It is, I suspect, the poor and the elderly who will suffer most from this scandalous but authorised theft. I have no doubt that the bosses who benefit from this sort of chicanery sleep well at night.

16

The so-called captains of industry now regard themselves as special in some way. But most have created nothing and have, by and large, contributed little or nothing to the success of the company they run. Moreover, their greed and extravagance have usually done little or nothing for the wealth and well-being of investors, pension fund holders and employees. It is difficult to avoid the conclusion that the bosses of large companies are driven not by a desire to see a better world (or even a better company) but by a yearning to grab as much money as they can for themselves. And that's simple, old-fashioned detestable greed. Gluttony. Our corporate entities are run by people corrupted by financial lust. These are the new corporate heroes; the men and women who tell us that it is our duty to buy things, that pillaging the earth is good for the economy and that exploiting the poor and the disadvantaged around the world is in some curious way `for their own benefit'.

17

Bonuses (or tips) used to be something that posh people gave to poor people. Taxi drivers, waiters and hotel doormen got tips because they were poorly paid and it was a way for their temporary employers to show their gratitude (and superiority). Factory workers making things on a production line were given bonuses if they made things faster than expected (or faster than time and motion experts thought was possible). Today, everyone with a job expects a bonus and vast bonuses are paid out to people who haven't even done what they have been paid to do - let alone done something special. Bizarrely, even public sector workers, following enthusiastically in the greedy footsteps of company directors and executives, now demand bonuses simply for turning up and doing their jobs.

Just a decade or two ago no self-respecting banker, company director or civil servant would have accepted a tip (or a bonus) for doing their job. They would have been as unwilling to accept the idea that they needed fiscal encouragement as would a doctor or priest. (Try offering £50 to your surgeon as an incentive for him to make a neat scar and I hope you'll see what I mean.) Bonuses were popular in the Soviet Union where it was generally believed that they helped increase productivity. They were also used to encourage informers to snitch on their neighbours.

But bankers and public sector workers have lowered their social vision of themselves. These days they are quite happy to be lumped in with cabbies and bellhops and very pleased indeed to be able to trouser extra cash for doing what they get paid to do anyway. If bank staff had pocketed just 10% less in pay and bonuses over the last decade the banks would have had £50 billion more in capital. If they'd taken just slightly less in undeserved bonuses the banks would have been awash with cash when the crisis hit. Was it any wonder that in Greece demonstrators set fire to a bank? The only wonder is that banks all over the world aren't all still smouldering.

The big myth about bonuses is that giving people bonuses encourages them to work harder and better. The Labour Government of 1997 (the one which led England down the road to ruin) believed that our world could be transformed by targets, awards and bonuses. They were right. But it has not been transformed in a good way.

The bonus system works for production line staff whose productivity can easily be measured but it doesn't work for most other people. Giving a doorman a tip may mean that he remembers your name. Giving a waiter a tip may mean that (if you visit often enough and he remembers you) you will get a smile when he hands you the menu. But the door won't be opened any more effectively. And the tea and crumpets won't taste any better.

In order to check the effect of bonuses on performance, four North American professors conducted two experiments. In one they gave subjects tasks that demanded attention, memory, concentration and creativity. A third of the subjects were promised a day's pay if they performed well. A third were promised two weeks' pay. The final third were promised five months' pay. The result was that the low and medium bonus groups performed the same. The group offered the big bonus performed worst of the three. In a second experiment graduate students were given an opportunity to earn either $600 or $60 by performing one four minute task. The result again showed that a big carrot led to poorer performance.

Bonuses clearly don't work. They cost employers (and when the people receiving the bonuses are public sector workers that means taxpayers) a good deal of money and they result in less effective work being done. But banks, big companies and the civil service will, without a shadow of doubt, ignore this evidence and continue to hand out big bonuses. Civil servants now expect bonuses for not having holidays all the time. They regard their bonus as another part of their salary - for turning up and doing their jobs. They will protest vigorously if any government tries to take away their new perks.

And the money for the bonuses will be provided by shareholders and taxpayers.

In America, between 90% and 100% of the earnings achieved by the major banks are now being shared among employees as salaries, bonuses and benefits. Nothing is being put aside for a rainy day and nothing is left for shareholders. Bonuses were originally designed to encourage but today they are often paid to directors, civil servants and executives just for breathing and turning up occasionally. Bosses and civil servants who have, by any conceivable standard, failed miserably, still get their bonuses. Today, even tax inspectors receive bonuses for doing the work they are well paid to do.

The bonus system has, for decades now been destroying our world in every imaginable way. The My Lai massacre of 128 civilians during the Vietnam War occurred because the USA army was giving awards for the number of deaths that could be filed. 'Kill more of the enemy and get a medal or a bonus.'

The bonus culture has helped create a thousand inequalities and injustices. Much of the banking crisis can be traced back to the enthusiasm of bankers for bonuses acquired by gambling with other people's money. Endless public sector workers receive huge bonuses for being pathetic. In June 2012, it was merrily announced that the boss of Royal Mail (surely the most badly run organisation on the entire planet) would receive a bonus of over £300,000. What the hell for? Turning up? Wearing a nice suit? Not falling down the stairs? I hope he wasn't given it for running an organisation efficiently and for providing the public with a reliable, competent service.

The problem, of course, is that the bonus system is here to stay. The people who decide whether or not bonuses are given all receive bonuses.

Within corporate structures the shareholders (who own the company in which they have shares) cannot vote against absurd bonus schemes because nominee accounts pool shareholdings in the name of the nominee company. The individual shareholders cannot vote. And the fund managers, who represent investment trusts, unit trusts and pension funds won't vote against excess because they are part of the problem. They hardly ever vote against remuneration reports because they don't want to rock the boat. After all they too are enjoying the same delights. They too receive bonuses for failing to do their job properly.

Until the bonus culture is destroyed (or employees are, at the very least, prepared to accept bonuses only when they have done something clearly very special) the economy will continue to be sucked dry. Money that could have been used to create jobs will be used to sustain jobs that, in many cases, should never have been created in the first place and in other cases involve employees who are already overpaid and underworked.

Conclusion

During the last 30 years the real incomes of the richest 1% of Americans has risen by 300% and their share of the national income has more than trebled. In the same period the median household income has risen by just 40% and that rise has been largely a result of the fact that there are now two people working instead of one). The assets of the top 400 people in the USA are equal to the assets of the lowest 140 million. The situation in England is identical. We live in an unequal society which is ripe for a revolution.

Chapter 8

The Story Of Hitler's Bastard Love Child

Introduction

It is difficult to think of any aspect of our lives which has not already been adversely affected by the EU and it is difficult to think of any way in which the EU has contributed positive values to our health, wealth or well being. The EU as we now know it, the modern super-bureaucratic fascist version, was conceived by Adolf Hitler. Anyone who doubts this has only to check the history books. Talk of the EU being a result of Mitterand and Khol honourably attempting to prevent another war (the sort of explanation you're likely to hear on the BBC) is entirely fanciful and a result either of woeful ignorance or politically motivated deceit. Today, the eurocrats who run the

EU ignore democracy and reality and impose their will upon the European population without allowing their malignant megalomania to be disrupted by good sense, respect or compassion. They are too swamped with conceit to entertain the idea that they can ever be wrong; they are overwhelmed by a conviction that they always know best what we should do with our lives, how we should live and how we should behave. Like all true fascists, eager to obey the strictures of Mussolini, they have discovered ways to meld corporate power with political power for the benefit of all those directly involved.

I have already described the extraordinary evils of the European Union in previous books (most recently in *OFPIS*) and this chapter is merely intended as an updated summary of a few of the ways in which the EU is ruining our lives, our country, our future and our hopes.

1

Two decades ago, when the EU fanatics decided that the best way to seal their slightly dodgy union was to create a single currency, the euro, just about every economist on the planet warned that the new currency wouldn't work.

But the hubristic EU fanatics didn't care. When they asked economists to give their opinions they rejected the views of those who warned that the euro was flawed and listened only to craven fools who supported the idea.

The euro was designed to glue disparate European countries and to force them to work together. And the people who designed the new currency knew that in doing so they were messing around with people's lives. They knew that unless they could arrange complete fiscal union there was a very real risk that the new currency would collapse; they knew that people and companies would be at great risk. They knew that if one nation collapsed then its citizens would be in dire trouble if their debts were outside their country and their savings and assets were within a bankrupt nation. They knew that banks would collapse and that there would be utter chaos, civil unrest and probably deaths.

The EU has always been the European version of the USSR, more closely allied to the old Soviet Union than the USA. The EU imposes a way of life on people who don't want it. Most citizens of Europe want nothing to do with the EU. But they have no choice. Democracy has been suspended indefinitely.

And the eurocrats and europhiles are going to use the weakness of the euro to take the one big step forward that they are dreaming of.

There are only two things that can happen to the euro.

Either it disappears (and all the constituent countries of the EU go back to using their francs and marks and whatever) or else the countries which use the euro join together in complete fiscal harmony with a single exchequer. That, of course, will mark the formation of Hitler's dream: the United States of Europe.

2

The European Commission's economic directorate, which issues policy recommendations which have the force of law, employs 544 staff. There are just a dozen or so English citizens among these employees. There are more Romanians than Englishmen making the laws which rule our lives.

3

There is so much corruption and deceit practised by and within the EU that it is impossible for one man to keep track of it all. The EU has made freedom a dirty word and has turned patriotism into a sin. When MPs voted to approve the signing of the Treaty of Lisbon (which Gordon Brown had signed in December 2007) they signed the final death warrant for England. I am certain now that it is no exaggeration to say that almost everything bad that has happened to England in the last few decades is the fault of the EU.

There is no doubt that the Lisbon Treaty diluted (yet again) English sovereignty. Indeed, the Lisbon Treaty formally gave the EU the characteristics that international law recognises as the usual attributes of statehood. Thanks to Gordon Brown and the other signatories, the EU now has a head of state, a foreign office, a criminal justice system and the right to sign international treaties.

The Treaty also gave the EU the authority to abolish any controls on individuals, whatever their nationality, when crossing internal borders. If 20 million Russians manage to enter the EU then our Government will be powerless to stop them from entering England and staying there. The Labour Government, headed by a Scotsman, broke its promise to hold a referendum because it would have had to reveal just how much of our sovereignty had been ceded to Brussels and how much more it was giving away. Brown knew that if he had a referendum he - and the EU - would lose. And so, just as he had chickened out of holding an election in the autumn of 2007 because he had been frightened that he would lose, so he broke his party's promise about a referendum.

The new Treaty which Brown signed in December 2007 extended the powers of the EU in every conceivable direction. The treaty gave the EU `primacy' over the laws of the member states, it gave the EU power over England's economic and employment policies (despite the fact that we are not in the euro) and it abolished national vetoes. The Treaty created a full European criminal justice system, with a European public prosecutor and an EU legal code. (The new EU legal codes run directly counter to our own common law traditions.). The treaty Brown signed gave the EU jurisdiction over transport, energy, public health, trade, employment, social policy, competition, agriculture, fisheries, defence, foreign affairs, space exploration, and asylum and immigration. The EU now has ownership and command of our police, army, Royal Navy, RAF, currency reserves, North Sea oil and nuclear weapons. Serving officers in the forces will have to take an oath of allegiance to the EU instead of the Queen. It is now illegal to criticise the EU.

Oh, and the Lisbon Treaty gave the EU the right to make up any new laws it wants and to change the Treaty that Brown signed if it wants to do so. The Lisbon Treaty is `self-amending'. It can be altered for any purpose, at any time. Neither you nor Gordon Brown can do anything about it.

On the day that the Lisbon Treaty was signed the EU stopped being an association of states and became a state in its own right.

Among other things, the EU constitution which Gordon Brown signed in Lisbon in 2007, proposed:

* Europe wide taxes (probably on top of national taxes).

* Massive increases in workers' rights - even guaranteeing a job for life.

* A Europe-wide minimum wage.

* A common education curriculum throughout the EU (which must include pro EU propaganda).

* A more powerful EU army.

* The abolition of national sovereignty.

* A huge rise in the EU budget.

* Recognition that the new constitution be regarded as the first step towards political unity.

I feel sure that the Labour Government meant to tell you about these things. Perhaps they just forgot.

The Lisbon Treaty is, according to EU insiders, the last EU treaty. It is the last EU treaty because it provides the EU with all the powers it will ever need.

4

`Despite the political, economic and cultural legacy that has perpetuated its name, England no longer officially exists as a country and enjoys no separate political status within the United Kingdom.' - Encyclopaedia Britannica

5

Europhile fascists (something of a tautology I know, but I like the phrase so please humour me) often dismiss those who want England to leave the EU as Little Englanders. Those who use this term in a pejorative fashion clearly don't understand its origin or meaning. But the euro aficionados are not renowned for their understanding of history, their sense of culture or their intelligence. (The term Little Englander dates from the Boer War and refers to people who were, at the time, opposed to the English Empire and were anti-Imperialist. The Little Englanders wanted the English to stop taking over the world. Such folk were regarded as unpatriotic. Today, ignorant pro EU fascists use the term as one of abuse; it is usually applied to those who are aware that removing England from maps and history books is an essential part of the EU project and who don't want England to disappear and be converted into nine EU regions. Europhiles, who also tend to know nothing much about European history, are also usually woefully ignorant about the word `fascist'. I have described the definition (in Mussolini's words) in previous books. It is, I hope, sufficient here to say that Mussolini would, like Hitler, have been an enthusiastic supporter of the European Union.

6

When, at the turn of the millennium, other nations all celebrated their history and their culture, the English celebrations were pathetically multi-ethnic, cravenly politically correct, appallingly embarrassing and an insult to our history, our culture, our ancestors and the millions who have died to help make the world a better, safer place. Since then the English establishment has done everything in its power to diminish English history and to apologise unnecessarily for past, redefined sins.

The result, of course, is a nation which has lost its way in the world and a nation whose citizens no longer have pride in who they are. The authorities have even decided that `English' is not a nationality. You can be Welsh,

Irish or Scottish but you cannot be English. Without an identity, without an ethnicity (what an awful word that is), the English are lost souls in a regimented, bureaucratic world.

7

The EU has supposedly made it easier for us to travel around Europe. This is a lie. It is now far more difficult to travel to France than it was a year ago. And then it was far more difficult than it had been ten years earlier. And then it was far more difficult than it had been a generation before. The truth is that the EU's absurd immigration policies have resulted in our Government having to introduce stricter controls at our borders. And so, thanks entirely to the European Union, it is now far, far more difficult for English folk to travel to foreign lands. And far, far more difficult for foreign tourists to come to England.

8

Making a speech or writing a book which criticises the EU (or the laws of the EU) may be regarded as a crime if it is considered subversive. It is, of course, up to the bureaucrats of the EU to decide whether or not something is 'subversive'.

9

Fascist supporters of the EU (which I prefer to call Hitler's Bastard Love Child) claim that membership of the EU is essential for the English economy. To put it diplomatically, this is a barefaced lie. According to official Government figures, membership of the EU costs us a fortune - both in terms of direct contributions to the EU and the indirect costs of high levels of regulation and red tape. A 2005 Treasury report suggested 'that the likely EU cost was around 7% of GDP'. This would be well over £100 billion in today's money. Other studies have suggested that the cost of our membership of the EU is around 10% of GDP. If we were not members of the EU we would have at least an extra £100 billion to spend on ourselves. And that, to save you the bother of working it out, is around £2,000 for every man, woman and child in England. Put another way, the average family in England would be £8,000 a year better off if we left the EU. And then, of course, we would be free to do what we should have done all along: enhance our ties with the Commonwealth. Those who favour the EU forget that the members of the Commonwealth (including India, South Africa and Australia) are among the strongest and fastest growing countries in the world. Many are rich in essential commodities. Growth rate in the eurozone will probably be stagnant for years to come (assuming that things go better than forecast and better than expected) whereas the countries of the Commonwealth have a combined growth rate of 7.3%.

10

The English don't like to complain. We put up with our statist society because it's what we have. We put up with gold plated EU regulations that the French won't accept even in their original vanilla flavour. We obey the rules, politely and obediently. We allow our pavements to be made pink and knobbly and we spend untold millions making unnecessary and disruptive changes to our motorways. We cope with absurd rules about rubbish collection and we sit quietly by as our history and our culture are slowly but efficiently dismantled. We have sleepwalked into statism, communism and fascism - which are all the same thing. If the EU survives, the organisation will presumably build statues to the founding father: Adolf Hitler. (Hitler had a house in Saltzberg. The EU now has offices in Saltzberg. Just a coincidence? Well, there are several thousand towns and cities of comparable size in Europe.)

11

European Commission Bureaucrats (our new rulers) want to introduce a Tobin tax on all financial transactions. The EU says that the new Tobin tax is being introduced to punish the banks for making such a mess of Europe's economy. The tax has been welcomed by experts such as the Archbishop of Canterbury. But the tax will consist of a tax of 0.1% on all share dealings. So it will not be financial institutions which suffer but small savers and investors and pension holders. This is a typical EU trick - an inverted Robin Hood scheme - which takes money from the poor to give to the rich. For English investors this will be particularly unfair since they already pay stamp duty on many transactions and so will be paying two lots of tax on every financial decision they make. And where will the money go? To the EU bureaucrats of course. To pay for more expensive dinners and weekends away and private planes.

12

Cameron has become ever more gutless. He is now apparently considering getting rid of Greenwich Mean Time and making us all match our clocks to those of the rest of the EU. I suspect that he is doing this to please the awful Clegg. Clegg, a former EU employee (who will receive an EU pension until he dies), is of course mad keen on

Hitler's Bastard Love Child and has threatened to walk out of the Coalition if England stands up for its national interest. (I suspect that the Deputy Prime Minister isn't much of a patriot.) Clegg seems to think that the boys and girls in Brussels can do no wrong. His arrogance matches that of all the EU lovers. It is because of them that extremist, populist, nationalistic parties are springing up all over Europe (precisely as I predicted they would in my book *England Our England*).

13

I sometimes suspect that not all politicians are entirely au fait with what is going on in the world. This is true of national politicians but it is also true of regional and local politicians. For example, the English county of Cornwall has its own political party - Mebyon Kernow - which wants independence for Cornwall. Mebyon Kernow supports the European Union. Fair enough. They're entitled to support anyone they like and since it is one of the poorer parts of England, Cornwall has, from time to time, received money from the EU. (`Here's some of your own money to build a bridge. But make sure you put a big sign on it saying `Money donated by the EU'. And don't mention that the money originally came from English taxpayers.'). But I can't help wondering if the members of Mebyon Kernow are aware that the EU plans to abolish Cornwall completely. Cornwall will be part of the South West Region which will stretch from Lands End and include Gloucestershire and Wiltshire. Its regional capital will be Exeter.

By supporting the EU, the Cornish party has, in my view, helped sign Cornwall's death warrant.

Whoops.

14

For some time now one of the strongest currencies in the world has been the Norwegian krone. Norway is not of course a member of the EU.

15

Back in 1995, an economist with the European Commission published a book entitled *The Rotten Heart of Europe*. He was fired because his book was seen as an attack on the EU and the euro. You don't get fired for fraud or misconduct in the EU. But you do get fired for telling the truth. The author, a brave man called Connolly, brought an action against the EU and in May 2011 (after 16 years deliberations) the European Court of Justice finally decreed that the EU Commission can restrict dissent in order to `protect the rights of others' and `punish individuals who damage the institutions's image and reputation'.

16

The EU, Hitler's Bastard Love Child, represents intellectual terrorism, power, bureaucracy and regulation. It exists to give power to those who work for the organisation and to force responsibility on those who don't. The only people who support the EU are the ones who don't understand what it is, and what it is for. The vast majority of its supporters are bureaucrats. Creative and productive individuals loathe the EU for the barrage of pointless, self-serving and restrictive legislation it has forced us to accept. The EU is run by nerdy, geeky, incompetent buffoons (think Caroline Ashton, the Queen of Geeks) who never seem to question their own competence and so do not recognise their shortcomings. If a film were ever made about the EU the title would surely be *The Revenge Of The Nerds*. There hasn't been a statesman in Europe since the whole damned fiasco started. I hope that the mean-spirited nerds working for the EU do not regard this paragraph as a criticism.

17

The EU has introduced a new law called `droit de suite' whereby artists receive extra money every time their paintings are resold. This only happens to art sold within the EU and will, therefore, do permanent, serious damage to auction houses operating within the EU. (The biggest and most successful auction houses in the EU operate in London.)

18

The EU is introducing more regulations which will increase bank charges and red tape. It will be increasingly difficult for customers to get hold of their own money or to move it around or, indeed, to do anything with it other than let it just sit where it is.

19

`The British deputies to Strasbourg will derive their authority from the same electorate and by the same process as Members of Parliament derive theirs. It will soon be perceived that whatever they decide or approve along with the directly elected members representing the rest of the inhabitants of the Community can no more be reviewed or overturned by the British House of Commons than the Worcestershire County Council can reject an Act of

Parliament. There will be an end to the fiction that British ministers in the council of ministers will have to take their orders from the House of Commons or accept its censure. They will say to the House of Commons thereafter 'What we have done has already been approved under the constitution of the Community (which England has accepted) by the representatives of the English people, directly elected and sent precisely for that purpose, being duly authorised thereto by the electorate from the very fact of their being elected. Who are you, and what is your authority to interfere, you minnows of Westminster? Did you not yourself authorise, back in 1972, the supremacy of the Community and its laws over your own assembly and its laws? Be off with you and mind what little business we are good enough to leave for you to do...We take no orders from you...we take them from the representatives of the whole people of the Community.' - Enoch Powell, in a speech to the Croydon Monday Club 27.2.1975

20

In December 2010 the leaders of England, Germany, France, the Netherlands and Finland wrote to Jose Barroso, the president of the European Commission (all genuflect in the direction of Brussels, please) demanding that the EU increase its spending by no more than inflation from the year 2013. Cameron and the others suggested that the EU might perhaps consider making a few cuts - reducing the absurdly high salaries for EU officials, increasing the working week, increasing the retirement age and even cutting a few jobs.

The EU bureaucrats (who are overpaid, underworked and immune to taxes) thought about this and have replied with what can only be described as an artfully displayed two fingers.

The EU has decided that it will be spending around £1,000 billion between 2014 and 2020. And since the unelected EU bureaucrats run things that is what will happen. While individual countries are cutting back and struggling to deal with their debts the unelected bureaucrats will be on a spending mission. Spend, spend, spend is the new EU theme song.

The bureaucrats are introducing an EU wide tax on financial transactions to top up their coffers even further. (Yes, that means that you and I will be paying a new tax direct to Brussels. On top of all the other multi-billion contributions. No chance of voting on this, of course.)

None of this should come as a surprise to any of us. And it certainly shouldn't come as a surprise to readers of my book *OFPIS*. When the Treaty of Lisbon was signed we became citizens of the new EU state. Our politicians handed over all rights and responsibilities to the unelected bureaucrats. The most important thing politicians sitting in the House of Commons have to deal with these days are expenses forms. (Admittedly, this is something at which they have become very adept.)

The EU rules. OK?

Naturally, Cameron and the rest will not complain about any of this since the EU rules mean that even if they want to they can't.

21

Those of us who loathe the EU and everything it stands for can only hope that the Greek debt fiasco gets worse because if Greece goes bankrupt (as it really should) then the euro will quite probably collapse. (If Greek bankruptcy doesn't trigger a euro collapse then maybe the bankruptcies of Ireland, Spain, Portugal or Italy will do the job. As I write this in early summer 2012, unemployment in Spain has risen above 25%. Among the under 25s unemployment has topped 50%)

And (as forecast in my book *2020*) if the euro goes then the banks will go down all across Europe and the EU itself will quite probably also collapse.

Let's keep our fingers crossed.

There could be good times ahead for those of us who loathe the Fascist State of the EU.

But there is a snag.

The EU bosses also know this and so they will bail out Greece (and, if necessary, Portugal, Spain, Ireland and wherever) until they run out of money.

And when things get really bad they will take the opportunity to explain to us that it is necessary, for our own good, to create a more closely linked United States of Europe. And, as all this happens, so the resentment will grow among those hard-working tax-paying populations (expected to retire at 67 years of age) who are being forced to subsidise lazy, tax-evading populations (allowed to retire at 60 years of age or even earlier).

The fascist politicians who love the EU are so devoted to Hitler's Bastard Love Child that they do not understand that you cannot build a new state (or, indeed, anything very much) upon a basis of unfairness and resentment. The result will be a political and economic catastrophe.

22

A new plan to rescue the euro means handing over enormous powers to the European Commission and the European Central Bank without bothering to ask for the approval of the voters. The series of treaties which have been signed, without voters' approval, have given the EU bureaucrats the power to damned well do whatever they please. If they want to ban football, chips and television they can.

23

The eurocrats aren't the only people making a fortune out of the EU. The politicians are doing well too. MEPs' salaries and allowances have risen 78% in the last seven years.

24

The euro was never going to work and to be honest I doubt if the people who thought it up expected it to work. The euro was set up for entirely political reasons by fascists whose only aim was the acquisition of power and who didn't give a damn what happened to the countries whose currencies were being destroyed. The euro fanatics were (and are) perfectly prepared to screw up the lives of hundreds of millions of Europeans in order to get what they wanted. Hitler would have admired such ruthlessness, such efficiency and such singlemindedness.

25

The eurocrats can bend the rules as much as they like. When EU bosses find something inconvenient (such as the debt levels of member countries) they ignore the problem, they suspend the laws and they carry on regardless. These are the actions of hubristic, deceitful, corrupt and irresponsible fascists. Bailing out Greece was against the law but, in their desperation to save their manufactured currency, the eurocrats ignored reality. However, the same eurocrats force you and I to obey every single one of their laws. If we don't then we go to prison.

26

Every survey done shows that the vast majority of English citizens want to leave the EU. (Actually, similar surveys have shown that the citizens of France, Germany and just about every one of the early joiners want to leave.) If any one of the three major parties campaigned on a `We will take England out of the EU' slogan they would win hands down. So, why don't they? Simple. Bribery, corruption and orders from Brussels.

27

The euro should have been allowed to die. It is only being kept alive in order to protect Hitler's political dream of a European superstate. The euro was a stupid idea (designed for political rather than economic reasons) and, like everything else the EU does, it was badly planned. If the EU were run by sensible, thoughtful, intelligent people who gave a damn for the lives of the European people, the euro would have been killed off a year or two ago, and individual countries allowed to revert to their original currencies. Allowing the euro to die would result in some immediate pain but the pain would soon be followed by recovery and growth. Maintaining the euro simply prolongs the agony and causes needless real suffering. But the EU and its servants will fight to the last breath to save the euro.

28

The EU's environment levies, designed to support inefficient and uneconomic energy sources such as wind and solar power, are destroying English industry. Companies are having to pay far more money for electricity than companies in other countries (including France and Germany which may also be in the EU but which do not take the EU's regulations so seriously). Our Government takes all EU nonsenses more seriously than any other government. The result will be that many large companies will close their factories in England and move them to Germany and other EU countries. This was, I suspect, all part of the original plan. (Remember, please, that the two most powerful countries in the EU, Germany and France, hate England. We beat Germany twice at war and we humiliated the French by saving them.)

29

'He perceived that he was up against French red tape, compared to which that of Great Britain and America is only pinkish. Where in the matter of rules and regulations London and New York merely scratch the surface, these Gauls plumb the depths. It is estimated that a French minor official, with his heart really in his work, can turn more hairs grey and have more clients tearing those hairs than any six of his opposite numbers on the pay rolls of other nations.' - P. G. Wodehouse, Frozen Assets

(NB The French no longer take their red tape seriously. But we gold plate it. And take it very seriously indeed).

30

The European Court has decided that England must allow prisoners to vote. It is, apparently, unfair to prisoners to deprive them of their liberty and their vote. I look forward to seeing who is elected the next MP for the Dartmoor District.

31

Under the terms of the Greek bailout, the ECB and various national banks will take no losses on their Greek debt but private investors (through pension funds and insurance funds) will lose 75% of their money.

The ECB I should mention includes no elected officials and is not subject to any real democratic oversight. It's a bunch of hybrid bureaucrat-bankers with all the authority in the world and none of the responsibility. These are the people who believe that you can always solve a debt problem by throwing more money at it. If a country is in debt, give it more money. If a bank is in debt, give it more money. This is utter, unbridled madness. But the money they use belongs to ordinary, small investors and pensioners so they care not one jot. Pure fascism in action. The EU staff are constantly changing the goalposts, the referee and the rules as they go along. But there is one constant: official creditors are spared any pain, the banker-gamblers who bet against Greece are protected and 'small' investors pay all the bills.

32

According to every definition of 'fascism' the EU (Hitler's Bastard Love Child) is the most fascist state ever invented. (Commentators who don't understand what fascism means happily jump on the EU's propaganda bandwagon and claim that anyone who criticises the EU is a fascist.)

Here are some of the things all fascist regimes have in common:

1. Enthusiasm for the State is encouraged. (In our case we are encouraged to be enthusiastic about the EU rather than our real countries.)

2. There is an obsession with national security. There is constant talk about the need for vigilance. Armed police patrol airports.

3. Elections are dodgy. Candidates are imposed on the electorate and questions are often asked about the results. But nothing much ever changes.

4. Fascist countries need enemies in order to keep the people frightened. In a fascist country there is usually at least one war going on.

5. Huge amounts of money are spent on the military.

6. Politicians and bureaucrats have contempt for the rights of ordinary citizens.

7. There is control of the mass media. Critics are silenced. Serious opponents of the regime's activities are labelled `terrorists'.

8. Public money is spent to protect corporate power. Bankers, for example, are given public money even though their businesses are run along private lines. The lines between public and corporate money are blurred.

9. Money is transferred in huge quantities to those loyal supporters who work for large organisations such as banks which support the `leadership'.

10. There is an obsession with creating new laws. (Within the EU, these are usually described as `rules', `regulations' and `guidelines' but any `rules', `regulations' and `guidelines' which are enforced with severe penalties, including imprisonment, are, in my view, best described as laws.)

11. The police have almost unlimited powers - and constantly demand greater powers. Remember: the police regularly shoot people in England - and get away with it.

12. Cronyism and corruption are rife among those in power.

33

England is a fascist country. Or, rather, it would be if it still existed. Officially, England is now just a series of EU regions. And although idiotic Scottish nationalists believe that they have acquired quasi independence, Scotland and Wales are EU regions too.

34

The number of trials for which we have the right to be tried by a jury will, in the future, be dramatically reduced. Instead individuals will be tried by EU approved state appointed functionaries.

35

In an attempt to reduce heavy drinking (and the rapidly growing incidence of alcoholism among the young of both sexes) politicians wanted to introduce legislation forbidding supermarkets to sell lager and beer at absurdly low prices. (At the moment they are cheaper than water). Unelected, anonymous bureaucrats working at the European Union forbad the Government to introduce any sort of minimum pricing policy, thereby guaranteeing an ever higher incidence of alcoholism.

36

In March 2012, the Hungarian Prime Minister told a rally in Budapest that he would not bow to EU pressure to amend legislation on the country's central bank. He compared European bureaucrats to Soviet apparatchiks (as a Hungarian he should know) and said his country was still fighting for freedom. 'Hungary will not be a colony,' he told a rally. 'We are more than familiar with the character of unsolicited comradely assistance, even if it comes wearing a finely tailored suit.'

I have for many years compared the EU to the USSR and it seems that even some nations are now recognising the truth of this.

37

There are 4.5 million businesses in England but three quarters of them have no employees at all: they are sole traders. Politicians and commentators seem puzzled by this. I am not. Sensible businessmen no longer want to grow their businesses because it means hiring staff and, thanks to the EU's employment rules and regulations, no one who wants to run a business, make a living and stay sane wants to employ people.

38

Diplomats working in Baroness Ashton's European Union foreign service are entitled to 17 weeks holiday a year. They are also entitled to two weeks off for 'professional training' (reading menus, wine lists and so forth). So that's 19 weeks away from work. As if all that wasn't enough, diplomats working in the 30 EU delegations in the Far East, Asia and Africa (I bet you didn't know we were paying for 30 EU delegations in the Far East, Asia and Africa) are also entitled to another four or five weeks off work. That means that they have 24 weeks holiday (by which time even school teachers are probably feeling envious). And if they have to go somewhere further than the nearest five star restaurant they are entitled to two days travelling time and paid business class tickets for themselves and their families. With all this free time the EU officials obviously need lots of money to spend on hobbies and having fun and so they receive very high net salaries (largely tax free) and their accommodation is provided free of charge.

39

The EU has always been deeply opposed to the basic principles of democracy. Remember when the Danes held a referendum in 1992? Vast amounts of money were spent by the EU on propaganda. There were leaflets, magazines, newspaper advertising, radio and television programmes and a massive door to door canvassing campaign. All this was paid for by the EU. Those who opposed Denmark joining the EU had to rely on what meagre resources they could scrape together. Despite this unfairness, the Danes voted against joining the European Union. The EU panjandrums did not accept this. The EU simply ordered another referendum. This time they spent ever more money on lies and deceits. It was the sort of political propaganda the Nazis created. And this time, by a narrow vote, the Danish people were conned into voting `yes' for slavery and fascist control.

Just under a decade later much the same thing happened in Ireland. The first vote was won massively by those who opposed the European Union and who did not want to give up the remains of their national independence. Naturally, the EU demanded that another referendum be organised. By this time the EU's opponents had spent all their money. And the EU propaganda machine won. Within just a few years Ireland had been led by the EU into virtual bankruptcy.

The EU's supporters don't believe in democracy

Whatever we do, short of a bloody revolution (a civil war), will make no difference. They won't allow us to vote. There will be no clear cut `in or out' referendum. And if we did ever get the chance to vote and they didn't like the result, they would simply make us vote again. And again. It's what they do. And if we still get it wrong, or they suspect that democracy is getting out of hand, they will simply impose a dictatorship. As they have done in Greece and Italy. Politicians who offer the hope of protest will be bought or silenced. The media will be bought and controlled. Dissident writers will be suppressed and oppressed. News and feature programmes on broadcasters such as the BBC will be turned into propaganda broadcasts.

40

Despite the fact that the bureaucrats working in Brussels are hardly ever in their offices, new laws are being introduced by the minute. Here's one: firms with over 15 employees cannot get rid of staff without risking legal proceedings which can last for years. Not surprisingly this makes companies loathe to take on new staff. And so unemployment soars. Here's another: Shops and supermarkets can now be fined £5,000 for failing to hide tobacco products from public view. Smokers who want to buy these products have to ask for them. And staff aren't allowed to show customers what choices are available.

41

Every time a workman visits our home they tell us about some daft new rule (they don't usually know that it originated in Brussels) which means that we must pay to have a chimney moved, a flue opened or perfectly good wiring replaced. Millions of people are forced to have their homes knocked about to satisfy the utterly pointless and absurd requirements of a bunch of faceless, brainless EU bureaucrats.

It all started with MOTs for cars, which were introduced not to make our roads safer (they haven't) but to make more work for motor manufacturers and garages. Now every industry is at it. All they have to do is take a few EU idiots out to lunch and persuade them that there is a real health and safety risk if (fill in the blanks). Then, before you know it and without any discussion, the new regulation is introduced and everyone in the world has to wear steel capped bedroom slippers in case they stub a toe against the bed or drop a tooth glass onto the bathroom floor. The uselessness of all these regulations is proved by the fact that despite the vast number of rules and regulations designed to stop people tap dancing on the top of stepladders, or standing on the window ledge of their 19th floor flat to clean the windows, the incidence of accidental injury continues to rise remorselessly. Our legions of health and safety professionals are useless because (having been misdirected by the EU) they allow themselves to concentrate on the wrong things and because the existence of too many rules means that everyone concentrates on the rules and forgets about common sense.

42

When the euro was founded, the eurocrats were creating a monetary union and not a political one. The participating States (the ones which agreed to abandon their own currencies and to join the euro) established a common central bank but refused to give up the right to tax their own citizens.

This was really stupid. Why did the eurofanatics start monetary union before political union? My guess is that they did it deliberately (knowing that it would fail) because they hoped that it would allow them to push through the tricky stage of creating a full political union; the United States of Europe. The eurofanatics knew that they were creating future problems but believed that they could use the inevitable chaos as an excuse to push through their plans for a united Europe.

The EU is a dysfunctional organisation and the euro is a dysfunctional currency. What most people don't realise is that they were designed that way; they were designed to fail in their present form. The people who set them up knew that if they tried to get all the power they wanted right at the start they would encounter great opposition and that Hitler's project would fail.

43

The EU was brought into existence by what Karl Popper called `piecemeal social engineering'. A group of megalomaniacs, inspired by Hitler's vision of a United States of Europe, and realising that their dream could only be approached little by little, set limited objectives, mobilised the political will needed to achieve them, ignored public opposition and prepared treaties which required individual states to relinquish only a little of their sovereignty at a time. This enabled local politicians to sell the latest development to their reluctant and suspicious citizens.

And so a relatively innocuous Coal and Steel Community was slowly transformed into the EU.

The whole project was built on dishonesty. It was never wanted by the people of Europe and it was always based on deceit, corruption and a whole library of hidden agendas. German politicians who favoured the EU realised that Germany could only be reunified within the context of a greater European unification. The French EU fanatics wanted support for their farmers through the CAP. England entered the EU to please the USA. (There is more detail about this in my book *OFPIS*.)

44

A reader wrote to me about *OFPIS* saying `I can see why you are so unhappy with England in the EU. However, writing such a book and upsetting so many readers is not likely to change the situation is it? Perhaps you could develop a happier attitude by applying the wonderful pattern for happy living in the Serenity Prayer.'

45

The EU is very short of money. The eurocrats have their eyes on English pension funds. English savers who aren't civil servants (and who will not, therefore, receive a fat pension) have around £2,000,000,000,000 invested in their pension funds. That is more than all the investors have saved in the rest of the EU. The French have just £25,000 million. The Germans have £120,000 million. The EU wants our savings. And they are determined to have them.

46

Within the EU, democracy is regarded as an irrelevant nuisance. Elected governments in Greece and Italy were summarily dismissed as surplus to requirements by our bureaucratic masters. EU-approved ex Goldman Sachs administrators were put in charge (bypassing inconvenient non EU-acceptable concepts such as voting). The Prime Minister of Greece was thrown out of office after he suggested that asking the public what they thought about things might be the honourable thing to do. (It was, of course, Goldman Sachs who helped Greece fiddle the books and get into trouble in the first place.) In Italy the Government which replaced Berlusconi contained not one elected official. Not one.

47

The pain the EU has caused by its attempts to protect the euro and the bankers is vast. When I last looked, youth employment in Greece was over 50%. It was 35% in Portugal. The suicide rate in Greece has doubled and psychiatric helplines can hardly cope. They are 20,000 homeless people on the streets of Athens and crime rates are soaring. There are soup kitchens everywhere in Greece. (The Archbishop of Athens runs 73.) In Lisbon 200,000 people rely on soup kitchens to stay alive. The eurocrats don't care about any of this. They are fighting for Hitler's dream: the United States of Europe.

48

`One day the whole of Europe will be one vast socialist state...even England.' - Lenin

49

I have mentioned Hitler a good deal. There may be some readers who doubt my assertion that the European Union is Hitler's Bastard Love Child.

They should read these paragraphs carefully.

In 1936, Hitler told the Reichstag: `It is not very intelligent to imagine that in such a cramped house like that of Europe, a community of peoples can maintain different legal systems and different concepts of law for long.' His pal Mussolini, the father of fascism, said in 1933 that: `Europe may once again grasp the helm of world civilisation if it can develop a modicum of political unity.' Oswald Mosley, England's leading fascist in the 1930s, also supported the idea of a European Union.

In 1941, Walter Funk, Hitler's economics Minister, launched the Europaische Wirtschafts Gemeinschaft (the European Economic Community - EEC) to establish a single European currency - the reichsmark. Hitler's plan was to integrate the European economy into a single market.

In 1945 Hitler's Masterplan (captured by the Allies) included a scheme to create an economic integration of Europe and to found a European Union on a federal basis. The Nazi plan for a federal Europe was based on Lenin's belief that: `Federation is a transitional form towards complete union of all nations.'

No more doubts please.

The European Union is Hitler's Bastard Love Child.

(I was going to add a line here to the effect that anyone who supports the EU, and who knows anything at all about history, must be a Nazi at heart but my Princess advised me that if I did so men in sharply pressed uniforms might be inclined to seek out our front door and kick it down. So, with great reluctance, I will cut that bit out.)

50

Decisions used to be made by those who showed up and took an interest. No more. Today, the big decisions are made by Goldman Sachs and the European Union (and it is not always easy to tell where one ends and the other starts).

51

In a letter to the *Daily Telegraph* in January 2012, the President of the Royal College of Surgeons and the President of the Royal College of Physicians complained that EU laws are having unintended consequences on health care and putting patients at risk. They were particularly worried by the EU laws which result in doctors from other countries within the EU being able to work in England without being able to speak English and by the legislation which reduces the time that young doctors have available for looking after patients and learning. I'm so pleased that these eminent leaders of the profession have noticed. But what took them so long? And why didn't someone representing GPs mention that GPs are still preening themselves at having used EU legislation to opt out of 24 hour cover and to wriggle out of their traditional responsibility of doctors to patients. As a result of EU legislation today's GPs are simply uncivil servants, public sector workers committed to feathering their own nests and supporting the needs and demands of the State.

52

The NHS pays people £50,000 a year to make sure that young doctors in hospital don't break EU rules and spend too much time with their patients. How absurd can you get? Other EU countries simply ignore the dafter EU laws.

53

The weight of a huge, intolerant and committed eurocracy lies behind every order and every form. Every institutional demand, however meaningless and trivial, pointless and wrong-headed in concept, is carved in stone and delivered by truck. There is never room for dissent, discussion or such old-fashioned luxuries as logic and common sense.

54

Many years ago I forecast the rise, rise and rise again of nationalism. It is happening.

Inevitably, there is much fear that nationalism will affect the success of Hitler's dream.

In England politicians and unions have spoken about banning pro-nationalist organisations which dare to promote England (or Britain).

55

The EU is run by people who are probably among the world's most stupid. They are there because they fit certain criteria: the right nationality; an outstanding ability to please an appointments committee by making the right oink and moo noises; the ability to kiss ass; no knowledge whatsoever of anything and a complete absence of moral compass or common sense.

56

In April 2012, it was revealed that the EU was forcing England to allow member states to store waste carbon dioxide in the North Sea off the English coast. Experts admitted that England risked unknown levels of environmental damage if the gas leaked. Germany and other European countries have banned the storage of the waste in their countries because of safety fears. So the EU has ordered that England must store the stuff instead.

57

The French regard EU legislation as optional. The Princess and I saw a splendid example of this the other day while driving through the heart of Paris. We drew up alongside a police van. Inside the van there were around a dozen policemen. Half of them were puffing on cigarettes.

I suspect that the French regard EU legislation as a menu. They go through the list of laws, tick the ones they will take and ignore the rest. 'Ah this one looks useful, we will adopt this one. But no, no, no this one is absurd. This one we will not take thank you.'

58

Two psychologists, Leif Nelson and Tom Meyvis, asked a group of students to listen to a very loud industrial vacuum cleaner. Some had to listen to it for 40 seconds, others for just five seconds. They found that the students who endured the 40 seconds of noise rated the last five seconds of the experience as significantly less unpleasant than those who heard only the five seconds. The explanation is simple: people adapt to unpleasant experiences. Nasty experiences become tolerable. And that's why so many people put up with the EU.

59

Occasionally, we hear a refreshing voice from a politician who opposes the European Union and the euro. He or she will make great promises and talk loudly about how and why the organisation must be opposed. There will be promises and threats and talk of serious opposition. And then: silence.

Such opponents are silenced by threats or bribes. They are never heard from again. After politicians in Slovakia voted against the EU giving boat loads of money to Europe's impoverished bankers the parliament was told to think again. Within hours they had changed their minds and voted for the EU to give away tons of money to the bankers. It took just hours for an entire parliament of determined, committed parliamentarians to change their minds completely.

60

Early in 2009, the regulators in England suggested that house buyers needed protection from bank failure in the weeks during which they were buying a new home. They suggested that the Government should provide security for temporary balances of up to £500,000 (presumably deciding that anyone buying a more valuable house was too rich to deserve help). Three years later the EU had still not decided whether or not this would be allowed. And so, house buyers who have enough money to purchase a house without a mortgage (perhaps because they have sold their previous home) will lose everything if the bank they are using for the house purchase decides to go bust while the money is sitting in an account.

61

The eurocrats have designed employment laws to suit themselves. The problem is that the eurocrats don't do essential work. They can have a year off without anyone noticing. They can turn up for half an hour a day without anyone going bust. They can take long holidays and enjoy vast expense accounts without their employer going bust. Sadly, however, these laws make life extraordinarily difficult for people trying to run real businesses in the real world. The arrogance of the eurocrats is well illustrated by the absurd working hours directive (in real life a 'directive' is a law which has not been passed by any democrat body) which forces Tour de France cyclists to have rest days. The cyclists don't want to stop (because their muscles seize up) and so they spend their rest day riding anyway.

62

Here's a thought: was the economic chaos suffocating Europe deliberately devised? Did the EU's proponents want economic instability so that they could force us to accept a United States of Europe? I wouldn't put it past them. I wouldn't put *anything* past them. And if the Americans can fly aeroplanes into their own high rise buildings why shouldn't the EU create poverty, unemployment and fear throughout Europe? Even the most conservative of historians now accept that it was the Nazis, the founding fathers of the EU, who burned down the Reichstag in order to obtain more control of pre-war Germany.

63

I have detailed the idiocy of the EU at length e.g. in my book *OFPIS* but few things illustrate the idiocy of the EU more effectively than the replacing of our safe, effective and inexpensive light bulbs with costly, dangerous and ineffective bulbs.

64

Anyone who doesn't believe that the Lisbon Treaty took away our sovereignty probably believes that there were weapons of mass destruction in Iraq.

65

The EU is run by unelected, incompetent, arrogant, sanctimonious bureaucratic Cleggies who have never done anything useful, practical or creative in their miserable useless lives and whose skills are in obtaining jobs, manipulating expense accounts and ordering a good wine to go with a taxpayer funded luncheon. The eurocrats want a bigger EU so that they can justify bigger budgets, bigger salaries and longer lunches. Eurocrats have loads of authority but no responsibility; endless arrogance and no empathy. They are the storm troopers of Europe.

66

The EU's carbon emission policies mean that power bills in England will double in the next decade (in real terms). And there will be frequent power outages.

67

During demonstrations in 2011 there was much talk on television about demonstrators attacking the 'centuries old' Supreme Court, our ultimate court.

Actually, although it may sound very old and very important, the Supreme Court was established in October 2009. It was authorised by the Constitutional Reform Act 2005 and is just another bit of EU junk. The building may be old but the Supreme Court isn't yet old enough to start school. The legislation allowed the Supreme Court to take over the Law Lords, part of the Privy Council, and remove the functions of the centuries old Lord Chancellor.

The changes were made because of the European Convention of Human Rights.

68

At the beginning of March 2012, the EU ruled that staff who fall ill while they are on holiday have to be given extra holiday to make up for the holiday they have lost. The Liberal Democrat part of the Coalition welcomed the proposal as a really good idea.

69

`If England had sided with Germany in World War II we would be much better off financially than we are. The Americans would be much poorer and we, with the Germans, would be running the European Union.'- Reader's letter

70

Lorries designed for trans-European autobahns are allowed to enter England and to struggle through small towns and villages, knocking bits off centuries old houses and cottages and destroying the foundations as they rumble by. The EU says it must be and so it must be.

71

In April 2012, it was announced that rather than take a cut in its income, or even hold down costs, the EU was demanding an extra £900 million - an effective pay rise for every employee of 7%.

72

The EU is opposed to copyright. They are planning to regard anyone who tries to protect the copyright of their work as a criminal.

73

EU policies have destroyed the quality of products and services. Every manufacturer and every service industry now spends a huge proportion of its income not on improving quality but on satisfying the EU's unending stream of rules and regulations.

74

The high costs of dealing with bureaucracy and buying licenses mean that small companies and sole traders now really struggle to stay in business. This is no accident. Most of the new regulations and licenses are introduced at the behest of, or with the approval of, large international corporations. The lobbyists working for these companies ensure that any new rules which are introduced are designed to suit their own corporate interests. These corporations know that a large company, with a special department of people hired to do nothing but fill in forms, can cope much better with newly introduced regulations than a small, growing company. According to the official definition of fascism (as composed by Mussolini himself) this is pure, practical fascism in action.

75

In September 2011, it was announced that EU staff were refusing to work a 40 hour week. They claimed that having to work so hard would ruin the attractiveness of their jobs. The 55,000 officials refused even to discuss working as many as 40 hours a week, despite the fact that people in ordinary jobs all over Europe are having to work harder for less money, or have no jobs at all.

A large proportion of EU officials earn between £104,000 and £185,000 and have three months holiday a year. Among their perks they are given an extra 24 days off work every year if they put in an extra 45 minutes at the office chatting or surfing the Web. And in addition to the additional 24 days of annual holiday they also get seven days of public holidays and an additional 11 non-working days when the offices are closed at Christmas.

A union representative, explaining the long holidays, said that `the principle of recuperation needs to be consolidated'.

76

During World War II, England was ruled by eleven regional commissioners.

77

The world is full of people who claim they know better than I do how I should run my life. Most of those people live in another country and know nothing whatsoever about my life.

78

The Government plans to knock down perfectly well-built Victorian houses because they are too expensive to renovate to modern EU-acceptable environmental standards.

79

We are oppressed by a secret fascist state which dare not give its name to its orders. Our politicians are prevented from admitting that new laws come from the EU. Instead, they pretend to be the originators of the legislation (however unpopular it may be).

80

At the start of 2012, as the EU started to crumble, a spokesidiot announced that if the EU collapsed there would be a European war.

81

`It was decided some years ago that we didn't have enough goons in England, telling us what to do, so we went offshore and hired goons working in Brussels. Now these goons tell us how to run our lives - and charge us huge fees for the privilege. Is the EU some sort of joke?' - Reader's letter

82

The EU is introducing licences for just about every job imaginable. Even agents handling professional cyclists have to have a licence. What next? Licences for strippers? Licences for beggars, perhaps? Everyone who wants a job has to attend a degree course in their chosen speciality, pass an examination and then pay an annual licence fee. I think the begging course will be particularly popular.

83

When you see lorries with `limited to 56 mph' labels on their tailgate do you ever wonder why anyone would pick such an odd number? Convert it into kph for the answer. And lo, you will suddenly remember all those continental lorries you've seen whizzing along the French motorways with 90 kph labels on their tailgates.

84

School children are taught to be ashamed of England and indoctrinated with EU validated, politically correct McNuggets of history, designed to make anyone English feel guilty about their heritage.

85

EU bureaucrats have 380 billion euros in unused structural funds to help out poor countries such as Greece but those countries can only access the money if they match the EU money with their own funds. But they don't have any money (that's why they need EU help) and they can't access the funds the EU has available. So the EU bureaucrats keep the money, and hand it out to their pals at the big banks. Or they spend it on expensive lunches.

86

Turkey used to be very keen to join the EU. But they've seen the mess the EU has made of things and, surprise, surprise, the Turks are no longer keen to be part of the chaos. (And they probably don't much fancy being asked to bail out Greece.)

87

Thanks to the EU, we are no longer living in a civilised country. Justice, honours and access to power can all be bought.

88

The Greeks spent their money on having a good time but, with the help of Goldman Sachs, fiddled the accounts to suggest that they were behaving responsibly and spending their loot on roads and sensible underwear. When it became clear that the Greeks had spent their money on booze, dancing and having a good time the EU, worried about the banks losing money, and the bankers being embarrassed, lent the Greeks even more money (taken, in one way or another, from unwilling taxpayers throughout the rest of Europe in a way that would be called highway robbery if done by a man in a mask on a horse). The theory behind this was that if someone is in debt and you lend them more money then they will be able to pay off the interest on the first debt and so one will notice that they are now in even more debt that before. This is a technique not widely favoured by bankers when dealing with small businesses but it is now popular with the EU when dealing with bankrupt sovereign nations. The bankers love this sort of arrangement because whenever they do a deal to lend out money they can give themselves another bonus. They borrow money from the ECB and that triggers bonus no 1. They then lend that money to a bankrupt country and that triggers bonus no 2. Brilliant.

89

Whenever the EU adds to the debt pile it is always the middle classes who lose money. The poor don't have anything to lose and so they are the same as before. And the really rich have all their money in Singapore, the Turks and Caicos islands and Delaware and so they don't suffer at all either.

90

It takes the average citizen an extra hour a week to sort out their rubbish, put out the bins, bring them back in again and, in general, obey the EU laws about rubbish disposal. So, if 20 million people a week do this that's 20,000,000 hours wasted a week. And that's around a billion hours a year. If we assume that the average person is worth £20 an hour (some charge less but bankers push up the average) then the EU's rubbish directives cost the nation £20 billion a year. But that's not the whole of the cost. There are also massive risks in having rubbish lying around in kitchens, back gardens and streets for weeks at a time. In addition, the EU has scarred our streets with huge plastic rubbish containers; so large and so numerous that they never disappear. In towns they stand permanent guard outside terraced houses because no sensible householder is going to drag the bins through their home.

Scariest of all, however, the billions of gallons of water wasted on washing out tin cans, yoghurt cartons and jam jars will contribute to the planet's growing water shortage problem. Our most valuable natural resource is in short supply and, thanks to the European Union, millions of people are using it to wash out empty containers that will, scrubbed and shiny bright, end up as landfill in China. Plus there's another problem that the bureaucrats, in their bottomless ignorance, haven't considered. Most people go on holiday in the summer. Even non EU bureaucrats usually manage to grab a fortnight away from work. (EU bureaucrats measure their holidays in months rather than weeks.) Many of those will miss their fortnightly rubbish collection with the result that stinking, rotting household refuse will stay in the bin for four weeks. Does no one working for the EU realise that this is a huge health hazard?

91

It is impossible for any entrepreneur or investor to plan properly because the rules are constantly changing. And, to make things even more challenging, the rules are changing retrospectively. So, what might have been legal last week may, in six months time, become illegal. The constant changing of regulations also means that house buyers are constantly being forced to spend money hiring builders to redesign their homes. For example, new regulations being introduced in 2013 mean that many home owners will have to rip apart ceilings and walls so that flues from gas boilers, etc., can be fitted with inspection hatches. Rarely a month goes by without a new regulation being introduced. The building industry welcomes these changes, of course, for the same reason that the motorcar industry welcomes changes to the regulations governing motor vehicles. Within the EU, and among those who now control the minutiae of our lives, `different' is a synonym for `better' and `change' a synonym for `progress'.

92

It is no exaggeration to say that nearly everything bad that has happened to England in the last decade or so has happened as a result of our membership of the EU. The legislation may have been `accepted' and put into place by Blair, Brown or Cameron (the BBC of modern politics) but it originated in Brussels. (The bad stuff that didn't come from the EU came from the USA.) Regulations which have come from the EU have led to a dramatically reduced quality of products and service and to reduced corporate profits (leading to smaller dividends and more inadequate pensions for those not fortunate enough to have public sector pensions or, better still, EU pensions).

93

In general, people do bad things because they can. The bad people of the EU do bad things because we let them.

And we let them because their propaganda system is so good. (It should be. It seems to be based on the work of ace Nazi propagandists led by Joseph Goebbels.)

94

English legal tradition is that everything is legal except that which is banned. The EU philosophy is that everything is banned unless it has been authorised. We are remorselessly moving towards the second.

95

As Machiavelli said, you can make someone fear you but you can't make someone love you. Creating fear among the people is the basic philosophy followed by the whole of the EU and its supporters. Anyone who attacks the EU is dismissed as an oddball, an extremist or, ironically, a fascist. One of most critical failings of the EU is that the officials do not understand that when you have too many regulations, people stop behaving morally. The existence of too many laws makes it seem that there is no need for good behaviour; morality, having been taken over by the State, is no longer the responsibility of the individual. And, in addition, the existence of so many laws means that people are so busy struggling to avoid breaking the law that they simply don't have time to think about their behaviour.

96

The people who run the European Union know well that the only way out of the economic crisis created by the chaos in Greece, Spain, Portugal, Italy, Ireland (and other countries) is for the birth of the true EU superstate to be brought forward. And that is what the devoted fans of Hitler's Bastard Lovechild will insist must happen. There will be firm calls for a Central Finance Ministry to manage the economies of all the countries using the euro currency. And such a Ministry will, I suspect, be born.

Conclusion

The EU was an evil idea. The euro was just a stupid idea and was a result of the pro EU fascists trying to speed up their process of political assimilation. The founders and supporters of the EU will not be satisfied, and will not have achieved their aims, until England and other individual member nations have disappeared and their identity has been merged into the United States of Europe; that is, and always has been, the aim. Hitler's plan was to produce a socialist superstate and there is, of course, no practical difference between that brand of socialism and fascism. The two are indistinguishable. The europhiles always believed that they could bleed capitalists (of every size, shape and nationality) and use the proceeds to pay for entitlements, regulatory regimes and Europe-wide social security. It was always an insane dream. (Or, more precisely, it was always their dream and our nightmare.) Meanwhile, the eurocrats in charge of the EU aren't fit to run a bus let alone an entire continent. And thanks to the parade of dishonourable, treacherous politicians who signed away our rights and our history, we have lost our liberty, our culture, our democracy and our self-respect and been taken over by a fascist organisation whose mantra is `control, regulate and tax'. May the politicians who betrayed us be forever flushed with embarrassment and shame. The europhiles will not allow the current European crisis to go to waste. They will take full advantage of the chaos to promote their cause and to expand the power of the new United States of Europe. But it will all be in vain. The single currency and the EU will collapse - though not until they both have done terrible damage to every country in Europe. Neither of these sad creations can survive. I don't know when they will go (the sooner the better) but they are doomed.

Chapter 9

Immigration: Out Of Control

Introduction

Having paid to bail out the Scottish banks, England is now bankrupt. We have six million citizens living on State benefits. Millions more are registered as disabled. Our infrastructure is creaking at the seams. And yet immigrants continue to pour into the country.

1

In July 2012, Ed Miliband, the leader of the Labour Party, finally admitted that Eastern Europeans had kept English youngsters out of work. (Those who say that there are no jobs available in England might like to ask themselves how 750,000 Poles managed to find employment.)

2

There is a Romanian woman in Bristol who sells the *Big Issue* magazine and claims £2,600 in housing benefit from the local council. In fact, in addition to whatever she makes out of flogging what must surely be the world's least readable magazine, she receives a total State handout of £28,000 a year. That is, of course, considerably more than the average wage in England. (I am puzzled by the fact that it is possible to sell the *Big Issue* magazine and have somewhere to live.) It is hardly surprising that Eastern Europeans are queuing up to come to England. They don't want to come here because they admire William Shakespeare or want to visit the Lake District or because they adore Yorkshire pudding. They aren't attracted by our culture, our history or our weather. They are attracted by the fact that we give away free money. Imported beggars make life infinitely harder for our home-grown homeless.

3

In one short period in early 2012 the Government lost track of 106,000 criminal immigrants and asylum seekers. This is equivalent to the population of Cambridge.

4

Criticism of immigration is always demonised as racist and those who politely ask if we haven't perhaps got enough people living on our crowded isle (and straining our already overstretched infrastructure) are likely to find themselves answering questions down at the nearest police station. The sting of this politically motivated calumny is removed by the fact that many of those calling for controls are immigrants themselves who realise that even in the five to ten years they have been in England everything has deteriorated enormously. The immigrants don't want any more immigrants cluttering up the countryside and competing for jobs, homes and hospital beds.

5

People who decide to move to France or Italy usually go because they approve of the lifestyle enjoyed by the locals. Many know more about the culture and history of the country to which they are moving than the indigenous population. But it is a sad but inescapable truth that many of the people who come to England come for what they can get out of it and have no interest in our culture or our way of life.

6

There are 18 million people with long-term health problems in England and more than 20% of the population are over 60. Our infrastructure simply cannot cope. And yet we are encouraging immigrants to pour into the country. After one new EU law was introduced the Government announced that around 10,000 people would come into the country as a result. A year or two later they admitted that 700,000 a year had poured in. Our small, overcrowded island is unable to cope with the needs of the indigenous population (a phrase which may, I suspect, be frowned upon if not downright illegal). Our infrastructure certainly cannot cope with the endless stream of immigrants pouring across our borders.

7

As a result of our immigration policies (which were kindly donated by the European Union) thousands of English born children now go to schools where English speakers are in a minority and where lessons are conducted in the language of the majority. This is utter madness. It doesn't happen anywhere else on our planet.

8

Fighting wars with Muslims while at the same time inviting them to immigrate is plain, unvarnished lunacy. We should, perhaps, choose one of the two.

9

Rich people such as politicians approve of immigration because the immigrants don't threaten their homes and jobs. On the contrary lots of low paid immigrants provide a steady supply of eager gardeners and nannies.

10

Citizens from Eastern European countries which are now members of the EU go straight through Europe like a severe case of diarrhoea. They don't hang around in France (where the weather and food are better). They much prefer to come to England, which has the best benefits system around. Many then head directly for a place with a high unemployment level where they can settle down and nurse their newly acquired long-term backache.

11

In the three months to December 2011 the number of English nationals in employment fell by 166,000 compared with the previous year. By one of those strange coincidences the number of non-English nationals in employment rose, in the same period, by 166,000.

12

Although it has clearly become much easier for foreigners to enter England, stay here and take full advantage of our absurdly and unaffordable generosity and our crumbling infrastructure it has, paradoxically, become considerably more difficult for the English to travel abroad. A decade or two ago it was relatively easy to go abroad (and come back again) as long as the traveller held a valid United Kingdom passport. I remember that my father used to make day trips to towns and cities throughout Europe without any difficulty. He certainly didn't have to spend hours queuing to leave and enter the country. These days the whole business of getting through customs has become absurdly time consuming. The official argument is, of course, that we must protect our borders against terrorists, money launderers and illegal immigrants. The reality is that we never catch any of these people and the systems, as they are designed, merely make life difficult for the honest, legal traveller. (In exactly the same way, of course, as our banking regulations don't prevent any illegal activity but do make life difficult for the honest citizen trying to access his own money.) It is now not at all uncommon for travellers passing through Heathrow to have to spend two to three hours queuing to pass through a customs post. The anger felt by travellers is often enhanced by the fact that immigration officials may be seen standing chatting to one another as the queues mount up. The problem has even spread to Eurostar with the result that trains are now frequently delayed as passengers wait in long queues to be processed by officials who seem to be suffering from some sort of disease which makes them work at a pace that even a lethargic snail would find embarrassingly slow. If the immigration officers worked in shops or banks (or any other real world concern) the queues would go three times round the world. The surly, French customs officers placed at St Pancras, to balance the English ones at the Gare du Nord, deal with passports as snappily as a baccarat dealer deals with cards but the surly, leaden fingered English officials at the Gare du Nord seem to delight in building up massive queues.

13

Many immigrants are now leaving England and going home. They have taken money out of our economy but now realise that the infrastructure is better back home. 'We are going back because health care and education are better back home,' said one Polish family. 'Crime rates in Romania are much lower than in England,' explained another family of returning exiles. 'There are too many immigrants in England,' admitted a spokesman for another Eastern European family. Countries which like to think of as rather poor are doing quite well, thank you. The average Russian now has at least two top end mobile telephones. Three quarters of the Chinese have at least one.

14

There have been many attempts to turn us all into multinationals but few of the attempts have been as blatant as the way our national cricket team has been altered. Just a few years ago all members of the team which represents England were born in England. A random, recent representative side included four players who were born in South Africa, one born in Ireland and one born in Australia. That means that more than half of the England cricket side were foreign born.

15

People who move to live in the USA are strongly encouraged to become American (and most do) but people who move to England are strongly encouraged to retain their traditional roots and to remain 'Scots', 'Pakistanis' or 'Poles' at heart. Such immigrants never become citizens. They simply live in England because it provides them with financial benefits they would not obtain if they had stayed at home.

16

Rich foreigners who want to move to England but have no links with our nation, or any interest in its past and future, can buy English citizenship and a passport. (Curiously, Government ministers don't often talk about this cute example of sovereign prostitution.) However, most rich foreigners who move to England don't bother taking out citizenship. It is far more profitable to stay in London as a non-resident, non-domiciled visitor because this turns England into a tax haven: a dream destination for tax dodgers.

17

Some countries (such as Greece) have porous borders which allow virtually anyone into the EU. And once people are in the EU they can travel to England.

18

Politicians, judges and many highly-paid commentators defend the right of Muslim extremists to live in England and to create communities which are set apart from the English. Curiously, the same people are often quick to want to ban people from promoting Christianity (though they are invariably happy to take time off to celebrate Christmas and Easter). And they are, of course, also eager to ban political parties such as the British National Party, which has a good many home-grown English supporters. (It does not, apparently, seem strange to these people that they should want to ban a political party which represents a large proportion of the population. The party, and its supporters, may not be to their taste but the fact is that when you ban or suppress political groups because you don't approve of them you are running a type of country which cannot possibly be described as a democracy.)

19

Immigrants complain a good deal about the way we run our country and they often have many fundamental ideas for improving our society. And yet their own societies, in the countries from which they have often fled, are frequently repressive, invariably misogynistic and often run as dictatorships. It is, I confess, sometimes difficult to understand why they are prepared to put up with living in our country. I suppose we should be grateful for their generosity in allowing us to give them money and houses and for encouraging them to make the effort to change our society, our culture and our way of life.

20

Now that rabid Scots want to be an EU region rather than a UK region one assumes that many of the most annoying and incomprehensible Scots (particularly those who have taken over our media) will be loading their ill-gotten gains into their motorcars and driving back to live in Glasgow. But we should warn them that they aren't getting what is left of the oil. Most of it lies off the English coast. And it was found with English money. When the separation papers are signed they can keep the haggis and the bagpipes. We'll keep the oil. Incidentally, during the 2102 London Olympic Games, Scottish (and Welsh) members of some teams were told that they did not have to sing the National Anthem.

Conclusion

Our immigration policies are outside our control. Until or unless we leave the European Union (or the European Union collapses in an explosion of hubris and ignorance) we will be forced to continue to accept boat, plane and trainloads full of immigrants - most of whom are coming not because they want to live in England but because they don't want to be where they were and England offers the best financial incentives. And there is another, infrequently discussed, side to this problem. One in three English born citizens is now considering emigration. Many have already gone; disappointed and frustrated by the decline of their country. England will soon be left with just the civil servants, the unemployed immigrants, the hard core scroungers, the international tax evaders and the money launderers. The producers and taxpayers will have gone. It may soon be time for us all to consider leaving.

Chapter 10

Education: Misdirected And Mismanaged

Introduction

Politicians talk about education a great deal. They say how important it is and they repeat this mantra as though saying it is enough. As with the health service there is much talk of targets and there are many managers. But if you measure the quality of education in England by the number of adults who can read and write then the quality of education is deteriorating rapidly. Our teachers and our schools are failing. Education has been dumbed down to suit the absence of ambition and enthusiasm among the laziest and greediest of our teachers. Schools are forced to try to hit targets and since the trick with targets is that those setting them always remember to make sure that they are always slightly lower than the latest set of results, everything gets worse. The EU has warned that our chances of fighting our way out of recession are being damaged by our poor educational standards.

1

We are taught to take education seriously. We are told that the quality and extent of our education will shape and govern our lives. We are told that if we work hard at school and at college then we will reap the benefits later. `Education, education, education' was an early communist mantra which was borrowed by the Labour Government in the 1990s.

`Study hard, pass your examinations and you will obtain a better job, earn more money and be able to enjoy a more luxurious lifestyle than those who spurn their educational opportunities.'

How many children hear that each year? It is the standard stuff of school speech days.

What we are told is, to a large extent, true. But there is another truth about education which is even more important and which is never talked about. We are never told the real price that we will have to pay for our years of education. We are never told the spiritual price that society expects us to pay in return for having our lives shaped and improved.

To understand the potential costs to the spirit and the soul it is necessary to understand the *purpose* of the education society offers us all. We must understand what society stands to gain from the deal we are offered.

Sadly, nothing that society offers ever comes free and an education is certainly no exception. The main reason society offers to educate us all is to prepare us for work. Society doesn't want to educate us so that we become more thoughtful, more creative or wiser individuals. Society doesn't want to broaden our horizons or enhance our sense of vision. Society doesn't want to instill passion in us (that can be troublesome and inconvenient) and it doesn't want us to know how to think for ourselves (that can be costly and disruptive).

What society really wants is obedience.

Society - the social structure which we have created but which has now acquired a strength and a force of its own - values obedience highly and rewards the obedient more than any other group. Society knows that the obedient will work hard without question. Society knows that the obedient can be relied upon to do work that is dull, repetitive and possibly even dangerous. Society knows that the obedient are unlikely to be troubled by spiritual or moral fears. Society knows that the obedient will fit neatly into whatever hierarchy may exist and society knows that the obedient will always put loyalty above honesty and integrity. Society will always reward those who are obedient because by doing so it can demonstrate to others the value of obedience!

The obedient are always prepared to do what others tell them to do. The obedient are allowed to climb higher up the ladder. But because they are obedient they always do what they are told - however high they climb. The obedient obey the politicians, the administrators and the bureaucrats. Millions of men and women are blindly obedient because of the lessons they learned at school. They do work they dislike. They listen to people they despise. They do what they are told without questioning. They are blindly obedient because that is what the educational system taught them to be.

The obedient also become good and reliable customers. The obedient obey the advertisers and buy things that they don't need. By doing so they help society to evolve and stay strong. The obedient accept shoddy workmanship and unreliability without complaint. They accept new fashions as necessary and they buy new clothes and new cars when society wants them to buy those things - not when they need them. The obedient customer is a passive customer and the passive customer is the best customer.

Think back to your own education and you'll see how important obedience was. With some honourable exceptions most courses which involve a textbook and a teacher, and conclude with an examination, are designed to prevent thought and to encourage obedience.

The educational system prepared us all for a life in a meritocracy where nothing is more meritorious than silent obedience.

If you were a good student then you will have been rewarded.

If your education was successful - on society's terms - then you will have been offered choices that marked you for life. Whatever profession you chose to follow, society will have taught you to feel special. You will have been encouraged to believe that you are superior to those who do not have your own specific skills. You will have been taught prejudices rather than truths.

You must remember that one aim of a modern education is to harness the minds of the imaginative or potentially disruptive. Such individuals are dangerous to a smooth running society.

Society's schoolteachers - the handmaidens of the system - are prepared and willing to manipulate the minds of the young because that is what society expects them to do in return for their own status in society.

Education, the most fundamental force of all, is designed to help produce a neat and layered world. But the price we pay for our education is a high one. And the more successful our education is in society's terms (and the higher our subsequent position in the meritocracy) the greater the price we must pay.

Our choices - or the choices that society helped us make - will have strictly defined the boundaries of our lives. We may be better rewarded (in material terms) than many of those who were less capable of satisfying the system but the price we pay will be higher too. The price we pay for educational success is intellectual constraint. We pay for our success with our freedom. We pay for our success with guilt, frustration, dissatisfaction and boredom.

The modern educational system is designed to support the structure of our society but it is also a major force in the development of stress and misery.

If it is true that our schooldays are the happiest days of our lives it is because by the time we leave school freedom is, for most of us, nothing more than a faint memory.

'The best part of every man's education, is that which he gives to himself,' wrote Sir Walter Scott

Regular, mass-market schooling for everyone was originally a by-product of the industrial revolution. Prior to the industrial revolution most people lived in villages and hamlets and only a relatively small percentage of the population lived in towns and cities. The first factories and industrial towns developed in England when industrial machinery such as spinning wheels which had been installed in cottages, barns and village halls were smashed by the Luddites; rebellious workers who believed that the introduction of machinery threatened their livelihoods. As a direct result of the Luddite activities the machine owners put their replacement equipment into specially built 'factories' so that they could be protected against vandalism. Since public transport did not exist this, inevitably, meant that the people who were going to work in those factories had to be housed nearby. In this way the first new, purpose built industrial towns developed.

The first schools were built not to educate or to inform but because unless some provision was made for looking after children, factory owners could not employ women as well as men. The development of the first towns had meant that family units had been splintered and it was no longer possible for young parents to turn to their own parents for help and support.

Either by purpose, design or simple good fortune it was quickly discovered that the development of formal schooling had an additional benefit. Employers found that children who got into the habit of attending a school for regular hours during the day adapted more readily to work in a factory. Many of their parents, who had been brought up working as farm labourers, found factory hours and discipline difficult to get used to. Children who were accustomed to school hours and discipline had no such problems.

Today a formal education is still primarily designed to occupy pupils, to keep them busy and out of mischief and to prepare them for an ordinary working life. Very little of the tedious by rote learning which goes on in schools has any practical purpose. Children are taught algebra, trigonometry and Latin - and then subjected to examinations designed to find out how well they have absorbed the entirely useless material they have been taught. The aim is to not to teach or impart learning but to produce school leavers who will feel comfortable with the standard working ritual of modern life.

Schooling is a disciplinary activity rather than an educational one (although the latest and most fashionable educational methods - those which are designed to educate without work, study, labour or pain - fail even to instil much discipline into pupils). Students are certainly not being given information which will enable them to live independent lives. They are being taught to fit into society's demands for them, rather than taught how to think.

Why, after all, would society want to teach young people how to think for themselves? People who can think for themselves are likely to be a nuisance rather than an asset to a closely structured society which depends more on discipline and routine than on innovation or imagination.

Students, at schools, colleges and universities, are trained to do as they are told. It is for this reason that rules play such a crucial part in all educational establishments. Learning to obey the rules and do as you are told is a more important part of any educational establishment than learning to create or to question. Most education and training is designed to make sure that people do not maximise or optimise their own skills but that they accept whatever life or fate offers. The `society' which we have created, which now has a purpose and an agenda of its own, does not want thinking citizens. People who think are likely to threaten the status quo.

And yet there are many citizens in our society who believe (with apparent sincerity) that once their formal education is over they can stop learning. They assume that when they leave school, college or university they do so as educationally complete individuals, and that they can, from that point in their lives onwards, stop expanding, exploring and discovering.

This is no accident. It is exactly what 'society' wants.

When graduating students believe that they no longer need to learn they inevitably become content and stable cogs in society's complex machinery.

The truth, of course, is very different. The truth is that a genuine education, one which encouraged original and creative thinking, would be merely a beginning.

The word 'educate' is derived from the word 'educo' which means to draw out and develop. Once a child has learned to read and write education should not be about learning and remembering dates and mathematical formulae. A truly educated man is one who has developed his mind to take advantage of his skills and talents and to get where he wants to be without hurting the innocent. An ignorant man who has been taught to think can get hold of all the knowledge he needs in order to deal with his ignorance - either from a library or from people who have the knowledge.

The truth is that a modern, formal education is irrelevant to life. And so it is not surprising that many people do well without any formal education and why many modern employers prefer to hire intelligent and enthusiastic staff who do not have any formal (and often stifling) education.

Knowledge is only valuable when it is used. The knowledge you have stored - but which you do not use - is of no value to you or anyone else. Knowledge is potential power and potential wealth. But knowledge and wisdom, unlike money, only really show their value when you put them to use. And knowledge and wisdom can, unlike money, be spent more than once. A good formal education should (in theory) show you how to acquire knowledge and how to use knowledge when you have acquired it. Sadly, however, very little modern formal education teaches people where or how to acquire more knowledge for themselves, and hardly any formal education is designed to show people how to use what they have learned.

Too many students assume that their education ends when they finish their formal schooling or university or college course. A frightening number of people who regard themselves as 'well-educated' have never read a non-fiction book since qualifying and leaving college. Too many teachers regard education as meaning 'acquiring skills and training'. Too many parents and politicians expect the educational system to teach children nothing more than the information they need to get a job - and how to obey the rules. It is a dangerous myth to assume that education is designed to teach wisdom. It certainly doesn't do that. And nor does it teach students how to think.

2

It is important to remember that schools were only ever invented so that parents could go to work and have somewhere safe and secure to leave their children. After the industrial revolution factories in England were in desperate need of hands and bodies to operate lathes and looms. Children were a nuisance to factory owners because the women who could be hired often felt they had to stay at home to make sure that Tom, Dick and Harry didn't fall on the fire and ate a slice of bread and dripping occasionally.

So the principle of education for all, including the poor and dirty, was born.

From this unpromising beginning has developed the idea that education is a universal right, more important than food, drinking water and a rain proof roof. In political terms education has become untouchable and fundamental.

Sadly, the quality of education has deteriorated massively in recent years. Naturally, the politicians have not allowed this uncomfortable truth to interfere. They have got round reality by making exams easier and easier to pass. It's known in the trade as grade inflation and it means that each year students get better marks than they would have done if they had taken their exams a year earlier. As a result many universities now set their own entrance examinations for prospective students.

Meanwhile, despite the high marks, illiteracy rates soar.

We now have a politically correct, distorted, manipulated education system which produces illiterates and semi-literates by the regiment. We have an education system which uses official EU propaganda and refuses to teach English history or English culture for fear of upsetting racists who feel full of resentment about England because they aren't English themselves and because their country (be it Scotland or Pakistan) doesn't have a comparable history or a comparable culture.

3

When asked why they are emigrating to France one of the first reasons English citizens give is `education'. They are, they say, leaving because they want to send their children to French schools.

4

Immigrants from developing countries in Europe (such as Poland and Romania) may come to England to take advantage of the financial benefits but they often send their children back home to be educated. (They also go back themselves if they need medical treatment. They know that our infrastructure and our basic services are now of Third World quality.)

5

Teachers are now so keen for their students to pass their exams (because if enough students pass enough exams the teacher can take home a financial bonus) that more and more of them are showing their students the questions beforehand. This may not quite be according to the Marquess of Queensberry rules but it does boost the success rate and increases the teachers take home pay.

6

Too many students now waste their time and money studying subjects that were never really designed to be anything more than a hobby. Just how many graduates in `gender studies' and `art history' does a country need?

7

Most people today are over-educated for the work they will be fit to do, will need to do and will do. The wild enthusiasm for further education (a phrase which rather ambitiously implies that those going into further education have already been educated to some degree) is inspired by the need to keep the unemployment figures low and is merely yet another example of political dishonesty.

8

Montaigne advised that pain should be part of every boy's education because of the risk of him one day having to undergo torture. Modern children are denied pain at the time when it will do them most good. No one is allowed to compete and fail. School sports days are banned because they are considered `elitist' by the politically correct (and, partly, too because the sports fields have been sold off by the local council and are now covered with a supermarket and low grade housing). The result is young adults who expect nothing but success from life, and who regard any sort of failure and disappointment as an unjustifiable personal affront, require counselling and lengthy courses of anti-depressant medication.

9

The Government is now paying for care for 15 hours a week for two-year-olds. It is called, rather pompously, `pre-school education' but is clearly really just childcare designed to enable women to go to work (or the park). Playschools and nursery schools were only invented so that mothers could go to work and avoid the responsibilities of parenthood. Why do women have children if they don't want to look after them?

10

Astonishingly, just under half of young people now go to University. This is a staggering notion. I have absolutely no doubt that most of those now officially described as attending university are neither attending an establishment that could properly be described as a university nor suited to a post-school education.

11

The Government is planning to make it possible for students to obtain a university degree within two years. They're doing this because the cost of a three year course is rapidly becoming scary. The Government has to keep students signing up for courses so that they can continue to disguise the unemployment figures (and save money on unemployment benefit). Hence the reduction in course time. Politicians don't give a damn about whether citizens are educated or not, and if the Government thought it would prove profitable they would give away degrees with packets of cornflakes. (Actually, that's not quite true. Politicians do care a bit about whether or not the citizens are educated. They prefer them to remain ignorant and unable to tell the difference between a sponsored website, keeping them on message, and a real website, offering genuine news and views.)

12

Exams have to be dumbed down because most of those who stay on for `further education' are neither keen on studying nor are they any good at it. The Government doesn't want thousands of students failing their exams and so they make the exams easier and easier to pass. And to persuade unwilling students to go to `university' they also insist that departments teaching dull, difficult subjects such as mathematics receive less money (even though a good country does rather need one or two people who can add up) and that oodles of boodle is given to departments which teach courses in attractive, intellectually less demanding subjects such as tourism, physical education (actually, I think they now call it Sport and Exercise Science but it still means shouting at the unwilling while they leap over wooden horses and run round the field in a singlet and shorts), hairdressing and nailcare. (I wonder if it is possible to do a PhD in nailcare. Probably.)

13

School discipline has declined since corporal punishment was outlawed in 1986. And attacks on pupils and teachers have increased. Officially this is, of course, merely one of those odd coincidences. Of course it is.

14

How long will it be before primary schoolchildren who attend school at least once a week are automatically given a degree in anything they can spell? Teachers will talk proudly of children aged 12 who have so many degrees that it takes them ten minutes to recite the list. Politicians will claim that news showing that our nation is awash with four-year-olds who have fistfuls of degrees proves conclusively that standards have been raised and teaching methods improved.

15

I rang a broker at one of the big State subsidised banks in order to buy some Exchange Traded Fund shares in silver. The price was 13$ U.S. and the 'broker' at the other end converted this first of all to 50 pence and then, after some giggling, to 90 pence. After yet more giggling she said she thought I ought to speak to someone more senior. I frequently find that dealing staff have no idea that the American dollar is a different currency to the English pound, that there are, in fact, several types of dollar and that the position of a decimal place can be of considerable significance when quoting a price. This was Lloyds TSB (the bank which was ruined by its links with one of the bankrupt Scottish institutions).

16

Why aren't children taught how to manage their money? Most schoolchildren would be better served by being taught basic accounts, domestic science, typing (now known rather pompously as keyboard skills) and basic plumbing. Girls should be taught to make curtains and boys to grow vegetables and mend bicycles. But these subjects are ignored - and my suggestion will be regarded by many as politically incorrect and sexist. Children are forcibly slotted into a pseudo academic environment and encouraged to waste their time and money studying subjects which will never be of any real value to them or to anyone else.

17

A reader recently told me that her (perfectly healthy) young son was being taught sign language at his nursery school. The teachers were, for example, teaching him to pretend to milk a cow when he wanted to say `milk'. What sort of lunacy is this?

18

Creativity, inventiveness and independence of thought are now regarded as dangerous and are, therefore, suppressed in schools and universities. Schools do, however, seem to have plenty of time for sex education, a subject which arrives on the curriculum when pupils are five or six-years-old and very easy to terrify, confuse and bewilder. Naturally, to satisfy the politically correct, there is much talk about homosexuality in these harmful sex education courses.

19

Teachers no longer seem to bother trying to make their pupils behave decently. The Princess and I always veer away if we see a party of schoolchildren under the supervision of their teachers. The children are invariably rowdy, undisciplined and rude. The teachers are far too busy chatting to give a damn. Pedestrians are frequently forced off the pavement by unruly snakes of venomous kids. I am ashamed to report that when we see unruly children in Paris we know, before we hear them speak, that they will be English. Neither the Princess nor I have much time for the French (the city and the country are wasted on them) but they do ensure that their children know how to behave decently.

20

School sex education programmes seem designed to teach children to say that they are homosexual even if they really aren't and our politicians and State-run television programmes reinforce the message at every opportunity. Could this be because politicians know that gay relationships tend to be short-term and that it is in their interests to break down the sort of long-term relationships which exist in marriage because individuals gain great strength from such relationships?

21

Teaching English children in languages other than English is racist and a form of child abuse. It creates ghettoes.

And yet it is increasingly common today in England.

22

Citizens in their 60s can add up the cost of their shopping in moments. It used to be called mental arithmetic and it was a consequence of old-fashioned, learning by rote. Younger people, trained in something called 'new maths', can't add up two and two without the aid of a calculator. But despite this clear evidence that the old methods were best, teachers (who clearly don't like listening to children chanting out their tables) insist that the new methods are preferable.

23

From September 2012, English universities can charge students up to £9,000 a year for tuition. (Scottish students don't pay a penny. They are generously subsidised by English taxpayers, most of whom have no idea they are being so generous.) The £9,000 a year is a rise of £6,000 on the £3,000 maximum that previously existed, and even Government ministers of the Clegg variety will doubtless be able to work out that this is slightly above the official inflation rate. Students also need to borrow money to pay for their accommodation costs since they are unlikely to receive grants. All this means that the average student attending a three year university course will leave with debts of around £40,000 give or take a textbook or two. Students who leave after a longer course (medicine, dentistry or veterinary science for example) will have much higher debts and will doubtless be disappointed to discover that it is no longer possible to avoid these debts by electing to go bankrupt. There is nothing wrong with the principle that students should pay for their education. Why, after all, should those who do not go to university pay for those who do? But there is a strong argument that the fees being charged are absurdly high and that universities and colleges are now in the exploitation rather than the education business. It is difficult to understand why students should pay £9,000 a year for the privilege of attending a few mouldy lectures.

It is only since 1998 that students in England have had to pay for their education but in America, where students have had to pay for many years there are now (literally) millions of students with huge debts. Amazingly, there are two million pensioners in the USA who are still paying off their student debts.

24

Blair and Brown worked out that by encouraging young people to go to university (on the spurious grounds that after being educated they would find it easier to obtain employment) the Government would be able to keep the unemployment figures down (because young people who are studying don't count as unemployed and cannot, of course, claim unemployment benefit, thereby saving the Government another ton and a half of money a week) and (if you're still following this sentence this is the really nasty bit) could actually make money out of unemployment by moving the cost of higher education from Central Government to the English students themselves. (The careful Scots ensured that Scottish students don't have to pay anything. Remember that Gordon Brown had signed The Scottish Claim of Rights, giving his eternal allegiance to Scotland over England.) This was short-term barrow boy politics. And it is difficult to see how it was not racist - other than for the fact that the English are almost alone on the planet as not officially allowed to describe themselves as a `race'.

25

Thanks to the appalling polices of the last few Governments, young people who choose to better themselves through education will not start their lives with a clean slate. Most are starting with huge university debts. And with housing still far too expensive (in historical terms) they have very little hope of clambering onto the housing ladder. They will, therefore, need to live with their parents or (if they can find the money) rent somewhere to live.

It is this debt problem which will stop the housing market recovering. It is, of course, usually younger people who buy houses at the cheapest end of the market. The people who sell those houses move up into something bigger and more expensive. And eventually, at the end of the chain, older folk, approaching retirement, sell their larger homes so that they can move into a little cottage in the country or at the seaside.

The inability of the young to buy means that no one can sell.

The young are also doomed because in addition to their personal debts they will have to pay back the nation's huge debts. England's debt, still rising as I write, is already well over a trillion pounds. That will have to be paid back through higher taxes. And higher taxes will mean lower growth, greater unemployment and a long-term economic depression. How many of today's teenagers realise that they will spend their entire lives suffering for Gordon Brown's stupidity? How many will, as they shiver their way through an ever-hungry old age, curse the memory of Gordon Brown?

And, as if all that were not bad enough, today's young people also have to pay the costs of pensions for tomorrow's old people. All those millions of public sector workers promised and expecting huge pensions will want their money to come from somewhere. Higher taxes and fewer public services will be the only answer.

The pain will be greater because young people are brought up expecting to become rich and famous, without realising that generally speaking you have to do something to acquire either or both. There is a great sense of entitlement and a lack of awareness of the realities of life (engendered by school policies which are designed by people who wrongly believe that a child who fails anything will be scarred for life and will grow up to become a psychopathic mass murderer). Children grow up unable to understand the meaning of words such as `honour' and `gratitude' and with a sense of entitlement that would embarrass Royal Princes.

There is going to be much anger, frustration, disappointment and resentment.

At what point will there be a revolution?

At what point will young people refuse point blank to pay all those pensions for all those greedy public sector workers?

26

A new survey shows that three out of ten students believe it is their right to work from home once they get jobs (if they get jobs). This rather reminds me of a survey conducted at the height of the dot-com madness in America. The survey showed that a majority of American college students planned to retire as millionaires at the age of 25.

27

When they reach the grand old age of 50, today's 20-year-olds will have the debts of several generations to worry about. They will have to pay off their own student loan debts. They will have to help out their starving and shivering parents (struggling to survive without employment or pension) and they will have to help feed, shelter and clothe their own children.

28

Children don't learn much these days because school terms are getting shorter and shorter. Even when the children are supposed to be at school they are hardly ever learning. There are days off for snow, days off so that teachers can be trained and days out on coaches so that the teachers can get out of the classroom and visit places they enjoy.

Conclusion

Nothing will change until there is a real revolution forcing teachers to put children first and their own interests second. Until things change, the incidence of illiteracy and innumeracy will continue to rise. The basic problem is that education is organised and run by and for teachers - just as health care is now run by and for health care professionals.

Chapter 11

The Growing Shortage Of Oil, Metals, Food And Other Commodities

Introduction

Reserves of all commodities are falling by 6% a year and replacements are expensive and difficult to find. There seems to be some public resistance to the idea that all the earth's resources are, inevitably, limited and there seems to be little or no understanding of the fact that, for non renewable commodities, the easy to obtain stuff has been obtained. Everything left is difficult to get at and, therefore, expensive. For England there are three serious problems. First, we import most of our essential commodities. Second, EU regulators are constantly bringing in onerous new laws governing the extraction and use of energy. Third, environmental campaigners protest about all the possible energy sources - whether they be oil, coal, nuclear or windpower.

1

The cost of all utility bills (water, sewage, gas and electricity) will rocket in the next ten years. Be prepared to pay a good deal more for these services than you pay now.

Gas and electricity bills will soar because the price of energy will go up. And because our infrastructure providing us with these things is old, falling apart and totally inadequate. The amazingly short-sighted decision by the Germans to abandon nuclear power means that the price of natural gas must soar. There is absolutely no chance whatsoever of the Germans (or anyone else) obtaining all the electricity they need from windmills, wave power or the sun. Because it has turned governments away from nuclear power, the Japanese nuclear disaster will add thousands of pounds to the average annual energy bill.

Water and sewage bills will soar because our infrastructure in these areas was built in Victorian times and is now in need of repair. A conservative estimate suggests that bringing the system up-to-date will cost around £100 billion. The real cost will, of course, be considerably higher. Until the improvements are made, huge amounts of money will have to be spent on keeping the systems working. Once the improvements have been made huge amounts of money will have to be spent on servicing and repaying the related debt. Global water shortages won't help the price problem, either.

In addition, the costs of all services will rise because new EU regulations require water to be treated in a more energy efficient manner in the future. Sadly, the more energy efficient treatment programmes are less acceptable from an environmental point of view. But the EU will doubtless introduce a new system of fines to ensure that the industry pays extra for adopting the new treatment programmes.

The shortage of energy supplies, combined with the constant introduction of new EU laws, mean that utility bills will soar. Anyone who has difficulty paying utility bills now should perhaps consider downsizing to a smaller property.

2

According to the latest figures, oil companies now have to spend nearly seven times as much to find, develop and 'commercialise' a barrel of oil as they had to spend in 1997. Finding new oil costs far more. And upstream spending has increased four fold as oil companies have to deal with every possible variety of inflation (including wage inflation in developing countries). Geology, geography and politics are all making oil more expensive. (The price of oil has risen about 1500% in the last 15 years.) And that's before we cover the fact that existing fields are running out. Or the fact that countries such as China are increasing their consumption.

3

Campaigners who protest about the ways in which we obtain our energy are among the biggest users of computers, which are massive users of electricity.

4

New driving tests are being introduced for the over 65s even though they are proven to be the safest drivers on the roads. The idea is simple: get pensioners off the roads and keep the oil for ministers, armed forces, public sector workers and taxpaying workers. This is age discrimination but politicians always ignore rules which they don't like when they seem inconvenient.

5

Those who claim that there is plenty of oil around will frequently claim that there are now many new ways of taking oil out of the ground. They're right, of course. Oil exploration companies do have new and improved ways to extract oil. The problem is that finding and obtaining this oil is expensive, dirty and dangerous work (and very likely to arouse indignant opposition from environmentalists). Here's a list of the new ways of finding oil. You will see that it is clear that the days of cheap oil are over. And they aren't coming back. Ever.

a) Oil Sands

The phrase `oil sands' refers to loose sand or sandstone that is saturated with a form of petroleum known as bitumen. The oil is obtained either by digging vast open mines or by processing the bitumen underground. The problem is that open pit mines leave huge piles of toxic waste that can pollute nearby water sources. Also, the petrol obtained from oil sands results in 10% to 15% more greenhouse gas emissions per barrel because of the extra energy needed to refine the bitumen. The cost of producing a barrel of oil this way is around $75 a barrel.

b) Oil Shale

Shale may include a solid material called kerogen which contains oil. The problem is that the rock has to be mined and then heated to a high temperature if the oil is to be released. Extracting this oil requires vast amounts of land and water and produces a great deal of toxic material. Vast amounts of energy are used in obtaining the oil. The cost of obtaining oil from shale is well in excess of $100 a barrel.

c) Deepwater Oil

There is oil beneath the ocean floor that was deposited there more than 150 million years ago. Obtaining this oil requires drilling down through two miles of water, then through rock and then through a mile of salt. There are huge environmental dangers involved in extracting this oil. And the oil is expensive - probably costing $60 to $70 dollars a barrel at least.

d) Arctic Oil

Vast areas of ice have melted in the Arctic. This means that the oil underneath can now be obtained by drilling. There are, however, huge difficulties and dangers. Oil from the Arctic is likely to cost well over $100 a barrel.

e) Tight oil

When light crude oil is bound into permaneable shale it can be released by a process known as hydraulic fracturing. The rock is broken up and the oil then flows up the well. (That's the theory anyway). Obtaining tight oil requires a process known as fracking in which millions of gallons of water are mixed with chemicals and injected deep into the ground. There are a number of problems. The process requires vast amounts of water (a scarce commodity in its own right. There is a real risk of contaminating other water supplies. Burning off excess methane can cause serious air pollution. And fracking seems to cause earthquakes. (These problems don't seem to worry the energy hungry hordes who talk with enthusiasm about fracking and who cannot bear the thought of life without regular access to Facebook, Twitter and the X Factor.) The cash cost of oil obtained this way is likely to be well over $50 per barrel.

6

The cost of adhering to absurd EU regulations controlling the production of energy will destroy what remains of our future prosperity. Other EU countries will, of course, ignore regulations which they consider inconvenient or expensive. And countries such as the USA and China (the countries which produce most of the world's pollution) are doing little or nothing to reduce their energy consumption.

7

The fact that the planet is running out of natural resources is exacerbated by the growth in the size of the world's population. (This was widely discussed in the 1960s but, since then, has been generally overlooked.)

Back at the start of the 19th century, the world population was, give or take a village or two, around one billion. Today, the world population, once again give or take a village or two, is seven billion.

The same area of land and sea is now expected to provide natural resources for seven times as many people.

And there's another problem (which I described in detail in my book *Oil Apocalypse*): for the last century or more we have survived the growth in the world's population because we learned how to harness the power of natural resources such as oil. It was oil that enabled us to create fertilisers increasing our food supplies. It was oil that enabled us to harvest and transport our food supplies. It was oil which enabled us to do everything we needed to do.

And now the oil is running out. It's not going to be gone by next Wednesday. But it's running out. The cheap, easy to get at stuff has all been burned up. Now we have to extract the difficult to reach, expensive stuff. And the environmentalists (even though they are in love with their energy-powered computers and mobile telephones) don't want us to get at it.

So we have to feed, clothe and house seven times as many people and we are heading, rapidly, for a world which will, in terms of energy availability, resemble the early 19th century.

Discovering the value of oil as an energy source changed the world. It gave us apparently endless access to relatively cheap power. Running out of oil will change the world again. As I described in *Oil Apocalypse* it will affect every aspect of our lives. Sadly, we have made no plans for the oil running out because our politicians are either in denial or they don't want to think about the problem in private, let alone in public. And yet there are things we could be doing to plan for the future. We should, for example, be reopening our network of canals. Along with bicycles, canals were one of the greatest of man's inventions. They enabled one man with a horse to move vast amounts of material easily and cheaply. No need for coal, oil, nuclear power or hideous solar panels.

8

All around the world, governments run by half-wits are taking every opportunity to increase taxes on oil exploration companies. (Our Government has, of course, already done this with predictably disastrous results). When the profits to be obtained from finding oil are dramatically reduced the incentive to look for oil is also reduced.

9

The cheap oil has gone for ever. Not all barrels of oil are equal. A barrel of oil taken out of the desert in Saudi

Arabia is a damned sight cheaper to acquire than a barrel hidden a few miles under the water in the Gulf of Mexico or beneath massive ice floes in the Arctic.

10

In 2012, the EU imposed a ban on oil imports from Iran to please Israel. This was, of course, breathtakingly stupid (unless the EU officials are all individually long on oil shares) since the one thing guaranteed to prevent the EU's economy from recovering is a shortage of oil and a high oil price.

11

The global demand for energy is going to grow as the developing economies grow. In 2009, China overtook the USA and became the world's largest energy consumer.

12

The cost of alternative fuels will only fall if a great deal of money is spent exploring ways to make them cheaper and more effective. But governments no longer have the money to spend on research. And neither have energy companies. Meanwhile, the cost of our disappearing, traditional energy supplies will continue to rise remorselessly.

13

Windmills in Wales are frequently net users of electricity. When there isn't enough wind to turn them round they have to be kept turning using electricity taken from the National Grid. (If they aren't kept turning then they seize up and need expensive maintenance.) Other attempts to replace oil, coal and gas as energy sources have been equally disastrous. And the absurd plan to replace petrol with biofuels has resulted in soaring food prices and the destruction of huge areas of woodland - inevitably causing massive environmental damage.

14

Global warming may turn out to be a real phenomenon (though the scientific evidence is confusing and has been deliberately made more confusing by scientists peddling a particular line) but there is no evidence that global warming is a result of man-made activities and it is unlikely that any evidence will be produced because scientists who are paid to favour the hypothesis now claim that the subject is beyond debate. (This is a common fault among scientists. For example, medical scientists frequently claim that vivisection and vaccination should not be debated because they are 'known' to be of value. The reality is that the evidence proves the exact opposite to be true.) I believe that the oft-repeated and fashionable warnings about global warming and climate change were politically motivated and designed to encourage us to use less energy in general and oil in particular. The enthusiastic support for the paper-thin man-made-global-warming argument is merely an excuse for preparing us for a world in which oil is a scarce and increasingly expensive commodity. Politicians are using the global warming argument in the same way that a magician attracts attention to his left hand when he is about to do something with his right hand (or uses an under-dressed assistant to distract attention from himself completely). They want us to worry about the global warming argument because the oil is running out and all (or at least most of) the things they want us to do 'to protect the planet' will also help them to deal with the inevitable reduction in the supply of available oil.

The problem for England is that successive Governments have decided that we must accept the unproven theory that the world is getting hotter because of our bad habits and they have decided that we must lead the way in controlling our energy usage. And so, while big users such as China and the USA do little or nothing to curb their polluting habits, England is obeying and gold plating nonsensical and economically damaging rules from the EU. The result is that whatever happens to the planet, England is doomed.

15

As a knee-jerk response to the unfortunate incident in Japan in 2011, Germany decided to dump all its nuclear energy by the year 2022. They closed one nuclear power station immediately and electricity prices immediately rose by 17%. There was much talk of replacing the nuclear power stations with windmills but protestors immediately announced that they would campaign against the proposal. If the Germans go ahead with this plan it will be the end of the German manufacturing miracle. I wonder how the protestors will persuade their computers to work without electricity.

16

Solar energy sounds wonderful. But most of the world just isn't sunny enough and the cost of making and fitting solar panels means that solar power is at least four times more costly than energy produced by fossil fuels. And there are a few snags. It doesn't work at night or for much of the winter. And since environmentalists like to e-mail one another at night and throughout the winter this means that electricity for heating and cooking becomes very expensive. Every country that has tried solar power has given up. Only if you live in the middle of the Sahara do solar panels work.

17

Food is running out and prices are going to soar. There are several reasons for this. But, here's one: the average age of farmers in England is around 60 and in some parts of the world it is higher. Farming is hard work (there are massively high suicide rates among farmers) and young people simply don't want to do it. In addition, as people in Asia become richer, so they want to enjoy a Western-style diet of hamburgers and hot dogs. And providing all that meat needs a lot of grain. Inevitably, the genetic engineering industry has sold itself as our saviour - and has managed to convince a number of people that it has the answers. Bill Gates (the well-known expert on food and vaccines) seems to believe that genetic engineering, along with vaccines, can save the world. I think he's a fool. The enthusiastic supporters of genetic engineering (most of whom, it has to be said, have been bought by big companies) point out that according to the United Nations and the Food and Agriculture Organisation there are over one billion people in the world today who don't have enough food to eat. Genetic engineering is, they say, the answer. They avoid the fact that there is a much, much simpler and safer answer: persuade more people to become vegetarian. If the world stopped eating meat there would be more than enough food to go round. But the meat industry wouldn't like that.

I've discussed my many objections to genetic engineering in previous books but my biggest objection is the fact that there is no evidence that genetically modified food is safe and plenty of reasons to suspect that it isn't. And, in a world which relies completely on one variety of genetically modified seed, a problem would be a big problem.

Meanwhile it is also worth remembering that food production is being affected by a dramatic reduction in the number of bees and my bet is that in the end it will be clear that genetically engineered and genetically modified crops are the problem. I've been warning about the dangers of genetic engineering for many, many years (and Monsanto has regularly been high up on my list of the world's worst companies) but no one has ever wanted to listen. The word `Luddite' has been widely used. The GM enthusiasts will perhaps listen when the bees have gone and pollination has to be done by hand. (Just what other problems genetic engineering will bring are yet to be seen. The main danger is that by persuading farmers to grow exactly the same crops the big multinational companies will create a problem which will make the Irish potato famine look like a minor menu malfunction.

18

Expensive, scarce resources are being wasted on building tatty new homes (with tiny rooms and walls made of plaster board) while beautiful, well-proportioned Victorian and Edwardian homes with solid walls are being knocked down because they don't satisfy the EU's absurd requirements.

19

As countries which have resources discover environmental concerns, decent wages and sovereign rights so they will insist on taking a closer control of their copper, uranium, rare earths or food growing capacity. They will insist that foreign countries and companies pay far more for the privilege of using those resources. It is worth noting that 60% of all the uncultivated arable land in the world is in the sub Saharan region which has good rainfall and sunshine and a big labour force. The proprietors are more determined than ever to keep their natural resource wealth instead of allowing the Americans to steal it.

20

Forty years ago there were 700 listed plantation owners in London. These companies made up 10% of the FTSE. Today there are hardly any plantation owners left. Food is in the hands of countries and huge international conglomerates. England has been left out of the loop.

21

It isn't just oil that is running out, of course. Just about every basic commodity you can think of is running out. As China and India use up greater and greater quantities of basic commercial ingredients such as copper so shortages appear and prices rise.

But there is one commodity which is running out that very few people take seriously; and yet it is the one commodity that matters more than any other: water.

In March 2012, all intelligence agencies in the USA got together to produce a semi-secret report warning about what they defined as the big future threat to America: water shortage.

They argued that the reducing availability of useable water, and the problem of pollution in drinking water, will lead to the collapse of governments and a rise in the number of extremist groups. The big, big problem for tomorrow is water shortage. And there is a massive need for more money to be spent on water infrastructure programmes.

There is, of course, plenty of water on the planet. Two thirds of the earth is covered in the stuff. But less than 1% of the water available is accessible, fresh and useable.

And there are several reasons why the world is facing a water shortage crisis and why England is facing a bigger problem than almost anywhere else.

First, the world's population is constantly growing and constantly pushing up the demand for water. In the year 2000 there were six billion of us sharing the planet. Today, just a decade or so later, there are seven billion. There is only so much useable water on the planet and the demand for that water is growing dramatically. Suddenly, millions of people who didn't use flush toilets or baths because they didn't have them now have them and use them regularly. The result is that around the world lakes and reservoirs are running low and rivers are running dry. Some nations are already towing icebergs half way across the world in order to obtain fresh water. (Much, but not all, of the ice will melt before it reaches its destination but there will be enough ice remaining to make the exercise worthwhile commercially.) Others (particularly rich Arab countries) are experimenting with desalination plants. These are expensive and use up a lot of energy but as the water shortage grows, and the price of water rises, so it will become an increasingly viable solution. The problem, of course, is that the oil (and therefore the energy) is also running out.

Second, as the population has grown so the amount of water needed for farming has increased. And as the number of people eating meat has increased so the need for water has increased still faster. A diet that is 20% meat uses twice as much water as a purely vegetarian diet. Agriculture already uses over two thirds of our fresh water. And farms need more and more water to grow the crops their cattle need. (And, of course, to give the cattle to drink directly.)

Third, industry uses up vast quantities of water. It takes around 20 gallons of water to make a pound of plastic. Making electricity uses up vast amounts of water - even if only as a coolant. Amazingly, around half of all the water used each day is spent cooling power plants.

Fourth, much of the world's drinking water is now polluted. In China around 90% of the freshwater has been contaminated by industry. Even in America, where there are strict rules about contaminating rivers and lakes, around 40% of all the water is dangerously polluted. And, of course, polluted water is of no use for drinking, growing plants or feeding to animals. You can't even use the damned stuff for industrial purposes. In England too, much of our drinking water is polluted. And the number of pollutants is rising rapidly. Decades ago I warned that our drinking water is polluted with prescription drug residues (which pass into the drinking water supplies when waste water from sewage farms is recycled but not properly filtered). This problem is getting worse.

Fifth, many of England's water companies are owned by foreigners whose primary concern is profits and who don't really give a damn about whether or not our drinking water is fresh or is reliably supplied. It is, sadly, perfectly possible to make huge profits without providing a good service. (If you have difficulty accepting this notion just think of English airports which provide an appalling service, are largely foreign owned and make plenty of money.)

Sixth, planners in England just don't understand how serious the water shortage already is and have no idea how really serious it is about to become. It makes sense to build new reservoirs to capture and store rain. But when Thames Water applied for permission to spend £1 billion building a new reservoir the company was turned down. In Singapore they are planning to build underground reservoirs (like the huge one in Istanbul) but in England the planners won't even allow empty land to be used for water collecting.

Seventh, more and more people live in cities and towns. In England the water supplies (like the sewage facilities) were largely built by the Victorians. As the number of people moving to towns and cities grows so the demand for a better infrastructure will rise. Private companies aren't prepared to spend the money and so eventually the Government is going to have to do something - or stand by as millions of people die of thirst or infections caused by polluted water. The cost to taxpayers will be vast as money which could be spent on growing the economy will have to be spent on standing still.

Eighth, our problems in England are exacerbated by the fact that our water supplies are managed by a number of different companies which don't work together very well. This means that there can be a shortage of water in one part of the country and a glut just a few miles away.

And finally, much of the water we have is wasted. Around 30% of our fresh water is used for flushing lavatories (surely it cannot be beyond the wit of the water companies to find a way to recycle used shower and bath water for flushing purposes). In England around 25% of the water sent out by the water companies never reaches its destination. It is lost through leaky pipes. In America the nation's water systems were recently awarded a D- by the American Society of Civil Engineers. As their economy crumbles the Americans need to spend trillions on upgrading their water supplies.

22

In May 2012, the International Monetary Fund warned that within ten years the price of oil would have doubled. They explained that the world's oil was running out and that demand was rising. This warning was, I repeat, issued in May 2012. I first made exactly the same points in my book *Living in a Fascist Country*, which was published in 2006, just six years earlier. My book *Oil Apocalypse* was dismissed as scaremongering by those who bothered to read it. Proof, yet again, that those who claim to lead us are in truth wallowing in ignorance and bewilderment.

23

We're coming to the end of an oil coloured age but there are a number of silver linings to the coming oil shortage. There will be less aeroplane travel, and so the risk of bacteria and viruses spreading around the world will be reduced. We will have to walk or cycle more, and so we will be healthier.

Conclusion

It is an unarguable truth that all commodities are becoming scarcer. We face a mass of commodity shortages and our supplies of natural energy are running out. The chances of there being an interruption to world oil supplies in each twelve month period are better than good - there is always likely to be a crisis somewhere. Supplies of drinking water and food are both scarce. No one is doing anything to deal with these problems. The cost of extracting commodities is rising for three main reasons. First, many essentials are running out. The supplies that are left are increasingly difficult to reach and extract. Second, the energy costs involved in running mines, ships and tractors are rising rapidly. Third, governments everywhere are insisting on sharing in the profits made by commodity companies. This puts up the cost of extracting materials and means that only the most profitable mines will still be worked. The overall result will be shortages, outages and constant, steep price rises. None of these will have an advantageous effect on our economy. And it's all going to get worse. Much worse.

Chapter 12

Tax, Tax And More Taxes

Introduction

Thanks to decades of tinkering and micromanaging, contradictory complications and retrospective legislation, England's tax system is now a great brake on the economy. It is the tax system (allied to an utterly absurd benefits system) which encourages the rich to emigrate or retire early and the would-be lower paid to stay at home and watch television.

1

Governments waste money because the people in charge of the purse strings aren't spending real money. They're spending monopoly money and they really don't care about it. Over a quarter of a century ago I exposed the fact that the NHS was spending more on such items as toilet rolls, washing powder and envelopes than I would pay if I bought them at a local supermarket. (I was writing a column for the *Daily Star* newspaper and an NHS employee had sent me a print-out listing all the prices paid by the NHS for standard items). After my exposé, NHS bosses launched an enquiry but, inevitably, the enquiry was not to look at their purchasing processes but to find out how I had obtained my information. I was not at all surprised when, in May 2012, newspapers reported that a survey had shown that the NHS still spent considerably more on staple items of stationery than you or I would pay if we bought the same items at a local retail store.

What is true of the NHS is true of all government departments. They all waste billions of pounds of taxpayers' money.

And nothing will ever change.

For one simple reason.

The money being wasted isn't their money.

2

A number of basic questions are never asked by those who collect and spend our money. It may well be that there are sensible answers to these questions. But that is not the point. The point is that the questions should be asked and debated and the voters given a chance to make their views known.

Here are just a few of the questions which are never asked because our `leaders' assume that they already know all the answers.

Why should the State provide people with free education? (The Nation doesn't provide people with free food which is patently more important). Why do we give foreign aid to countries such as India which don't want it and don't need it? Why do we run a National Health Service which is more expensive and less efficient than a private system would be?

Why should people pay more tax when they earn more money - and yet receive the same benefits as everyone else? Why is there no tax on lottery winnings? Why should people pay tax on the income from money they have earned, paid tax on, and saved? Why should people be punished by inflation for holding onto shares for a long time and then allowed nothing for the inflation part of their profit? Why should people work, earn and save and their estate then pay tax on what they leave when they die?

There may well be sensible and honourable answers to these questions. Or they may just be things we accept because it's the way things are done.

3

I doubt if any organisation in England makes anywhere near as many mistakes as Her Majesty's Revenue and Customs (HMRC). For incompetence the taxmen are in a league of their own. HMRC has admitted that they aim for a 75% accuracy rate when calculating bills. Their excuse for this pathetic target is that tax is a very complicated subject these days. Indeed, tax is now so complicated that the advice given by HMRC employees is often inaccurate or misleading and HMRC's technical advisers are often unable to answer simple queries. One in six tax bills is wrong. (A level of extraordinary incompetence that would result in an employee being fired from any normal institution.) Apparently none of this matters a damn. The Court of Appeal has confirmed that HMRC is not liable for administrative errors and does not owe a duty of care to process tax forms with reasonable expedition

4

If I have to pay the VAT man it takes three days for the money to get to them. If they have to pay me I have to allow 30 days for the money to reach me.

5

Tax collectors have always been loathed and despised, not just because they do an unpopular job but because they are, like traffic wardens, intrinsically unpleasant people. It is a self-selection process. No one with a beating heart wants to be a taxman or a traffic warden. And here's an idle thought: are HMRC employees born with an air of condescending authority and a delight in lightly restrained bureaucratic violence (HMRC Motto: `We can screw up your life and it will be a pleasure') or is it something they acquire at a special indoctrination course?

6

`The baseness of the English land-owners surpasses that of any other men that ever lived in the world. The cowards know well that labourers that give value to their land are skin and bone. They are not such brutes as not to know that this starvation is produced by taxation.' - William Cobbett, in Rural Rides

7

The Government gives charities nearly £13 billion a year of taxpayers' money. Shouldn't it be up to us to decide which charities to support? Charities which rely on Government grants are just quangos by another name. I am similarly annoyed by company bosses who give vast amounts of money which isn't theirs to charities and political parties. The bosses then receive honours and awards while the shareholders (whose money it was) are merely impoverished.

8

`The only difference between a tax man and a taxidermist is that the taxidermist leaves the skin.' - Mark Twain

9

A growing number of previously honourable people now feel that they have a moral responsibility to pay as little tax as possible - not because most of the money is wasted (although that is a small reason in itself) but because so much of it is spent on bad things (such as waging illegal wars and supporting Hitler's Bastard Love Child). Politicians claim they have a right to spend an increasing proportion of our money for us because, they say, they know better than we do how it should be spent. This is now a provable nonsense. Very few taxpayers are content with the way that their Government now uses their money to support private banking companies and to ensure that overpaid bankers continue to receive their undeserved multi-million pound salaries and their equally undeserved multi-million pound bonuses.

10

`Every man is entitled, if he can, to order his affairs so that the tax attaching under the appropriate Act is less than it would otherwise be.' - Lord Tomlin

11

We desperately need to simplify taxes and cut red tape but neither of these things will ever be done because the people who would have to make the necessary decisions are the people who complicate taxes and generate red tape. And they know that the more complicated things are, and the more red tape there is, the bigger their departments will become. And bigger departments mean greater security, more chances of promotion and bigger bonuses.

12

Why do so many people let HMRC employees get away with being so damned rude? People who work for HMRC are civil servants. We pay them. We are entitled to expect that HMRC employees behave politely and with respect.

If they don't then we are entitled to complain about them and to use such pleasantries as the Human Rights Act to help us defend ourselves. (Always remember: the taxman has a job and can be fired.) After many years of experience with HMRC I am convinced that honest folk who kneel before them, and grovel before their arrogance, are far more likely to end up broken and weeping than people who stand up for themselves, refuse to be bullied and demand to be treated with respect.

13

Every time I have to visit the HMRC website to complete my VAT return, or an employer's return, I am reminded that the official tax and customs website is the worst designed piece of rubbish on the planet. It is now compulsory to fill in these forms online and it always takes me far longer to make my way through the HMRC's badly designed website than it ever took to fill in paper forms. (The Government's enthusiasm for forcing people to fill in forms online has been followed by most utilities and other large companies. Since it is difficult for non-governmental organisations to `force' customers to conduct their business online these companies usually charge those who *don't* go online a substantial penalty for preferring old-fashioned paperwork. Web based accounting is always promoted as advantageous for the customer when it is, of course, always the company concerned with benefits.) The HMRC website appears to have been written by Kafka with a little help from the Marx Brothers. I have seen deliberately complicated computer games which are easier to work my way through than the HMRC website. I do as little online as I have to and I have refused to give them an e-mail address. (I also refuse to give them a telephone number so if they want to get in touch with me they have to send me a letter. And, naturally, they don't have my home address.)

14

The Government is planning to make tax avoidance illegal. I wonder when the half wits at The Treasury will realise that this will mean that it will be illegal to invest in National Savings schemes (such as Premium Bonds) which offer tax free prizes. It will be illegal to buy gifts (because they are exempt from capital gains tax). Those politicians who publicly excoriate members of the public who sensibly take advantage of perfectly legal tax avoidance schemes (while themselves fiddling their expenses) should perhaps understand that citizens would pay their taxes with far more enthusiasm if the money collected were spent usefully, instead of being wasted on illegal wars and supporting Hitler's Bastard Love Child.

15

Everywhere you look there are hidden taxes. For example, whenever more roadworks are planned the first thing that will happen will be the installation of speed cameras. These will go up (and become operational) weeks or even months before any work actually starts. And the cameras will remain in position long after the last workman has screwed the top back on his thermos and folded up his copy of *The Sun*. No one in Government understands, or gives a damn, that these unnecessary speed restrictions mean that billions of pounds are lost to the economy as people struggling to do business waste hours on journeys that become ever longer and more tedious.

Every Government department has become adept at gouging extra money out of the voters. The Royal Mail, possibly the worst run organisation on the planet (and the most incompetently run in the history of the world) offers many examples of this brand of aggravated meanness. For example, a reader sent me a letter in an old envelope which he had carefully sealed with sticky tape. Unfortunately, the sticky tape had extended the length of the envelope by approximately a millimetre. When I collected my mail I had to pay a fine and an additional fee because the letter did not conform to standard sizes.

16

In May 2012, HMRC introduced a new online tax gizmo designed to enable taxpayers to find out how and where their taxes had been spent. The new tool crashed on the first day.

17

Some of the taxes introduced recently have been so unfair (and so little understood by the people introducing them) that they make me want to weep. When, in the spring of 2012, it was announced that the Government was putting a 20% VAT tax on the sale price of static caravans, increasing the average price of £35,000 by a massive £7,000, the idiotic Cameron explained that it was unfair for there to be a tax on mobile caravans but no tax on static caravans. How stupid can you get and still be able to put on your own socks in the morning? The people who buy static caravans tend to buy them so that they will have somewhere to live. They cannot afford to buy their own home because politicians have deliberately pushed up the price of houses to stratospheric levels. And so they want to buy a static caravan. The people who buy mobile caravans want to tow them behind their Range Rover or their Volvo estate car so that they can spend weekends causing traffic jams in the lanes of Cornwall, Devon and Wales. It's not as if this was a big money maker for the Government. It certainly wouldn't go anywhere near covering the cost of the tax cut for bankers (reducing the top rate of tax from 50% to 45%). The Chancellor could, I suspect, have made far more money for the economy by cancelling Fred Goodwin's obscene pension.

18

Looking for examples of taxes that are unfair? Try this one: the cost of driving is not related to the time travelled on the roads. If you have a car and use it every other Sunday for a three mile drive to your granny's you will (assuming that you own the same sort of car) pay the same annual car tax as the road warrior who travels 100,000 miles a year racing up and down the motorways on business. And what about foreign haulage drivers, the ones who block our roads and knock the corners off our ancient buildings so that they can bring cheap imports into the country? They don't pay a penny for the privilege of using our roads. We let them wreck our roads and our economy entirely without charge. Barking.

19

More annoying than almost anything else they do is the fact that HMRC makes sweetheart deals with large companies (so that they don't have to pay too much tax) although they will, of course, go after private individuals with abrasive enthusiasm bordering on vindictiveness. The taxman let evil American company Goldman Sachs off some of its taxes (after a multi million pound `mistake') as a result of some very cosy chats over rather expensive meals. The latest annual accounts for Goldman Sachs show that the world's most evil company paid just £4.1 million in corporation tax despite making profits of £1.9 billion. `These are people who are at the heart of the problem in the financial world, who've paid extraordinary bonuses to their partners and aren't prepared to pay a fair amount of tax,' said a member of the Commons Treasury select committee. `It's pure unadulterated greed.' Naturally, no one did anything about this outrage. Goldman Sachs can, it seems, do anything it likes. It was revealed that Goldman Sachs hadn't even been charged interest by HMRC when settling a tax dispute. The company was, according to the chairman of the Public Accounts Committee, `let off'. Next time I receive a nasty letter from HMRC I intend to reply demanding that I be given the same treatment as Goldman Sachs.

When an HMRC boss, `Call me Dave' Hartnett, was questioned by a Commons committee, he played around with words in a way that would be considered reprehensible if done by a taxpayer being investigated by HMRC. It seemed to me that he was covering up huge multi million losses and shaky deals with his dining chums at Goldman Sachs. After it was announced that Hartnett (who allegedly had 107 free lunches and dinners with big company staffers) would retire early on a huge pension I wrote to my local tax office asking if the taxman would let me off what I owed if I took him out for egg and chips and a mug of tea.

20

You can still see the evidence of the windows which were bricked up when the window tax was introduced in the late 17th century. (Property owners had to pay double the regular tax if they had more than 10 windows and quadruple the regular tax if they had more than 20 windows). Will the window tax come back? Well, in a way it is with the various types of mansion tax now being proposed by the Coalition. Those advocating these taxes should take note of the bricked up windows. People will always find ways round silly taxes and doubtless mansion owners will simply knock down a wing or two or find some other way to devalue their properties. (The owners of empty factories and warehouses who have found themselves forced to pay council taxes have avoided this absurdity by having their buildings demolished.)

21

There are plans to charge houseowners a new tax called 'net imputed rental income' on their homes. The tax (another piece of legislation from the EU) will be equivalent to the rent you would get if you were not living in your house but renting it out to other people. Taxes such as these are designed to help the Government pay its debts by gouging money out of middle class families.

22

Inheritance tax is exquisitely absurd. If you inherit a house you have to pay tax on the proceeds before you are allowed to sell the house.

23

Here's a quick way to end terrorism: put a tax on bombs and bombers. Put a small tax on small bombs and a big tax on big bombs and make all bombs subject to VAT. The red tape would bring terrorism to a grinding halt.

24

HMRC employees never say `thank you' at the end of an investigation, even when they've found that the person under investigation is entirely innocent, and that they have been wasting his time. Instead they invariably lose poorly by sending a bad tempered letter saying `we can reopen this whenever we like'. My experience (after two lengthy investigations) is that HMRC employees are far more ignorant than anyone would believe, far more stupid than any living creature deserves to be, and ruder and more vengeful than the nastiest, meanest psychopathic hoodie.

25

Even Einstein found doing his income tax impossibly complicated. And he didn't have to try dealing with HMRCs 21st century nonsenses.

26

Don't tell friends or relatives anything about your tax affairs. One HMRC trick is to offer someone under investigation a lighter ride if they dob in someone they know.

27

If there is a post strike (caused by one government department) and tax returns are late then the taxman (another government department) fines people.

28

Most taxpayers have little or no idea how their money is spent. But from 2013 the taxman will send us all statements showing how much money has gone where. Lots of people are going to get a shock. A taxpayer whose earnings are £60,000 a year will pay a total of £18,401.24 in tax. Of this £6,127 goes towards paying out benefits, £3,201.82 goes on health care (private health insurance would be about a third of the cost), £368 goes on housing and local services (council tax has to be added to this, of course), £1,060 goes on defence, £920 goes on recreation, culture and religion, £400 is spent on administration and £1,177 is spent on paying the interest on the national debt (so you can see what Gordon Brown and the banks are costing us). This isn't the end of the story of course. Most of the Government's income comes from VAT and in addition there are business rates, council taxes, corporation taxes (which affect all shareholders and pensioners), excise duties and all the rest.

29

High-grade taxmen who make huge mistakes aren't usually fired. They are allowed to resign and to take with them their multi-million pound pensions and their contacts book.

30

If the taxman owes you money you will probably have to wait a long time to receive it. You are unlikely to receive much or any interest. If you owe the taxman money you will have to pay interest and huge penalties if you don't pay it immediately. And you may go to prison.

31

I invariably receive an HMRC demand on Christmas Eve. I am convinced they do this out of sheer nastiness. I now avoid this unpleasantness by not collecting any mail for a week before Christmas and a week after the New Year holiday.

32

The tax rules are designed to discourage marriage. For example, two unmarried people can have two residences, both of which are exempt from capital gains tax, but a married couple can only have one such residence. This illogical and unreasonable tax on marriage can be worth hundreds of thousands of pounds to unmarried couples.

33

High inflation rates, combined with capital gains taxes, mean that there is a huge incentive for investors to take big risks when selecting investments.

34

It's not personal,' said an HMRC inspector when I chided him for his department's behaviour. Of course, it's bloody personal. It's always bloody personal.

35

f the Government introduced a simple consumption tax they could get rid of all other forms of taxation. To make things fair there could be two or three different rates (one low rate for bread and bicycles and another high rate for yachts and caviar). Taxing through consumption works and is very simple to operate. It makes dishonesty pretty well impossible. And it gets rid of the need for millions of inspectors and accountants. There would be no need for financial records and form filling in. What's the problem? It would, of course, be too straightforward and too simple and would require the turkeys to vote for Christmas. So meanwhile tax continues to become ever more complex. *Tolley's Tax Handbook* is now 17,795 pages long. During Gordon Brown's disastrous reign as Chancellor of the Exchequer, the book nearly tripled in size.

36

Politicians have a loose attitude to tax avoidance. Ken Livingstone, the left wing former Mayor of London, has criticised personal tax avoidance through company structures. But, Livingstone set up a personal company (he and his wife are shareholders) and in one recent year Livingstone (who has said that tax avoiders should not be allowed to vote) avoided paying £50,000 in tax by having his writing and speaking fees paid into a company.

37

HMRC now wants to change the self-employment tax system. The new, proposed, system gives taxpayers online access to their own tax records. New tax returns will be completed by HMRC with data collected from all the sources it can find. The taxpayer will then be expected to sign or correct the return. HMRC can do this because it now has access to masses of information from banks, businesses, public companies. Big brother. HMRC wants to introduce this new system for several reasons. First, HMRC will reduce its costs because it will be the taxpayer's responsibility to check all the data submitted. (HMRC will be saved the responsibility of doing the checking). Second, many taxpayers will sign and pay and won't spot the errors. Third, the whole damned scheme will be run on the Internet. Fourth, it will be the taxpayer's responsibility to argue about any of the figures of which they disapprove. (Trying to get banks and public companies to correct information will be the responsibility of the taxpayer). And finally, taxpayers will be forced to complete their forms on the Internet and so HMRC will save money on printing forms and sending them out. Anyone who doesn't have access to the Internet will be stuffed. I object to this proposal on many grounds. But my main one is that since HMRC's idea of confidentiality is not the same as mine I believe that this scheme will result in a complete end to financial privacy.

38

If we must have an income tax, a flat rate tax of 10% on everything earned would be better than the present system It would remove all the paperwork and zillion pointless jobs and many regulators. It would ensure that everyone paid the same rate of tax and it would be fair. There would be no deductions. The tax would be paid on overal income. Many countries have already introduced a flat tax of 10% and it has proved simple, effective and inescapable. The 10% is charged on absolutely every penny earned by individuals or companies. Such a simple method of taxation (which would bring in just as much Government income as our absurdly overcomplicated system) would be unwelcome only with HMRC employees and accountants.

39

The politicians and the Hectors at HMRC want a law saying that 'anyone who does anything to save tax will be taxed as if he hadn't taken this action'. That's really well thought out. Anyone who gives up smoking will, presumably, still have to pay the tax on the cigarettes he no longer smokes. Anyone can no longer afford to drive a car will still have to pay the tax on the petrol he can no longer afford to buy.

40

Retrospective tax clampdowns are now common. When the laws change retrospectively something which is proper and legal becomes improper and illegal. Honest, decent folk can find, overnight, that they have become criminals. Retrospective tax legislation makes it impossible for anyone to make plans. All retrospective legislation is grossly unfair. And yet governments everywhere are becoming increasing enthusiastic about introducing retrospective legislation.

41

HMRC staff can claim hundreds of pounds in generous expenses without producing any receipts. Hard-working businessmen who want to claim for expenses incurred in their work must always produce receipts.

42

Tax inspectors are now offered bonuses of up to £2,000 (3% of their salary) if they succeed in forcing taxpayers to give more money to the Government. The money paid by the taxpayers doesn't actually have to be owed, of course. The tax inspector must merely bully the taxpayer into believing that it is owed.

Giving tax inspectors bonuses creates a conflict of interest by encouraging inspectors to pursue questionable investigations in order to boost tax receipts and give themselves a bonus.

43

HMRC employees are like attack dogs. Anyone who lets them know that they are sensitive or delicate will be attacked twice as hard. HMRC employees, like dogs, can smell weakness and fear. In the same way that policemen prefer to harass middle class motorists rather than real thugs (there is less chance of being hit on the head or knifed in the stomach) and journalists prefer to harass small businessmen rather than huge conglomerates (there is less chance of advertising being withdrawn, or writs being delivered) so HMRC prefers to target the mild, the honest and the easily bullied.

44

HMRC recently paid £100,000 to a convicted thief for the information he had stolen about bank customers (there was no evidence that the customers had done anything wrong, HMRC just wanted the information). If you or I paid money for stolen information we would doubtless be arrested, charged and imprisoned. HMRC employees are clearly operating outside the law.

45

Taxpayers will soon be forced to file all their returns electronically because the Internet makes life much easier and more cost effective for HMRC. (Naturally, HMRC will claim that they are doing it for our convenience). Online filing enables HMRC to compare taxpayers in similar lines of work. HMRC assumes that all plumbers, café owners, dentists or stand-up comedians have exactly the same expenses, exactly the same earnings and exactly the same level of profits.

46

A few years ago the Inland Revenue sold properties to a private company based in the tax haven of Bermuda and owned by George Soros. Mr Soros did not live in England and was not, therefore, liable to pay any capital gains tax on the properties. The contract to sell HMRC's entire 600 property portfolio was signed despite a Treasury crackdown on tax dodges using offshore islands. HMRC deliberately conspired to lose the nation millions in lost tax revenues. No one was fired or punished.

47

Overbearing, interventionist State employees want to control, regulate and tax every human activity in order to protect and extend their budgetary turf. The more regulations you introduce the more fees and fines you can collect and so your department gets bigger. A bigger department means a higher salary and more perks. The civil servants never understand that the rules and regulations they are introducing are destroying the goose that lays the golden eggs.

48

All the evidence shows clearly that reducing the tax rate will, quite quickly, result in an increase in economic growth. When tax rates are high people make a real effort to reduce their burden; they reduce their earnings by taking more time off, they enter into complicated tax planning plans, they use National Savings schemes or they simply pack their bags and move abroad. When, in the wake of the 2008 economic crisis, most countries started printing money and increasing taxes (in order to avoid having to make cuts in public spending) the Swedish Government reacted differently. Taxes were cut for everyone and welfare spending was cut to pay for the tax cuts. The result was a dramatic increase in economic growth. Everyone got richer. Once again a Government had proved that cutting taxes is the only logical, sensible way out of debt and economic disaster.

Sadly, none of this is going to happen in England because there are too many people who have a vested interest in maintaining the status quo.

49

How curious that the people promoting the Inland Revenue should invent a little character called Hector as a mascot. To `hector' someone is, of course, to talk to them in a bullying way.

50

I don't trust financial advisers. On two occasions I have been subjected to a lengthy investigation by HMRC. Both times I was, I suspect, dobbed in by people who were working for me. These days the primary loyalty of accountants, and other financial advisors, is to the Government. Accountants, like solicitors, are required by law to make secret reports to the Government - and are not allowed to tell their clients that they are doing this.

51

It annoys me enormously to hear politicians describe the interest I receive on my savings (or the dividends on investments) as `unearned income'. The money I save and invest is just as `earned' as the money I save and spend. For politicians to decide that they are entitled to take bigger chunks of it by describing it as `unearned' is offensive.

52

When politicians introduced plans to put a cap on bonuses paid to bankers, and related the cap to the bankers' salaries, the banks immediately got around this by increasing basic salaries. Neither the politicians nor their advisors had thought of this. The quality of financial advice available through HMRC and The Treasury is appalling.

53

It is not widely understood (especially by politicians and civil servants who, together, have little or no experience of poverty or industry) that higher taxes on companies actually hurt the poorest people. The higher taxes don't affect the salaries, bonuses or perks of bosses (which remain the same) but affect lower paid employees in several ways. First, the number of jobs will be cut. Second, wages will be reduced (or productivity increased). Generally speaking, it will be lower paid employees who will suffer most when corporate taxes go up. A study of European countries found that £1 of additional corporate tax reduced wages by 92p. Trade unions might do well to remember this next time they campaign for higher company taxes. Third, prices will be increased. Fourth, dividends will be cut with the result that pensioners will suffer.

54

It sometimes seems that half the nation's energy is spent avoiding tax and a half of what is left is spent filling in forms and discussing tax problems. This is particularly bad for small businesses which need to be concentrating their energies on trying to make a profit.

55

The Government will attack the middle classes because the poor have no money and the rich will simply leave the country if they are threatened (and, moreover, they will stop acting as benefactors to the political parties).

56

The Government realises that income is already taxed to the hilt (to pay for all those scroungers and unnecessary public sector workers) and so, with the official encouragement of the EU, they will now turn to taxing wealth. If by this they meant taxing billionaires (no one makes a billion by entirely honest means) there would be few complaints. But billionaires (and bankers) have clout and power and anyway there aren't really enough of them to make much of a difference so politicians will instead tax the thrifty and the prudent; they will take from those who have saved, not bought the flashy car or taken the endless foreign holidays; they will target those who have put a few pounds away into the building society or a pension plan. Those are the people who will be targeted with the new wealth taxes.

57

Billions of pounds worth of labour is wasted on filling in tax forms. In America it has been estimated that filling in tax forms wastes the equivalent of three million full-time jobs a year. Our tax forms are worse.

58

The Coalition (seemingly quite unable to grasp how business works and determined to put entrepreneurs at a disadvantage when compared with big companies) is planning to limit the tax relief for losses incurred either on trading activities or in unsuccessful investments in unquoted companies. The result will be that entrepreneurs will no longer be willing to take risks. The man who owns one shop will stick with the one shop instead of trying to build up a business. The businessman tempted to invest in a small company will realise that if the company is successful he will have to pay tax but that if the company fails he won't be able to claim tax relief on the loss. Just how that will help the country grow its way out of its debts is something HMRC and the Chancellor haven't been prepared to share. The problem, of course, is that these rules (and many similar ones) are devised by politicians and civil servants who have never, ever had to meet a payroll or run a business. Such laws are ultimately short-term. They may increase the tax take for a while but in the long-term they will damage entrepreneurial activity and destroy the nation's growth and productivity. Many businessmen will give up plans to expand, or decide to retire early, because of these laws.

59

The Government is planning to introduce a tax on house values. This will mean that people in retirement who have spent their lives building up equity in their home and who suddenly find themselves asset rich and income poor will suddenly find themselves in a sticky position. Their home will have been bought with taxed income. Now, with little income, they will find themselves faced with a tax on the home their taxed income bought. Many will be unable to pay the new tax and will be forced to sell their homes. This is, undoubtedly, the sort of tax that would have gone down well with the communist aristocracy in the USSR. It will undoubtedly suit very nicely the union leader on £140,000 a year who lives in a council owned property and who is guaranteed lifetime occupation.

60

The EU harmonisation of tax is coming but until then more complexities and unfairnesses are inevitable as EU legislation is layered upon English law.

61

Increasingly, these days, HMRC is insisting that taxpayers must prove that they have not done something. So, for example, taxpayers who have foreign property must prove that they have not let it out to anyone else. And just how do you do that? It is, of course, impossible.

62

HMRC has recently announced that it is not bound by its own published guidance. (So, why waste money publishing any guidance?)

63

Every year tax legislation is made more confusing, more complex and more absurd. `Yes it seems unclear...I think it means...' said one HMRC employee whom I had telephoned to ask for advice. `We're not always perfect,' protested another when I pointed out that he had just contradicted himself. Still, I suppose I was lucky, or persistent. Over a quarter of all the people who ring the tax helpline never have their call answered. HMRC, aware of this, says that they are aiming to answer 90% of calls by 2014/15. That's good of them.

64

HMRC claims that its website is there `to save you time and paperwork'. Is it hell. Using the website is compulsory for all employers and small businesses. And the site is surely the worst organised on the Web. It takes HMRC six days to send an automatic response e-mail. And the site actually warns users to beware of security problems.

65

HMRC inspectors can change their minds, act retrospectively and ignore inconvenient evidence. They can and do ignore correspondence, behave with no respect for common sense or the spirit of the law, bully and bend the rules in order to boost their own bonuses. They do all this with arrogance and a clear belief that everyone they meet is a criminal to be despised and treated like dirt.

66

Fees and fines have become an essential part of national and local government income. They are new taxes, not punishments or payments for services rendered. No fee is ever withdrawn or reduced.

67

Our tax system encourages companies to borrow money and take risks. Interest on loans is a tax deductible expense for banks and other companies and so loans are subsidised by taxpayers.

68

When a government puts taxes up too high the system doesn't work properly. An economist called Arther Laffer pointed out that at 0% rate of tax you raise no money and that at 100% you also raise no money because no one works. Somewhere in the middle is a point where taxes and earnings are in balance.

69

A group of senior tax consultants recently criticised HMRC for introducing secondary legislation (e.g. in press releases put out after the budget) which had not been scrutinised by Parliament; for constantly requesting new powers, without showing why they were necessary; and for making errors and failing to answer mail (or treat taxpayers, their employers, with any respect at all). HMRC was also criticised for pushing for retrospective legislation and for interpreting the law in a selective and erratic way with the result that many `grey' areas are produced.

70

Every chancellor promises to make tax rules simpler and every one makes them more complex. George Osbourne actually had the nerve to claim his granny tax (punishing pensioners for being alive) was merely a 'simplification'. And as if in compensation he then made child benefit unbelievably complex. Do they do this through mischief and a sense of fun? Or a toxic mixture of arrogance and stupidity? I leave you to answer that yourself. If you told me that our tax system had been devised by lunatics I would believe you.

71

HMRC receives around 200,000 tip offs a year - many vindictive or trouble making. All result in investigations.

72

HMRC has asked for power to take money from bank accounts, or to freeze assets such as houses without any legal proceedings. If they are given these rights the taxman will become investigator, prosecutor, judge, jury and executioner. And just think of those bonuses. (How fair do you think judges would be if they received a bonus every time they sentenced someone - and if their bonuses depended upon the length of the sentence?)

73

HMRC can now intercept letters and bug phone calls and e-mails and can visit homes and premises to inspect whatever they want to inspect.

74

A survey of HMRC staff found that 30% of all employees had no idea that HMRC's role was `to administer England's tax and custom systems'. Just what they thought they were hired to do was never released (or, probably, ever discovered).

75

Two thirds of businessmen and women say that they find dealing with HMRC more burdensome than five years ago. Not surprisingly, 88% say that simplifying the tax system would improve things. Half say that HMRC staff have inadequate commercial knowledge and two thirds are so confused that they no longer know what is legitimate tax planning and what might result in their being charged with tax evasion.

76

In 2011, a former tax inspector, giving evidence to an employment tribunal, claimed that tax inspectors exaggerated business tax bills in order to increase their own bonuses.

77

HMRC has, like the NHS, been especially criticised for its dealings with older people. It is always the elderly who get screwed by public sector workers because they are an easy target.

78

If tax levels had been kept at 1960 levels (30% of GDP instead of half) England would now be twice as rich.

79

The second most stupid thing people say is: `If you are being investigated by HMRC you must have done something wrong'. (The first most stupid thing folk say is: 'If you don't have anything to hide you don't need to worry about privacy'.) The fact is that tax investigations can be triggered by ex-employees, neighbours, ex-spouses or anyone with half a grudge. They can also be started at random.

It used to be said that ignorance was no defence. These days innocence is not much of a defence either.

80

As governments everywhere struggle to balance their books they will introduce yet more taxes. Windfall taxes, designed to take advantage of companies or groups of companies which have defied austerity and managed to continue to make profits, will become increasingly popular. These new taxes will make life almost impossible for investors and pensioners.

Conclusion

Our tax system has become so complex and intrusive that it has become counterproductive; it is cumbersome, unfair, expensive and unwieldy. Much of it exists not to collect money but as a sort of organised vengeance. Taxes are devised which actually cost money to collect and, increasingly, HMRC is seen as an organisation of thugs hired to demand money with menaces. In the future, anyone with any money will be targeted by the tax collectors.

Chapter 13

Public Sector Workers: Greedy And Out Of Touch With Reality

Introduction

Few things have ever better illustrated the divide between private and public sector workers than the sight of striking Government employees demanding that their absurdly generous and unaffordable pensions remain untouched.

England has become two nations, divided not by race, sex or age but by employment. On the one hand there are those who work for themselves or for private employers. They tend to work long, hard hours, they have little job security and many know that in their retirement years they will probably struggle to make ends meet. On the other hand there are those who are public sector workers. They tend to work short hours, their work is invariably undemanding (the ideal Government department does something for which there is absolutely no demand), they have tremendous job security and they can look forward to early retirement and a generous, inflation-proofed pension paid for largely by taxpayers. These employees are, like bank executives, greedy and selfish. And they will fight tooth and nail to preserve their undeserved standard and style of living.

We have acquired as overladen a public sector as France. (My Princess and I once travelled on an SNCF train in France which had 11 ticket collectors. They walked up and down the train in a bunch and examined the tickets one at a time, each checking on the other's work. Our tickets looked exhausted when the inspectors had finished with them. I would not have believed that so many people could have taken so much apparently genuine interest in such small pieces of paper. England has followed France. In recent years public sector employment as a percentage of total employment has risen dramatically. In Wales, for example, a third of all employment is public sector work. To keep the Welsh employment figures looking close to respectable, all vehicle, driving licence, pension and tax records now seem to be mismanaged in Wales. Swansea and Cardiff have become public sector ghettoes where private companies have enormous difficulty in hiring employees because they cannot compete with the advantages offered by the public sector (higher pay, pension perks and not much work). The inhabitants of the north east of England, Northern Ireland and the whole of Scotland are similarly reliant upon the Government for jobs. Even in London, where Government employment is at its lowest, just under a quarter of all the people with jobs are public sector workers.

1

The gap between public sector and private sector pay is now, on average, around 20% but in vast areas of the country (such as the north and west) it is well over 25%. In other words civil servants, who work short hours, enjoy the world's most generous pension (paid by other people), have longer holidays than anyone else and can stay at home to watch television without the risk of losing their jobs (or anyone noticing) are paid vastly better than the people whose work keeps the country alive. This is madness. Incidentally, the self-employed (who tend to earn even less than employees in the private sector) are excluded from these figures.

2

Unions, many of which are led by bosses paid over £100,000 a year, are threatening to cause chaos because the Government wants to limit absurdly over-generous public sector pensions. Ordinary teachers have taxpayer funded pension pots of £500,000. Headmasters and police chiefs have pension pots measured in millions. In contrast, millions of private sector workers can look forward to pensions which will just about pay for a twice weekly bowl of gruel.

I've been warning about the public sector pension crisis for nearly a decade and now I believe that the planned strikes could produce a social explosion and finally split the country. It's no exaggeration to say that we could be heading for a new civil war. Those who don't work for the Government are getting fed up with the wretches who do. And it's not surprising that the people who do the real, productive work find it offensive that greedy, selfish public sector workers should have the brass neck to go on strike to maintain their absurd pension rights. Moreover, teachers who close schools and force proper workers to take time off work to look after their children will do enormous damage to the state of the nation.

Public sector workers clearly don't give a fig about the country or the economy. Their strikes say it all. These are me me me me me people. Their strikes will lead to more redundancies and more real pain for the millions who live in the real world. Companies will close. And, inevitably, selfish, traitorous doctors, schoolteachers and all the rest of the public sector workforce will find themselves loathed in a way that strikers never have been hated before. These strikes are not for a living wage or a decent standard of living. These strikes are all about greed and selfishness. The people striking already have far more than their fair share. They are vastly overpaid. Their pensions are absurdly over-generous. And now they are fighting simply to keep their ill-gotten, undeserved gains.

I suspect that there will be some real resentment in the country during the coming months. People will begin to resent their neighbours who are overpaid, and who have unaffordable, taxpayer funded pensions, but who have the outrageous cheek to cause disruption by striking.

This could be the end of the Big State.

I suspect that these selfish strikes may eventually result in an awakening: a civil war that leads to a society in which the State plays a much smaller role. A society in which there are far fewer State employees. A society in which State employees are no longer overpaid.

There's a cheerful thought.

A happy ending, after all.

3

`Our contemporary Western society, in spite of its material, intellectual and political progress, is increasingly less conducive to mental health, and tends to undermine the inner security, happiness, reason and the capacity for life in the individual; it tends to turn him into an automaton who pays for his human failure with increasing mental sickness, and with despair hidden under a frantic drive for work and so-called pleasure.' - Dr Erich Fromm

4

It has been reported that civil servants who finish their work by 10.30 a.m. and then ask for something else to do are told to amuse themselves and shut up. Bosses don't want anyone to draw attention to the fact that civil servants are invariably under-employed. Public sector jobs are cushy and attractive jobs for the lazy, supercilious and unambitious and, perhaps most damaging of all, for those who have little or no interest in serving the public. The vast majority of public sector workers do jobs which require no more than a day or two of training.

5

One cannot blame young people for wanting to work for the Government. It's the safest place to work these days. And the pension and perks are better than anywhere else. But, sadly, the people who are now choosing to find work with the Government are making a big mistake. They have picked the wrong time to become public sector workers. The future for the public sector is extremely poor. There will, within the next decade, be many redundancies. And many who believe that they will be paid fat, inflation-proofed pensions are in for a big shock. Those pensions are not going to be paid.

6

Public sector fraud and incompetence will continue to go unpunished because the people who decide whether the fraud and incompetence should be punished are public sector employees. Why would incompetent and fraudulent people decide to punish themselves and their colleagues?

7

Between the years 2000 and 2010 State spending increased by a real 53% (that is to say that the figure is inflation adjusted) and much of that increase in spending went on hiring people who were given permanent jobs and paid huge sums to do trivial, unnecessary work. Many were hired to devise new rules and regulations designed to make life difficult or impossible for those in the private sector, and were encouraged to regard anyone struggling to make a living as in some way reprehensible.

8

Public sector workers may retire at 50 or 55, and receive huge pensions. They then take part time jobs for a little fun and pin money. Private sector workers must carry on working indefinitely. And they frequently find themselves competing with `rich', retired public sector workers for employment.

9

In the North East of England, paramedics (not the most highly paid of public sector workers) earn 60% above the average local wage. It is absurd to pay all public sector workers the same when wages and costs are so different around the country. The result of the national wage policy is that essential health workers in the South East can hardly survive while people doing the same job in the North can live like princes.

10

Private sector employees take around six sick days a year. Public sector workers take an average of ten. That, I suspect, is a fair representation of the effort the two sets of workers put into what they do. And yet the rewards are inverse to the effort. It cannot possibly last. Moreover, public sector workers are frequently allowed to retire, on a full pension, for the slightest of reasons. I know of a former fireman who retired in his 30s because he came out in a rash when exposed to heat. He now lives on a generous disability pension. He has a large, executive style home and a brand new sports car which he changes every two years. I know a former policeman who retired from the police force on full pay at the age of 41 because he had a skin rash which was made worse by wearing a uniform. He drives a Porsche Boxster. Police officers can retire at 50 (sitting in a luxury police saloon on motorway bridges is obviously considered more dangerous and tiring than one might imagine) and can only be made redundant after 30 years of service. Policemen and firemen who have to visit unpleasant scenes frequently claim that they are mentally scarred and unable to work. The words `post traumatic stress disorder' are steadily increasing in popularity. Surely, anyone who takes a job as a policeman or fireman must expect to come across unpleasant scenes? When I worked as a doctor I was occasionally called out by the police to certify dead bodies as, well, dead. On one occasion I unwrapped a woman in a black plastic bag. She had been murdered by her husband, put into a supersize black plastic bag and left out with the rubbish. The dustmen called the police because they couldn't lift the bag and they thought they could feel bits of bone. I certified a man who had been burnt to a crisp in a house fire (you could smell the burning flesh half a mile away) and a man and his dog who had been bludgeoned to death by two killers. I then examined the two killers, alone, in a police examination room. And so on. I was doing what I was paid to do.

11

The police, like members of the armed forces, are paid to take chances and put their lives on the line to protect us. That is why they are paid so well and, perhaps, why they are entitled to retire so early on such excellent pensions. In reality, therefore, the murder of a policeman is a minor crime compared to the murder of a citizen. Policemen are paid to protect the public and to take risks.

12

The people who work for the State have power of the State behind them and so they tend to behave badly. The police do things because they can (and because it gives them pleasure). So, for example, the police turn minor motorway incidents into five hour holdups with 20 mile queues in both directions because it makes them feel and look important. They clearly enjoy competing to see who can create the longest queues. They put up the cones, leave a car parked with flashing lights and wait for the chaos to ensue. You only have to look at them standing around with plastic gloves, clipboards, two way radios and bullet proof waistcoats to see how much they are enjoying themselves. They chat away like waiting mothers outside primary school gates. It is hardly surprising that the average driver spends 35-40 hours a year stuck in traffic.

The guards at border posts are invariably unbelievably rude. They bark instructions as though talking to concentration camp inmates. I am not so much surprised that the people in uniforms behave like that as I am that people obey them blindly and stupidly and without protest.

13

I once interviewed a potential new employee. He seemed bright and reasonably literate but he turned down my job offer and explained that he had decided to take a job with the council instead. He told me that he wanted an undemanding job with fixed hours, long holidays and a good pension. He was 24-years-old.

14

People with responsible jobs in the private sector live by their wits. Their daily aim is to make things happen. Civil servants and bureaucrats consider that their job is to prevent things happening. Our state functionaries exhibit undisguised contempt for everyone else and revel in their glorious inefficiency and incompetence. The main aim of civil servants is to avoid blame and deflect criticism. (That is why they aren't fit to run enterprises or organisations upon which the public rely). It is hardly surprising that if they leave the public sector, expecting to find employment in the private sector, they invariably find that no one wants to hire them.

15

Bureaucrats have all the time in the world to attend entirely pointless functions and meetings and to create incomprehensible forms (complete with accompanying thick books of notes). This would be fine if these time consuming activities kept them out of the hair of people struggling to do real work. But it doesn't work that way for the bureaucrats enjoy nothing more than to use their time and their form creating to interfere with the rest of the world. It makes them feel important.

16

It is almost impossible to get fired if you are a civil servant. Selling secrets to the enemy and not handing the money over to your superior will probably get you a reprimand and a delay in promotion but offences which would lead to an immediate sacking in the private world are ignored in the comforting tea and biscuits world which public sector employees inhabit. Civil servants can make multi-million pound errors without fear of censure. They probably won't even lose their bonus. On the very rare occasions when a civil servant resigns in disgrace he will still receive a generous pay off, his pension and, of course, a bonus. And within a month or so he will be rehired as a consultant.

17

Civil servants are parasites. But when parasites become too greedy, they kill their host. And then they themselves will also die.

18

In France students have for years dreamt of growing up to become civil servants - attracted by the money, the status, the power and the perks. Things are now the same in England.

19

During a recent spell of bad weather a Government spokesman announced that only essential civil servants needed to turn up for work. It was widely reported that many Government offices were completely empty. When civil servants go on strike (which they do with increasing frequency) the invariable response from the public is: `How will we know?'

20

Civil servants (such as tax inspectors) love conferences. When they go to a conference they can claim all sorts of generous per diem expenses. Naturally, very little work goes on at these expensive conferences, but people do tend to have a rather good time at public expense.

21

Civil servants have the power because when we come into contact with them we usually want something from them. In all our encounters with them they have the key to something we need to open. They have a form we need to complete. They have a licence we need in order to do our work. Or they may have access to the bedpans.

22

The average salary for a State employee is £28,802 compared to £25,000 for a private sector worker. The average pension for a State employee is a safe £7,800. In the private sector the average pension is £1,800. (Both sums are paid on top of the official old age pension). Public sector workers also enjoy greater job security, shorter working hours, longer holidays and unlimited sick pay. And they receive much grander perks (such as private health care, free car parking, subsidised food and generous travel and subsistence allowances).

23

Inside every uniform (even a cheap suit) there is an SS guard struggling to escape the confines of bureaucracy and jab his or her cheap biro into an eyeball.

24

When considering the number of public sector workers in England we must now include doctors and nurses who work for the National Health Service. They work for the State and their loyalty is to the State rather than to their patients. (Their primary loyalty is, of course, to themselves.). BBC employees are also civil servants, of course.

25

In February 2012, it was revealed that around £100 million was being paid in bonuses to civil servants. Despite egregious, collegiate incompetence hugely overpaid employees at the Ministry of Defence were taking home bonuses of up to £85,831 just for doing their jobs rather badly.

26

If a man bakes bread every day of his working life then it is reasonable to describe him as a baker; baking bread is what he does. Similarly, if a Government employee wastes money efficiently and with regularity it becomes difficult to argue with the thesis that the primary purpose of the civil servant concerned is just that: to waste money.

27

Government employees acquire a tendency to treat members of the public (their employers) as half-witted irritants who are interrupting their crossword, magazine reading or chat. They like to give the impression that they are bored and impatient and far too important to be doing whatever menial task they are doing ('My normal job is as a brain surgeon/racing driver/international film star but I'm just filling in as a local council planning office clerk/hospital trolley pusher/postman/doctor's receptionist/passport office employee'). The problem is that the people employed by the State have assumed the role and authority of the State, and the EU has given them (and indeed all employees) the confidence to know that they are effectively unsackable.

28

In the old days the best brains used to go into science or engineering. But in the early years of the 21st century the brightest students choose jobs with the Government (it's a safe, undemanding job with a good salary and a fantastic pension) or banking (it's a safe, undemanding job with a ridiculous salary and an incredible pension). Today, three quarters of young people say that they want to be public employees. That is their ambition.

29

When I see a throng of protesting public sector workers I am reminded of Nietzsche who foresaw much of what has happened in the last 100 years and who wrote: 'the great majority of men have no right to existence, but are a misfortune to higher men.'

30

Public sector workers will not work on bank holidays. And so, for example, public libraries are invariably closed at the very time when most people are likely to want to use them. It is as though amusement park employees refused to work on bank holidays.

31

To Government employees we are all enemies, available to be bullied, forced into queues and lied to. It seems that public sector workers have forgotten that they are our employees; paid to serve us. And although many existing utilities (such as gas and water companies and train companies) are public companies, they are often still run like Government departments (with rude and uncaring staff) because they still have the in-house culture that was devised when those companies were nationalised, and the employees worked for the State.

32

'People who hold positions of power or trust and violate them are probably a more serious danger to a democratic society than organised crime or crime in the streets.' - Robert Morgenthau, former New York District Attorney

33

In May 2012, it was announced that civil servants employed in London would be allowed to stay at home for a seven week period during the Olympics 'to reduce traffic congestion'.

This announcement was made just three days after a Government Minister had announced that everyone must work harder to pay off the national debt. Presumably, having suddenly noticed that London's infrastructure was not capable of coping with an influx of Olympic delegates and sponsoring executives all looking to have a good time with someone else paying the expenses, the Government had looked around looking for a group of people who could be kept at home without causing any inconvenience or, indeed, without anyone noticing. It wouldn't have taken them long to plump for civil servants as the obvious choice. And then someone had a brilliant idea. Instead of just telling the civil servants to stay at home for two weeks (so that they could watch the Olympics on television, or use their free Government tickets to go and watch them live) why not tell them to stay at home for longer? If they stayed at home until, say, the end of the school summer holidays then the Government would save a fortune on light, heat, air conditioning, private telephone calls and so on. And thus it was. `Will anyone think that the seven week period of extra holiday seems rather excessive when the Olympics are only lasting for two weeks?' asked a junior in the office. His fears were dismissed airily. `Don't be daft,' said a senior principal deputy adviser who had more wisdom than is common in such circles. `The common folk don't give a damn about the Olympics. They won't notice that they only last for two weeks.'

34

I can't remember the last time I had a holiday. A man I know who works for the Government told me recently that he has eight weeks holiday owing to him.

35

It is impossible to fight State employees because they have unlimited time and money and no personal liability.

36

'The standard of morality in the public sector frequently does not reach the very minimum that private industry would regard as essential to its survival.' - Lord Chandos, former chairman of AEI

Conclusion

Government expenditure now accounts for half the English economy. Over one fifth of all English workers have jobs in the public sector - with absurdly generous salaries, pensions, perks and employment conditions. Too many of the millions who are state employees behave like employees in old communist USSR - they don't care, or have any pride in the work they do. The country can no longer afford such a large workforce of under-productive civil servants. Things have to change. Until they do change the nation's economic situation will continue to get worse. Since turkeys never vote for Christmas the problem isn't going to be solved soon.

Chapter 14

The Pension Scandal

Introduction

The Government can no longer afford to pay the pensions it has promised to public sector workers. Nor can the Government afford to pay the State pension. And, just to make things worse, Government and EU policies have destroyed the attractiveness of private pensions. In a generation's time our streets will be packed with geriatric English beggars pleading to be given enough money to buy a little food.

1

A pension is (or should be) a fairly simple thing to understand. In his or her prime years a man or woman regularly puts aside some money so that when they are old, and either want to stop working or can no longer work, they will have money with which to pay heating bills, buy food and enjoy a few little luxuries. The money that is saved is put somewhere safe where it can grow quietly and consistently. You can't get any simpler than that. But governments and finance companies have made pensions unbearably complicated and, in financial terms, extremely unreliable. The main problem, of course, is that our governments have for years run a Ponzi scheme for pensioners. The money you pay in taxes and National Insurance (and which many people still think is being put safely on one side for their retirement years) is being used to pay today's generation of pensioners. Pensions for tomorrow's generation of pensioners will be paid by tomorrow's generation of workers. That is a Ponzi scheme. It's crooked, dishonest and downright illegal. The same sort of scheme is run for public sector workers. Their pensions will be paid by tomorrow's taxpayers. And the same is true for councils too. Tomorrow's council tax payers will pay the pensions for today's council workers. These too are Ponzi schemes and none of them is sustainable.

2

Although their Government may rely on Ponzi schemes to pay pensions, a number of Englishmen and women have saved for their older years in the proper, more traditional way. In fact, in no country in the world have citizens saved more money for their pensions. (We mustn't get too excited about this. The average English citizen with a private pension has saved around 90% of their annual salary. That is the pension pot from which an annuity must be taken. So, a man with a £20,000 salary may have £18,000 saved and will probably be lucky to receive a pension of £1,000 a year. Still it's something.) In contrast the people of the other EU countries have saved next to nothing. And therein lies a problem. You won't be surprised to hear that the EU wants our savings - and there is a scary chance that they'll find a way to get hold of them. If you have a private pension fund beware: the EU has had its eyes on your pension fund for years and your Government wants it too. Your savings would help pay off a large chunk of England's Gordon Brown debt. In the end they may just take it (by introducing some form of confiscatory legislation) but I suspect that for the time being they are more likely to nibble away at it by more changes to the rules.

3

The rules about private pensions (and company pensions) change so often that it is impossible to keep up with what is, and is not, allowed. Even the professionals get confused. The pension plan you thought you signed up to will have changed many times in scope and prospects by the time you eventually get to an age where you need to try to take the money. The complexities, made infinitely worse by retrospective legislation, are now so absurd that many professional advisers no longer recommend that people invest in a pension at all. There are better, safer ways to save money and to have some hope of being able to get hold of a little of the cash when you eventually need it. The end result is that the number of people putting money into a pension fund is falling rapidly and the amount people save for their old age is dropping by 5% a year. The Government has only itself to thank for creating yet another future disaster. Osbourne, Clegg and other public sector workers with vast, taxpayer funded pensions probably don't understand that for many people the State pension will be all that stands between them and penury. Those who struggle to cope on the meagre state pension (one of the meanest in the world) and who have difficulty finding any money for luxuries such as food after paying local taxes, the BBC television licence fee and heating bills will in the future find that they have even less money to spend.

4

In the 2012 budget, the Coalition Government stole £1 billion a year from poorer pensioners but took on a multi billion pound debt for Royal Mail employees. (The Government is desperate to sell the Royal Mail and the pension fund liabilities put off all prospective purchasers). And so taxpayers will in future be responsible for paying pensions to yet more public sector workers. I wonder if the postmen realise that the public sector pension bill will soon be impossible to pay - and their pensions too will simply melt away into nothingness. Naturally, this huge additional deficit won't appear on the nation's balance sheet.

5

English private sector workers used to have the world's best pensions but they were buggered by Gordon Brown who took £5 billion a year out of private pensions to help subsidise his massive spending spree. It was as though Brown (realising that he could use the cash on some of his absurd schemes) was deliberately creating a two-tone State - those on civil service pensions and those without. Brown's grab pushed millions of pensioners into needing State aid (which it will not be able to provide), created the makings of a civil war (between civil servants and the rest of the country) and made the whole idea of pensions brutally unattractive. Gordon isn't just a moron; he is a nasty man who seems to have been opposed to self-sufficiency and independence. Together with the war criminal Blair, I believe, he did more damage to England than anyone else in history. In a couple of decades time our streets will be knee deep in geriatric beggars. These won't be the professionals we are currently used to, whining *Big Issue* sellers imported from Romania by the lorry load, but home-grown grannies and granddads; starving, frightened and desperate; hard-working former taxpayers sitting on the pavement, watching bureaucrats driving past in expensive cars and tututting at the human mess on the streets.

6

Towards the end of 2011, I read in the *Financial Times* about a woman who had put £50,000 into a pension fund twenty years ago. Today, her fund, after the efforts and charges of hugely overpaid advisers, is worth just £8,000. Why aren't her advisers doing time? Sadly, this is neither exceptional nor unusual.

How long will it before there is huge resentment among private sector workers who realise that although they may have worked hard, and earned comparable sums to their former civil servant neighbour, he is receiving three, four, five times as much pension as they are - and they are paying for it.

One in six people already relies totally on the State pension. The number so doing is rising rapidly. And the value of the State pension is falling rapidly too. There will come a time (not far away) when almost all of those struggling to live on the State pension will slowly starve or freeze to death.

Two decades ago we, as a nation, saved around 12% of our disposable income. Today, that figure has pretty well halved. High inflation and low interest rates have made saving singularly unattractive.

Public sector workers who feel smug when they look around and see the way that successive governments have destroyed private pensions should know that their pensions are not as safe as they think they are. I have for several years been predicting that the Government will one day be unable to honour its pension obligations to public sector workers - and that day is getting closer. Those who believe that this cannot possibly ever happen should know that at the end of December 2011, almost 300,000 retired employees of SNCF, the French rail company, discovered that they had only been paid a third of their normal pension (the French Government normally pays pensions quarterly in advance). Similar situations were narrowly avoided at other public utility companies such as EdF (Electricity de France, the electricity utility) and GdF (Gaz de France). The Government eventually managed to find the necessary funds. But what will happen next year?

It is safe to assume that if you work for the Government (central or local) and are under the age of 50 your employer will not be able to pay you a pension at all. Public sector workers will not receive the pensions they are expecting. Let me put that another way: if you work for the Government or a quango (the same thing really), or a local council, then your chances of receiving the pension you were promised are directly related to your age. If you are over 50 then you have a good chance of getting your pension. If you are under 30 you have approximately no chance of receiving the pension you were promised and are expecting. Council workers may think that they have an enforceable contract with their employers. They may think that their union will look after them. Wrong. I suspect that councils will merely file for bankruptcy.

Central and local government officials in England are notoriously shy about revealing the figures relating to their pension debts but in America these figures are available. And those figures are scary.

The pension benefits that have been already promised to folk who work for the Government in Ohio will cost the State more than 50% of its future total tax revenues. Much the same is true of government employees in Colorado, Rhode Island and many other American states where pension benefits are projected to use up between a third and a half of total State tax revenues. Countless employees simply won't receive the pensions they thought they were entitled to. And exactly the same is true for England. The doctors and teachers and whoever else who voted to go on strike to defend indefensible pension rights might like to think about this. Their pensions aren't as safe as they think they are.

If public sector workers cannot rely on their occupational pensions what about the old aged pension? Surely they can rely on that?

Well, er, sadly, no.

The Government has been running a pension Ponzi scheme and sooner or later it is going to explode in exactly the way that all such schemes explode. Tax revenues are going to have to rise and expenditure is going to have be cut drastically just to keep the nation afloat financially. The chances of today's 30-year-olds receiving a State pension are approximately the same as the chances of England winning the World Cup ten times in a row (Actually, I suspect that the chances of England winning the World Cup are better. There is at least a chance, albeit remote, of that happening.) We all expect to receive our pension because we have been led to believe that it will be there, patiently waiting for us, when we retire. But there is no legal liability. The money isn't there. And if the Government cannot afford to pay out pensions (because it has given all the money to Fred Goodwin et al) then there won't be any pensions and there won't be a thing anyone can do about it. There is no contractual liability. Just hope and naive expectation.

10

`Retirement at 65 is ridiculous. When I was 65 I still had pimples.' - George Burns

11

In a final, desperate attempt to find the money to pay pensions to public sector workers, the Government will undoubtedly mess around still more with private section pensions. The age at which we can take our pensions will rise yet again. The amount we can save will fall yet again. (Any excess will be taxed at punitive rates). The size of the tax free lump sum we can take (promised as part of the original deal) will fall and fall and then disappear completely. If we save too much for our pensions the excess saving will be subject to a hefty tax charge and a huge lump sum levy of at least 55%.

12

Most private pensioners are forced to purchase an annuity when they want to access the money they have saved. Annuities are one of the great financial scandals of our time. The pensioner must hand over all his money to an insurance company. In return he will receive a small, annual payment. When he or she dies the insurance company gets to keep the lump sum.

Annuity rates collapsed when interest rates were brought down and new rules have cut the amount that can be taken still further. Pensioners are paying the bill for the greed of the American and Scottish bankers and the stupidity of Gordon Brown. Thanks to EU and Government policies, annuity rates are down 20% over the last year or two. And things are going to get worse. New EU legislation means that there will be yet another huge drop in annuity rates - with male customers hit particularly hard.

13

Here's a question no one ever asks: why should jobs come with a pension at all? Most people don't receive a house or any other form of accommodation with their job. Surely, it is patronising and misleading to link jobs and pensions. It is bad for companies (which end up running huge pension funds) and bad for individuals (who end up serf-like, reliant on the company they work for and afraid to move to another job because of what might happen to their pension).

14

In 2012, the Chancellor of the Exchequer claimed that pensioners could no longer expect young people to pay for the costs of their old age. He said that this was an intolerable burden on the young. The statement suggests to me that Osbourne does not understand that successive governments have, for decades, been running one of the world's largest Ponzi schemes. The people who now become pensioners (and who worked) paid taxes and National Insurance contributions all their lives. Many probably assumed that some of the money they paid was being put on one side to pay for their pensions. They were, of course, quite wrong. The money that they paid in taxes was always used to pay for the pensions of those who were elderly at the time. Today's pensioners are not taking advantage of today's youth any more than any other generation has done so.

The reality is that the Coalition Government's policies have hit pensioners hard. It has hit those relying on private pensions and savings particularly hard. Low interest rates, high inflation, increased taxes and drastic changes to private pension rates mean that the elderly have been forced to pay an unreasonably large part of the burden created by Gordon Brown's Scotland-friendly policies. If the Coalition stick to their current, morally repugnant policies then it seems likely that interest rates will stay low for many years to come.

Osbourne has turned out to be a hoodie in a posh suit: mugging the elderly because they are the easiest to mug. It is clear that the Conservatives and the Liberal Democrats regard people who are responsible, sensible and prudent with their money as easy targets.

15

When Osbourne changed tax law to hit pensioners in his 2012 Budget, he described the change as a 'simplification'. It seemed a misleading, uncaring, deceitful and stupid word to use. If Osbourne really wanted to raise money in a fair way he would have cut the absurdly overgenerous pension scheme enjoyed by MPs. Or taken a larger chunk of money from the greedy public sector workers whose pension demands are bleeding the economy dry. Instead he turned yet again to England's uncomplaining pensioners.

16

Much of the money you pay to your local council is spent on providing pensions for former council workers. Astonishingly, 4% of English council workers retire on an annual pension of £67,000 or more.

As the recession deepens (and turns into a chronic depression) councils are cutting vital services to save money. They never think of cutting the number of bureaucrats, the size of the expense accounts or the generosity of the staff pensions. Councils are cutting libraries and social services but the top layer of staff aren't suffering at all they still enjoy their big salaries, their big pensions, their generous expense accounts and their annual pay rises and bonuses. Councils all over England are reducing the frequency of rubbish collections, turning off street lights, closing libraries and reducing services for the elderly. But the bosses, ignoring requests from central Government to cut their own salaries, are giving themselves pay rises and bonuses.

Most of your council tax now goes towards paying the pensions of retired council workers. And things are going to get worse. Soon there won't be any money left to pay for services and council tax payers will merely be paying for someone else's pension fund.

17

Companies exist to make profits for their shareholders (the owners). That is it. There is no other primary purpose. Companies don't exist to provide jobs, to offer a service to customers or the community or to pay taxes. Companies exist to make a profit for the shareholders. It is certainly not the job of any company to provide pensions for workers. In a sane and sensible society, where individuals take responsibility for themselves, providing a pension would be the responsibility of each individual. Only in a statist or communist society, where individuals have lost their rights, should companies be expected to provide pensions. (It is similarly difficult to understand why companies should be expected to pay workers holiday pay or sick pay. Why should a company pay its employees not to do anything?)

18

When I telephoned the Government's Department of pensions to ask a question about my pension I was told (by a recorded machine: `If you don't speak English ring (another number) and an interpreter and adviser will phone you back.' I wonder how much that particular service costs.

19

A third of the over 50's have no savings whatsoever for their retirement. The figure is greater (and therefore worse) for those under 50 and it is likely to rise, rise and rise for the foreseeable future. For over a decade now Government policies have discouraged people from saving money or putting money into a pension fund.

20

Doctors, teachers and other public sector workers are so out of touch with reality, and stuffed with selfishness, that they are striking to retain pensions which were never fair or sustainable and are, indeed, so absurdly generous that it is akin to giving everyone working for the Government a winning lottery ticket. GPs were, at one point, threatening to protest against pension changes by prescribing branded drugs rather than generic drugs. Their aim was to deliberately damage the Government's attempt to save money and cut the budget deficit.

21

In June 2012, the Organisation for Economic Cooperation and Development (OECD) announced that English savers had suffered bigger losses from their workplace pensions in the last decade than the citizens of virtually every other nation in the developed world. The OECD said that returns on money invested by pension companies on behalf of savers fell every year between 2001 and 2010. That's pretty good going and suggests that the people managing the money were pretty high-grade incompetents. (To put their failure in perspective I will point out that I have made a return of an average of nearly 20% a year on our investment portfolios during that time. I have no qualifications relevant to the investment business. One of my bankers dismissed my investment record by saying: 'Ah, but you've been lucky. You've been holding a lot of gold through the bad years.') It is not surprising that many people have stopped contributing to their pension schemes. Poor stock market returns have been made worse by incompetent fund managers (who seem to spend most of their time thinking up new fees), by high management charges and by derisory annuity rates (deliberately brought to an all time low by Government and EU policies). People have also been put off pension funds by ever-changing regulations (many of them retrospective) affecting what savers can do with their money, what tax savings they might enjoy and when they might be allowed access to their own savings. Pension funds and investment companies, forced by the EU to invest in products which eurocrats regard as 'safe' have, for the last year or two, been piling into government bonds. They are buying these because they are told, and they believe, that they are safer than shares, property or gold. I think they're stark raving mad. These bonds are yielding 2% or less and inflation is already far higher than that. Governments everywhere are busy debasing their currency by printing more of it and it seems certain that anyone who holds sovereign bonds for several years will lose some of their capital. And with inflation running at 5% officially and at least 10% unofficially they're losing money annually as well. Craziest of all are those investment 'experts' buying US Treasury bonds in the belief that they are buying the safest of the safe. The truth is that America is bankrupt and the dollar is in long-term decline. There doesn't seem anything very safe about choosing an investment that is guaranteed to lose great chunks of its value on a regular basis.

22

There is something almost indecent about the fact that pension rule changes which affect non-public sector workers are made, without exception, by people who are public sector workers and who are, consequently entitled to pensions which are not affected by the absurd, unfair, unjust and damaging changes which they make. For example, it is clearly unfair for judges and MPs with unlimited, inflation-proof, taxpayer-guaranteed pensions to impose limits on the amounts the self-employed can save for their old age. But they do. Moreover, the public sector workers who mess with the pensions of the people in the private sector are perfectly happy to introduce destructive retrospective legislation when it comes to other people's pensions, but won't have their own pensions changed at any price. The fiasco involving Equitable Life pensions was caused by idiotic managers (who remain unpunished) but Government regulators did nothing to stop the financial mayhem which resulted in hundreds of thousands of private sector workers losing a great deal of their pension savings. Public sector workers did nothing to correct the problem for many years (waiting until many of the claimants had died or were impoverished and hungry). When it was finally agreed that a derisory amount of compensation would be paid it was announced that it would not be fair to taxpayers to pay more. Public sector workers don't worry about taxpayers when their obscenely generous pension schemes are under discussion.

23

Many retired State employees receive more money when they retire than they received in salary when they were working. Their pensions are heavily subsidised by taxpayers. This cannot continue indefinitely.

4

There is much call from civil servants at The Treasury (all of whom enjoy massive pension benefits at little or no cost to themselves) for all tax relief for private pension contributions to be stopped. Many advisers now agree that the charges and costs associated with private pensions mean that they aren't worth contributing to and so without tax relief they will be utterly pointless.

5

The age at which people can retire is going to rise, rise and rise again. Those who are now in their 40s will probably not receive any sort of pension until they are at least 70-years-old and the current generation of young people will have to work until they are in their 80s. The blame for this will fall at least in part on the reckless excesses of Gordon Brown's years as Chancellor and partly on the incompetence and greed of Scottish bankers.

Conclusion

The Government cannot afford to satisfy any of its pension obligations. Many public sector pensions will not be paid out. The State pension will have to be subject to dramatic cuts. And the age at which it is paid will have to rise dramatically. The nation will go bankrupt if we continue to try to pay out State pensions as we do at the moment. Part of the problem is caused by the fact that our population is ageing rapidly. There are, today, more people over 65 than under 16 and the demographic situation is rapidly deteriorating. Within a decade this population time bomb (which I first described in my book *The Health Scandal* in 1988) will explode.

Chapter 15

Wars Without End

Introduction

Not all our recent wars have been conducted on the instructions of Jewish American lobbyists. Some of our recent military excursions were (apparently) home-grown.

Since war criminal Tony Blair used imaginary weapons of mass destruction to drag us into an entirely unnecessary and immoral war on Iraq the English people have been constantly at war. We are, as I write, bombing and killing people in three different countries. (In all of which there is, by coincidence, a strong American oil interest.)

Within months of staggering into power, the Cameron-Clegg Fiasco started yet another bloody war - in

Libya. And this time they didn't seem to me to be desperately keen to stick to the ground rules laid down by the United Nations. The result was that the Libyan leader, Colonel Gaddafi was executed by rebel soldiers. The United Nations calls this execution unacceptable and suggested that if those responsible were caught they would find themselves before a war crimes tribunal.

(So why, I wonder, is Obama not before a war crimes tribunal? He is, after all, busy executing people all over the place without the inconvenience of trials. Two problems I suppose. First, America doesn't recognise international law. Second, Obama has acquired a taste for executing those who disagree with him. (Republican party presidential candidates might like to lock their windows at night.))

Cameron and Clegg's illegal excursion into Libya ensured that the English will continue to be the world's prime targets for terrorists. Even the Americans shied away from attacking Gaddafi too strenuously. But our brave and well-guarded leaders recklessly risked the lives of English nationals everywhere by making England the prime target for militant Muslims. And just why? Bad things happen in China, Zimbabwe and several dozen other countries around the globe. In what way is Gaddafi worse than Mugabe? Surely, it couldn't be the oil again?

The truth is that there is a bigger war our leaders should be fighting. And that's a war against the greed of global capitalism (led by corporate America). That's the war which would truly save millions of lives, make the world a better place and enable more people to enjoy physical, mental and spiritual good health. But that's a war our leaders will never fight. Because they are part of the problem.

Look at the big issues - and what our so-called leaders are doing to deal with them.

a) Every year several million people in America and Europe die from cancer. The vast majority of cancers are preventable. We know what causes eight out of ten cancers. The simplest and most obvious truth is that meat causes cancer. Simply persuading people to stop eating meat would save millions of lives. To that truth we must add the fact that current methods of cancer treatment are destructive and ineffective - the cancer `industry' has consistently suppressed new therapies which might work and promoted therapies (surgery, chemotherapy and radiotherapy) which often kill people. If politicians cared a damn they could reduce cancer deaths by 80% without any effort.

b) Heart disease is a major killer. Every day far more Britons die from heart disease than have ever died in terrorism attacks. Most cases of heart disease could be prevented. Most people with heart disease can be cured with a simple regime which costs almost nothing to follow and which is more effective than drugs and surgery. But food and tobacco companies (and drug companies) would stand to lose billions.

c) Infectious diseases are coming back in a big way, and antibiotics are no longer as effective as they were. One big reason is that farmers are allowed to put antibiotics into animal feed to boost farm profits.

d) The food available in our shops is bereft of essential ingredients and laden with additives. Poor and misleading labelling (approved by the EU) prevents consumers from eating healthily.

Our governments have chosen to put all their current (and, probably, future) effort into one target - terrorism - which will not cost them corporate friends. The politicians aren't fighting unending wars to preserve our freedom. They are fighting them for money and for oil. They are fighting wars to terrify us. And they are fighting them to distract us from the real wars we should be fighting. The loathsome duo, Cameron and Clegg, are fighting the wrong wars. If they really cared about people they would be fighting the global corporations which are destroying the world - and creating poverty, pain and illness on a massive scale. They should be fighting the global corporations which are knowingly killing millions through their ruthlessly wicked profit making policies. But the Coalition won't fight that war. For them the price (in perks and campaign contributions) would be far too high.

The ultimate irony is surely the fact that if this world really needs a war then multi-national banks and corporations should be on one side and the rest of us - Muslims and Christians - should be fighting shoulder to shoulder against them.

Our leaders have for years turned a blind eye to the world's real problems. They have forsaken the sick, the dying, the hungry and the bereaved so as not to distress their corporate masters. Now they want us to cheer them on in wars very few people understand, wars that will probably never end and wars that aren't even legal or just. Meanwhile they do nothing to protect us from the very real threats which affect all of us every day of our lives.

1

`Let us learn our lessons. Never, never, never believe any war will be smooth and easy, or that anyone who embarks on that strange voyage can measure the tides and hurricanes he will encounter. The statesman who

yields to war fever must realise that, once the signal is given, he is no longer the master of policy but the slave of unforeseeable and uncontrollable events. Antiquated war officers, weak, incompetent or arrogant commanders, untrustworthy allies, hostile neutrals, malignant fortune, ugly surprises, awful miscalculations - all take their seat on the morrow of a declaration of war.' - Winston Churchill

2

Ed Miliband, and other current leaders of the Labour party, say that if they had known then what they know now they would not have supported the invasion of Iraq. Unfortunately, we all knew then what we know now so this argument doesn't hold a good deal of water.

Ed Miliband served in the Labour Government under its war criminal leadership but says he is not guilty of anything because of `collective responsibility'.

I don't think that will be much of an argument when he is standing before a War Crimes Tribunal. It didn't do the Nazis much good and it won't help him. Collective responsibility just means that he can be hung alongside the others.

Miliband, who does what I thought impossible and makes Gordon Brown seem charismatic, admits that the Government of which he was a member destroyed the economy (`it was just an unfortunate mistake, honest guv; could have happened to anyone'), started two illegal wars and took away our civil liberties. So what the hell is he now doing leading the Opposition? The man isn't fit to confiscate nail files let alone run the country.

3

The war on terror has resulted in moral bankruptcy, it will also help lead both us and the Americans into economic bankruptcy. One cannot help feeling that bin Laden's aim all along was to bleed the USA until it was bankrupt; to obtain revenge for all the oil that has been stolen.

Today, the threat to our future from terrorism is extremely small but the threat to our future from our broken economy is massive.

4

In my book *Rogue Nation* (published before the invasion of Iraq but predicting that it would happen) I estimated that the Iraq War would cost over $1 trillion. This was far, far more than the official estimates and was dismissed as wild exaggeration. The Joint Economic Committee of Congress recently put the cost at $3.5 trillion (that's over $30,000 per American household). The cost of the war to England has never been officially estimated but it was certainly far too much.

5

Not content with being the only nation on earth to use nuclear weapons, chemical weapons and biological weapons, the Americans are now proud to have started something they call `cybergeddon'. Under the guidance of Nobel Peace Prize winner Obama, the Americans combined forces with the Israelis to create a computer virus which disables software systems. They have already used this to attack a nation with which neither of them is at war. Hacking and Internet vandalism are, it seems, acceptable if they are Obama approved. Where will this end? Well, it will pretty certainly end in tears. It cannot be long before Iranian software engineers have re-engineered the American bug and fed it back into American computers. Computer virus warfare will be neither expensive nor overtly dangerous for the participants. The result will, of course, be chaos, chaos and more chaos. America, England and the rest of the so-called developed world now depend entirely on computers. Remember the fear that was triggered by the thought that computers might stop working at the start of the 21st century? Millions of people watched the clocks tick to midnight, trembling lest their computers suddenly stopped working. A decade or so on and the damage done would be incalculably greater. All banking would stop. Shops would stop operating. Logistic operations would come to a halt. There would be no traffic controls, no aeroplanes, no trains and no petrol. There would be no fuel deliveries and the only food available would be whatever people had growing in their gardens. And this is the new American choice for modern warfare.

6

`Why of course the people don't want war. Why should some poor slob on a farm want to risk his life in a war when the best he can get out of it is to come back to his farm in one piece? Naturally the common people don't want war neither in Russia nor in England for that matter in our Germany. That is understood. But it is the leaders of a country who decide policy and it is always a simple matter to drag the people along, whether it is a democracy or a fascist dictatorship, a parliament or a communist dictatorship. Voice or no voice the people can always be brought to the bidding of the leaders. That is easy. All you have to do is tell them that they are being attacked and denounce

the peacemakers for lack of patriotism and exposing the country to danger. It works the same in any country.' - *Hermann Goering, President of the Reichstag, and Hitler's designated successor.*

7

In our recent military adventures our political strategies and military tactics have been woeful. Our expensive and illegal wars (expensive in both human and financial terms) have destabilised Iraq, Pakistan, Afghanistan and Libya and created states where terrorism has become popular and fashionable.

8

The war in Afghanistan will finish at the end of 2014 said Prime Minister Cameron in early 2012. If it is a war, how can he possibly know when it is going to end? Road building schemes and weddings can be given dates. But wars?

Conclusion

Our illegal wars have made us enormously unpopular around the world. Just check out our success in the Eurovision Song Contest since Blair started killing innocent foreigners. But there are, ahead of us, many wars and much rioting. The wars will be fought to distract us from our other concerns. The rioting, when it comes, will be home-grown, natural and a part of the coming revolution.

Chapter 16

The USA: A Dark Past And A Gloomy Future

Introduction

Our unswerving, unquestioning allegiance to America has damaged England in every imaginable way. (We are unique in suffering both from our relationship with the EU and from our relationship with the USA.) The so-called special relationship with the USA, so loved by politicians, has taken us into illegal wars, made us targets for terrorists, turned us into a nation which condones torture and assassination, contaminated our culture and impoverished us. The special relationship with America will be sustained for as long as politicians and advisers make money out of it. And, for as long as the special relationship is sustained, our status, reputation and wealth will continue to decline.

1

David Cameron, Conservative Prime Minister and leader of the utterly absurd Coalition which replaced the long running and never popular Gordon Brown financial fandango fiasco, has accepted (and gold plated) the age old post war doctrine, favoured by idiotic time-servers at the Foreign Office and the SIS, that without the USA we are nothing. Cameron was so desperate to ingratiate himself with the Americans that he has described England as having played a junior role in the Second World War - the one which made America rich and which damned near destroyed England.

And so, bit by bit, sin by sin, like the unfortunate frog in a pan of warming water, we have steadily demeaned and diminished ourselves until now it apparently seems right and proper to those who call themselves our leaders that we should accept the use of torture and illegal prisons, the kidnapping of suspects, the execution of individuals of whom the American President does not approve and the systematic denial of fundamental human rights to selected citizens of other nations (particularly if they are unfortunate enough to be neither Jewish nor Christian). If American citizens were denied these simple human rights the entire American Government would be up in arms but the wrong sort of citizens can, in American eyes, be treated like indentured slaves. (How ironic that a black American president should be the one to take these methods to their illogical and most inhuman conclusion.)

The use of torture (which now has full American approval and must, therefore, be tacitly approved by our politicians) is worth a short detour. People use torture to obtain information. But if you are doing it to find something out then, by definition, you are torturing people you only suspect of doing something wrong. And sometimes you must be torturing innocent people. That is bad. If you torture people when you are certain they did something bad then whatever you do will look like revenge. And that's bad. And when you torture, how do you know that you are being told the truth? That's bad too. Nothing about torture is good. The whole idea of it is repugnant to any civilised human being. But the Americans are our allies. And so we officially endorse torture and are deemed to be responsible too.

The bottom line truth is that our junior partnership with America has resulted in thousands of loyal and patriotic English citizens giving their lives to help America persuade the world that its oil grabbing wars are 'world peace making ventures'. We have wasted billions we cannot afford to spend on immoral, indefensible military adventures.

Why have our leaders bent over forwards to accommodate the leaders of a country which still believes in executing children?

In my book *Rogue Nation* I made the point that I believed that Blair would take England into the Iraq War in order to endear himself to the USA and, from a selfish point of view, to enhance his commercial value after his political career had ended. Everything that has happened subsequently confirms that I was being neither imaginative nor cynical.

History shows that America, the home of barbed wire, pantyhose and plastic Ken (the doll devised, designed and built to partner plastic Barbie), has never helped England (or any other country) unless there was a clear route via which the USA itself could profit financially.

America made huge amounts of money out of World War I and World War II (which it only entered when clear profit opportunities had been identified) and the sly greed of American politicians has left England permanently impoverished. (The bravery and courage of American service personnel in helping the English combat an early brand of EU fascism is not in question but is, in the wider picture, irrelevant.)

American treachery has known no bounds (they have fought against us as often as they have fought with us, and in the 1950's for example, the Americans used their financial muscle to stop us continuing with military action against Egypt after President Nasser nationalised the Suez Canal) but anyone looking for American treachery need look no further than Ireland.

Politicians, journalists and commentators have been careful to conceal the truth but America's long-established and unstinting support for the IRA was, to say the very least, the act of an enemy rather than a friend.

In his book *The Millennium: The Future of Democracy Through An Age Of Unreason* (1994), the distinguished Irish statesman and author, Conor Cruise O'Brien wrote: `Other terrorist organisations, some of them with designs on the United States itself, will have been studying the tactics through which the IRA has managed to enlist the support of the United States for their programme of destabilising Northern Ireland and disrupting the present United Kingdom. They will note the demonstrated potential of combining blandishments with blackmail. They will note the general vulnerability of democratic governments, in the field of security. And they will note how the word `peace' and the hopes associated with it can be made to serve a terrorist cause. They will note especially the artistry with which a conditional suspension of violence can be made to supplement the violence itself and enhance its effectiveness.'

3

`It is part of the general pattern of misguided policy that our country is now geared to an arms economy which was bred in an artificially induced psychosis of war hysteria and nurtured upon an incessant propaganda of fear.' - General Douglas MacArthur

4

It is common these days for American owned economists to claim that war boosts the economy of any country fighting one. This is, of course, a manipulated piece of nonsense designed to allow politicians to sell war in order to benefit their friends in the arms industry. The meagre benefits and high cost of war were first defined by Norman Angel in 1909 in a pamphlet called *Europe's Optical Illusion*.

War may mean that a country spends more on guns and bullets (which means fantastic profits for the companies making them and the salesmen flogging them) but it also means that it spends more on bandages and hospitals (which tend not to be terribly profitable) and on disability payments for men, women and children with no legs, no arms or no eyes (and unless you're in the artificial limb or glass eye business it's tricky to see those a profitable).

War means that young men, young women and children are killed. There is no nice neat, selective killing o he old economically inactive citizens. War means that buildings are destroyed and resources wasted making bombs and then repairing the damage that has been done.

Lots of people do make money out of war, of course. Arms companies and building repair companies do terribly well and crooks, racketeers and politicians can make fortunes as well as reputations. The Iraq war put $3,000 per second into the bloated bank accounts of American arms dealers. Politicians can also start wars to help them win elections and anyone who thinks Thatcher would have invaded the Falklands if she hadn't been struggling in the polls probably also believes that Mickey Mouse lives in the wainscoting and comes out only when the cameras are rolling. Countries (such as America) can make their fortunes too, by helping themselves to valuable resources such as oil which they steal from the countries they attack.

But the damage done by war far outweighs these modest gains. And our enthusiastic support for America's military adventures has cost us much (not least our reputation) and delivered nothing (in Iraq et al the Americans stole all the oil and all the antiquities and got the contracts for repairing the damage they had done, thereby enabling America to make big bucks out of killing babies and small children).

There is a feeling that the wars in which we have recently been involved at America's behest (and in which we are, indeed, still involved) are in some way not proper wars and so the fact that we have started them all doesn't really count. There is a feeling that proper wars should involve the whole nation and that proper wars should dominate the daily headlines and be in our thoughts when we get up in the morning and when we go to bed at night.

The wars given to us by Blair, and resulting from the sale of our nation's integrity to the Americans, may not seem real but I have no doubt that they are real enough to the people fighting them and dying in them. And I have no doubt they are real enough to the families and friends of those who are fighting and dying.

The bottom line is that most modern wars (the sort we allow ourselves to be dragged into as accomplices of America) sacrifice the young, the brave and the patriotic for the benefit of the middle aged, the craven and the treacherous. Were Blair and Brown worth one private, one lance corporal? Are the Coalition warmongers Cameron and Clegg worth the lives of all the people who have died in their almost certainly illegal military adventures?

The American President has given himself the right to kill or imprison anyone he wants to kill or imprison without bothering to ask the courts for permission. Obama is, in short, a President who has given himself a licence to kill. There's a name for Presidents who kill their enemies without bothering to ask for help from the judicial authorities and it isn't 'democrat'. After the excitement of killing Bin Laden and his family, Obama seems to have developed blood lust and to have become a serial killer. No trials. No convictions. Just execution because Obama thinks so. In September 2011, Obama had two American citizens officially murdered without bothering with the annoying trivialities of arrest, trial or conviction. The killings went almost unreported. The crime of the two assassinated citizens? They criticised the American Government. They were murdered because they hadn't broken any laws and so couldn't be taken to court and sent to prison. It is of course a fact that Americans have been killing people for decades (most of them foreigners) but presidents have, in the past, always denied any involvement. Everything has been done under the table. Now Obama has gone further than either Bush would have dared. He has become a murdering president. What a joy it must be to be able to deal with your critics by killing them. (This all sounds so scary that it seems as though I've made it up. I haven't. It's all true.)

Obama, Nobel Prize winner, the black prince of hypocrisy, and surely an Olympic standard serial deceiver merits consideration, in my view, as the most deceitful politician in modern history. (Readers of my book *What Happens Next?* would not have been surprised.) If Obama were the leader of any other country in the world he would, I suspect, be standing, shamed, before a war crimes tribunal. (Note that his predecessor, George W. Bush recently cancelled a trip to speak at a private event in Switzerland because he was frightened that he would be arrested as a war criminal, suggesting to me that he is not only a war criminal but also a coward.)

6

By the year 2040, white Americans will be a minority in the USA. And then the fun should start. Think about it.

7

The enthusiasm for 'targets' mean that American politicians now measure the success of their wars by the numerical relationship between their dead (defined as 'imports') and the other side's dead (defined as 'exports'). As long as exports exceed imports the politicians are happy. I kid you not.

8

Thanks to our links with the Americans we are now the aggressors, the bad guys our fathers warned us about, the cowboys in black hats whose deaths in the final reel are always greeted with much cheering and a great sense of relief.

9

When he had managed to cheat his way to President of the USA, George W. Bush found a unique way to deal with the decline of his nation's manufacturing industry. Bush suggested that fast food jobs be listed as manufacturing for the purposes of the official statistics. And thus it was. And is.

10

In the middle of the banking crisis, US Senator Dick Durbin said he was astonished at all the bankers and bank lobbyists running around the halls of Congress. He said: `I can't believe these guys - they act as if they own the place.' And then he added. `The fact is, it's not an act - they do own the place.'

11

Executives at America's most respected companies hire people at near slave wages to work in inhuman conditions in Asian sweatshops. Oil companies pump poisons into rain forest rivers, killing people, animals and plants without a second thought. (In contrast to the waste products and residues dumped in emerging countries, the BP leak which aroused such hostility in the USA was a coffee cup spill. Naturally, the Americans did well out of it, with otherwise unemployed and probably unemployable Americans being hired to wipe individual blades of oil stained grass with paper tissues.) Vast areas of rain forest have disappeared. Three Ecuadorian cultures have been made virtually extinct so that the Americans can obtain the oil they want. Clear rivers have been turned into dangerous, deadly, stagnant cesspools. Between 1971 and 1992 American oil giants dumped four million gallons of toxic waste water (containing carcinogens) into open holes and rivers. Every day. It's still there, killing people and animals. During the Ecuadorian Oil Boom the official poverty level grew from 50% to 70% and public debt increased from $240 million to $16 billion. The share of national resources allocated to the poorer parts of the nation fell from 20% to just 6%. The American controlled pharmaceutical industry sells products which probably kill more people than they save, and denies lifesaving drugs to the people who really need them by keeping prices obscenely high. Companies such as Enron and crooks like Madoff are not unusual and the people involved usually claim that they weren't well or didn't know what was going on or were in the bathroom when all the really evil deals were done. Accountants and ratings agencies cheat and lie and do anything for another buck.

Throughout its rise America has grown rich at the expense of other countries. During the First and Second World Wars America grew rich and fat by bleeding England dry. The First World War was, for example, a boon for the USA. The emerging nation entered late and suffered few casualties but was able to expand its exports of war supplies (including raw materials, weapons and food) in a way that provided a huge boost to economy. Before the Great War America's GDP was $40 billion per annum. By 1919 it was 50 per cent larger.

12

While in Paris recently I picked up a copy of a book entitled *The Inter-Ally Debts, - An analysis of War and Post-War Public Finance 1914-1923*. One of the fascinating items in this apparently dull book was a table of the relative cost of the war to the great powers, measured in 1913 dollars.

It is clear from this that the war was a far greater strain on England than any other nation involved. The Gross Cost of War per head for England was £524.85, for France it was £280.2, for Russia it was £44.01, for the USA it was £176.91 and for Germany it was £292.57. More crucially, the gross cost of the war as a percentage of national wealth was for England: 34.49%, for France 19.36%, for Russia 13.11%, for Germany 24.71% and for the USA a relatively minute 8.67%.

The accounts show clearly that England was by far the biggest loser in the Great War. No other country suffered anywhere near as big a charge on its Exchequer. In financial terms, the American contribution was negligible.

And the human cost?

Well, England lost 1.44% of its population whereas the USA lost 0.05% of its population.

England never really recovered from the First World War. The Second World War put the finishing touches to a battered economy. In economic terms England lost both wars.

American politicians learned an important lesson from the First World War; they applied those lessons and they did even better out of the Second World War.

The truth is that America only entered those global wars when it could see its way to making huge profits

And the Americans did so ruthlessly and without a shred of compassion. America was built upon greed and cruelty. Remember, the first settlers gave blankets impregnated with smallpox to the Native Americans. And Americans still shamelessly celebrate the theft of the land they call home with an annual event called `Thanksgiving Day'. American children are taught that European colonial powers were ruthless and wicked. But modern America makes the conquistadors look like missionaries. Modern Americans conquer and destroy resource rich countries with spreadsheets and power point presentations. They don't hand out glass beads and blankets. They give the leaders money to buy large cars and foreign apartments. The bribes are bigger because they are more concentrated. The American corporate salesmen claim to be altruistic and they talk about the humanitarian things they are doing. They have MBAs instead of swords but they kill far more effectively than any other generation of conquerors. If bribery and flattery doesn't work then unhelpful, honest politicians die in sudden, violent accidents and replacement, more pliable politicians are promoted.

3

The USA and England spent trillions of dollars on the war in Iraq. They could, if they had been so minded, have used the money to provide clean drinking water, decent food, sanitation services, schooling, health care and good roads for everyone on the planet. If we'd used the money we wasted on killing people in Afghanistan in the same way we could have also given everyone a TV set, a mobile telephone and a Play Station. And if the money had been used in such a way there wouldn't be a terrorist left on the planet and America and England would be smothered with love and respect. But modern wars are fought over commodities such as oil and the people organising the wars don't give a damn about the fact that their policies are creating terrorists.

4

America now has armies of besuited men and women around the world using international financial organisations such as the World Bank and the International Monetary Fund) to create conditions that will force whole nations to become slaves to American corporations. It is a world of favours. An American company arranges for a country to receive a loan to build roads, ports, airports, industrial parks or electric generating plants. But in each and every case it is a condition of the loan that American engineering and construction companies must build the projects. And so the money that is borrowed is transferred from the World Bank (or wherever) direct to the construction company. Bribes, kickbacks, agency fees, commissions and other generous (but relatively small) payments are handed over to the country's ruling politicians. The country which borrowed the money must then pay it all back to the World Bank. The principal and the interest. The loans will usually be so large that the debtor nation will inevitably default on its payments. And then America, the Shylock of nations, takes its pound of flesh. It demands control over the country's vote at the United Nations. It demands access for the building of military bases. It demands access to natural resources such as oil. It demands whatever the country has that America wants. And, of course, the debt remains and the poor people in the country are further impoverished while America's global empire grows. Leaders who protest and dare not to cooperate are either bought, overthrown (with the aid of a CIA fuelled coup), demonised (with the aid of American controlled media) or killed (either in an automobile accident or in some way which suggests that the deceased was in some way dishonourable and unreliable.)

The admitted aim, when America moves into a resource rich country (and the resource, remember, may be something as simple as a United Nation's vote) is to bankrupt the country, to make it beholden, to own it so that favours can be demanded as and when they are required. Naturally, the Americans also want to make an immediate profit on the deal. And they are prepared to make a handful of influential and ruthless locals fairly rich in the process. They arrange for huge loans to be given out (using money from other nations, of course), knowing that the unpayable debt will give America control and yet deprive the poor nation's most impoverished citizens of health education and even food and water for decades. The fact that America controls, and effectively owns, the World Bank, makes all this ridiculously easy. Naive employees of the American companies involved in building dams roads and generator plants may innocently believe that their company is being helpful. If they knew the truth some perhaps, might actually feel guilty at the part they have played in America's desperate, feudal, ruthless yearning to rule the world.

The result of all this frantic activity is that America gets richer and poor countries get poorer; with the poorest people in the poorest countries suffering most. But in America the wealth goes not to the people (most of whom are poorer today than they were a generation ago) but to the already rich. The wealth America has stolen from poor countries has been reserved for the lucky few.

Furthermore, as America has spread its activities around the world so the modern day American slave raders have been busy setting up factories so that they can exploit low paid workers. Time after time American companies have moved into impoverished countries and set up factories where susceptible, vulnerable, workers can be exploited and turned into slaves making pumps, jeans and mobile telephones. What is this if it isn't just a modern version of slavery?

This is the country that England has protected, supported and fawned over. And although America has become rich through these tawdry schemes England has been impoverished by them in every conceivable way. We have never made money out of them. And instead of gaining power and authority (through sovereign blackmail) we have lost popularity and risen to become the most favoured target nation of terrorists. It is no secret that America is without a doubt the most hated nation on the planet. Americans are, quite reasonably, reviled worldwide for their grasping, selfish nature. And, by allying England with America, our Prime Ministers have squandered our good name, our well-established respect and our reputation for fairness and integrity and, instead, made us hated too.

5

The Monroe Doctrine (the work of President James Monroe in 1823) and the Manifest Destiny of the 1840s led many Americans to believe that the taking of North America was divinely ordained and that it was God who ordered the destruction of the Native Indians and the theft of their resources. The Doctrine was used in the 1850s to assert that the United States had special rights over the whole hemisphere and that the USA had the right to invade any nation in Central or South America which refused to back USA policies. In the 20th century, Teddy Roosevelt invoked the Monroe Doctrine to justify American intervention in Venezuela, in the Dominican Republic and in Panama. Since then American presidents have used the same nonsense to justify interventions in Vietnam, Indonesia and much of the rest of the world (especially those bits of the world rich in oil and other valuable natural resources).

6

American politicians admit privately that Israel is a liability but they will never say this in public; they know that they have to placate the Jewish vote (and the Jewish money which buys political favours) and so America is only ever going to back one side in the Middle East. For the USA this is a relatively small problem. They have a small

Muslim population. For England, America's Number One Fall Guy, this is a huge problem - and a massive social and security headache. England has a huge, vocal and constantly growing Muslim population and our membership of the EU means that the number of Muslims in England is going to increase indefinitely.

17

The owner of the *Atlanta Jewish Times* recently called for Mossad to assassinate President Obama for having refused to go to war with Iran.

18

In Afghanistan, our allies (American soldiers) have been filmed urinating on dead soldiers. And they've burned copies of the Koran. And they have, of course, killed large numbers of entirely innocent women and children. It seems that whenever Americans occupy a country they simply cannot behave like civilised human beings.

19

The figures are impossible to obtain (probably because they do not exist) but I strongly suspect that in all the recent wars we have fought alongside the Americans the biggest threat to our troops has come not from the official enemy but from our alleged Allies. In other words, I believe that the number of our service personnel killed and injured by 'friendly fire' exceeds the number killed or injured by 'enemy fire'.

20

America's absurd War on Drugs, supported, endorsed and promoted by all recent Presidents, has done great work to help those who sell illegal drugs. As I pointed out many years ago in my book *The Drugs Myth*, the legalisation of drugs such as heroin and cocaine (or the slightly squirmy alternative 'decriminalisation') would have brought down prices, removed glamour and excitement, taken away the power of the drug czars (on both sides of the war and dramatically reduced the number of users. The war on drugs, which has been dutifully echoed in England, has been welcomed by the leading wholesalers of illegal drugs because they know that their empires have been built up and sustained by the activities of the expensive, public sector leaders of this absurd and badly managed war.

Conclusion

The absurd belief, fostered by our diplomats, spies and politicians, that England gains power and credibility by hanging around with the USA was never based on any credible arguments. Many of those who most enthusiastically promoted the `special relationship' were more concerned with their own `special relationships' with American corporations and lobbyists.

For the last few decades our close links with America have done us no good and a great deal of harm. We have been dragged into the murky world controlled by the CIA (a world of torture, kidnapping and assassination) and our reputation as a nation has been trashed.

And, if we must ally ourselves closely with another country, wouldn't it be wiser to find a winner? Encouraged by its own massive arms industry and by politicians searching for power and oil, America has been fighting wars for decades without actually winning one. Korea, Vietnam, Iraq, Afghanistan...it's not exactly a military roll of honour is it? So many wars and so much failure.

Finally, if you thought that Greece was in a financial mess then you should take a close look at the United States of America. They are (as we are) truly, totally, completely and definitely stuffed. The merry days of American hubris are strictly limited. Back in 2005, two economists called Jagadeesh Gokhale and Kent Smetters estimated that the real American debt was $65.9 trillion. That isn't just bigger than the American Gross Domestic Product - it's much bigger than the Gross Domestic Products of all the countries in the world added together. To reach that figure they simply looked at the USA, using the same accounting standards that any private sector company is obliged, by law, to use when it draws up a set of accounts. And if you are thinking, well the USA can't possibly default you might like to think again. They've already done it twice. (In 1790 and 1933 if you're interested.)

As Mitch Feierstein points out in his book *Planet Ponzi*, the United States of America's Government now owes over $75 trillion and the median household income in the USA is approximately $50,000 a year. (That's the combined income of all the members of each household). If everyone in every household gave all their earnings to pay off the American debt it would take them all 1.5 billion years to do it. And that is assuming that the American Government hasn't been lying and that the figures aren't worse than we've been told.

The bottom line is that the USA is bankrupt. Anyone who buys dollars, or American bonds or shares, because America is `safe', is heading for disaster.

Chapter 17

Disappearing Jobs And Rising Unemployment

Introduction

Unemployment figures are high and going to go higher. If the official unemployment figures included people in part time jobs, and people recently made redundant, the figure would be 6.3 million - more than double the official figures. If the figures included young people on pointless training schemes, and those avoiding work because of non-existent illnesses, the figure would be doubled again. The official figures now show that unemployment among 15-24 year olds in England is close to 25%. One in four young people doesn't have a job; they are being trained for life on the dole and learning to find a life outside society. The chances of those young people ever finding employment (or ever being able to hold down jobs) are as close to nil as you can get.

There are several reasons for this plague of unemployment. First, we are in a recession which is going to become a depression. The money has all gone to the bankers and speculators. And, instead of lending it out to entrepreneurs setting up widget factories, they are hoarding every penny they don't spend on yachts and champagne. Second, the EU has introduced a mass of legislation which has made life nigh on impossible for people running, or setting up, small companies.

1

An increasing number of people don't do jobs they actually want to do; instead they do jobs they don't like because they need the money. When people do jobs which provide them with little or no satisfaction, which are in a way forcing them into self-imposed exile from real life, they have to find their satisfaction in other ways: one result is that they borrow more money than they should and they spend more than they can afford to spend.

Ordinary workers (by which I mean the people in a business who do the hard work, and not the people who swan around the globe in private jets and chauffeur-driven limousines) have done very badly in the last few decades. Most earn less (in real money) than they did a generation ago. There are several reasons for this. First, company bosses are taking all the money. And so wages and salaries have to be cut. Second, Asian companies have lowered the going rate for many jobs. Globalisation (so loved by politicians) means that workers in Birmingham can be replaced by workers in Peking or Delhi at a fraction of the cost. Even service industry employees have discovered the significance of this sort of competition. Third, automation has made it possible for factories to manage with less people. Robots have taken over in many industries.

And, finally, of course, there is the wretched Internet which has destroyed zillions of real jobs and done far more than any other invention in history to destroy our quality of life.

People who lose their jobs almost always obtain less well-paid employment (if they find anything at all). And their children earn less too.

The unemployed, the underemployed, the pointlessly employed and the malemployed all suffer from loss of self-esteem because work is an essential part of our lives. The man who makes chairs or puts roofs on houses can, at the end of the week, take great pride in what he has done. Where is the pride and respect in selling motorcar insurance over the telephone, being a traffic warden or flipping burgers? The man in charge of nothing much at the local council will probably go home unsatisfied, frustrated and restless. Sadly, more and more people don't like their jobs; they don't want to do them and so they either find a way to refuse work (benefits have become a genuinely better career option for millions and faking stress illness or a bad back is easy) or they demand big money (as with doctors and bankers), do as little work as possible and plan to retire as soon as they can. When job dissatisfaction is low there is really only one reason to get out of bed in the morning and go to work: money. And when 'compensation' is no longer just one of a number of reasons to work its importance obviously rises. And the union representative who offers workers better pay and shorter working hours will receive a better hearing. Workers who are content don't need unions and don't contemplate taking industrial action. When Eiffel built his tower in Paris he put the names of the men who had helped him around the ironwork on the first floor. They can still be seen. Maybe modern employers should find ways to give a feeling of pride to their employees. Workers who have pride in what they do work harder and work better. Productivity is higher, there is less sickness, more happiness and fewer strikes. Sadly, a recent survey showed that well over half of all employees take no pride at all in their work.

5

Politicians puzzle about why young women are having particular difficulty in finding jobs with small and medium sized companies. If anyone is interested I have the answer. No employer with more then three functioning brain cells will employ a young woman because if she is pregnant when she starts work, or subsequently becomes pregnant, she will be entitled to stay at home for up to a year. The employer will have to continue to employ her and he will not be able to hire a replacement. Government departments can cope with this daft law because no one does very much work and the absence of a young mother won't be noticed. Large companies can cope because they have had to over-employ in order to deal with the problem. But small and medium sized companies cannot cope with it. If a shopkeeper has two employees and one of them becomes pregnant he will be in an impossible situation. He is forced by law to allow the pregnant woman to take a year off but the law does not allow him to hire a replacement. He has to keep the woman's job open for her. She can have ten children, one after the other, and the law still applies. And so people running small and medium sized businesses do their very best to ensure that they do not hire women of childbearing age. And now that there are new laws giving men the right to take huge amounts of time off work when their wives (or girlfriends) become pregnant it is a fair bet that employers will start avoiding young male employees too. The European Union has forced employers into discriminating against the fecund. Still, all this means that older job applicants now have a good chance of finding employment.

6

The EU is constantly bleating about equality. The eurocrats should be aware that among 22 to 29-year-olds women now earn more on average than their male counterparts. If the EU cares about equality then the eurocrat clearly need to introduce legislation forcing companies to pay young men as much as they pay young women. If any group of citizens needs help it is low-skilled males - who are now virtually unemployable.

f two candidates for a position have the same qualifications and one is black or brown and the other is white then he candidate who is black or brown will get the job. If one of the two candidates is a woman and the other is a man he woman will get the job. Officially, that's called positive discrimination. Personally, I call it racism and sexism. Incidentally, if the only two candidates are male then the one with the most hair will be appointed.)

Positive discrimination of all sorts is bad because it is nothing more than officially sanctioned prejudice; egalised bigotry. And just because prejudice is official it isn't right. Black or female candidates are appointed and iromoted ahead of white males because of some bizarre attempt to put right something that happened a century or nore ago. I don't quite understand how punishing one group of people today corrects discrimination against nother group of people a generation or two ago. The whole absurd thing goes on because no one dares criticise iecause they know that to protest about the discrimination and the prejudice will be regarded as racist or sexist. If nat isn't a perfect example of utter madness I don't know what is.

)ne of Japan's television manufacturers recently cut its workforce from 5,000 to 15 (yes, from five thousand to ifteen) after automating a plant. However many burger joints and call centres are opened those jobs will never be ccovered or even re-created. The bottom line is that, thanks to automation and computerisation, there will, in ıture, be less jobs available than there are now.

lany central and local government policies seem designed to prevent people getting jobs. For example, many rorkers travel to work by bus. But bus services are being cut and many of the cuts are a direct result of iovernment policies. There has been a 20% cut in fuel duty relief for bus operators. There have been cuts to bus ıbsidies. And cuts to concessionary fares. All these cuts mean that people who want to work but don't have iotorcars can't travel and so must stay at home and remain unemployed. It's difficult to see how cuts of this type elp the country grow. If the Government really wanted to help the poor (and especially the working poor) they ould subsidise local public transport. Many people cannot afford to take jobs because the cost of bus or rail fares e so high.

10

Even those who can find work no longer regard what they do as rewarding or worthwhile. Labour is too often demeaning; repetitive, uniform and without skill or pride. Men have become machine minders and instead of being allowed to acquire skills and master the materials with which they work they are now subordinated to serving machines stamping out parts. Or they are reduced to serving pre-prepared `food' that contains little of nutritional value.

The reward for all this is higher living standards for those who can find employment. Aeroplane journeys to foreign resorts (where fast food is available), huge television screens which dominate the home, constant access to the Internet (so that everyone can share their prejudices in a me, me, me way). We consume more. We throw away more. But are our standards of living higher? How much progress is progress?

11

Strikes used to be about making enough money to eat and live. These days strikers want money to buy a larger TV set, a third car and a foreign holiday home. The damage done by trade unions will increase as austerity really starts to bite. The selfishness of union members will further increase the damage done and increase the depth and length of the depression. The slow down in growth, productivity, efficiency, competence and quality of service has been caused by three things. First, a decline in corporate and general management quality. Second, an abundance of rules and regulations (largely emanating from the European Union). EU regulations mean that people work less than they used to do. Roads used to be busy between 5pm and 6pm, when everyone went home, these days they are at their busiest between 4pm and 5pm. Working hours have, thanks to the EU, fallen by a quarter in recent years. It is hardly surprising that productivity has fallen. Third, the rising power of trade unions. The labour market today is dominated by the vested interests of regulators, unions and big employers (especially governments). Too generous a welfare system, added in, helps to sustain the ultimately unsustainable.

The pound has fallen by 20% since 2007 but there has been no useful impact on growth through trade as a result because, thanks to the unions, our home-grown regulations (brought in by two Labour governments) and our habit of enthusiastically gold plating EU regulations, we no longer have much of an industry.

12

Productivity in England is terrible (pretty well the worst in the world). It seems to be a puzzle to our leaders. They cannot understand how productivity can be so low when we have more regulations than any other country, longer holidays, more tea breaks and a massive social security system which encourages laziness and a feeling that `I don't care if I lose my job because if I do the State will give me a ton of money to stay at home'.

Productivity has also been damaged by our enthusiasm for taking time off work. If an official bank holiday falls on a weekend we take another day off in lieu. In other countries it is simply regarded as hard luck if Christmas Day is on a Saturday. Over the Christmas period many businesses simply close down for a week or two. Isn't it about time that we abandoned bank holidays? They were introduced at a time when workers had very little holiday. Today, some employees (particularly public sector workers and EU employees) seem to be away from work more often than they are there. Many employees (particularly those with public sector jobs) insist that if they don't take their allowed sick days they should be allowed to take those days as extra holiday. And people with jobs which require training (such as teachers) always insist that the training is done when they are paid to be working.

3

When tradesmen and shopkeepers worked for themselves, the services they provided and the products they sold were better and cheaper. Today, the paperwork, the red tape, the health and safety regulations, the essential licensing, the insurance costs and so on and so on mean that small businessmen have to hire professional help to enable them to deal with the problems they face. The result is that everything has become infinitely more complicated. Prices have risen, product quality has fallen and service is poorer.

4

The Government is systematically destroying small business. Is this deliberate? Well, yes it is. But we have to remember that the rules which are destroying small businesses are being brought in by the EU on the instructions of international goliaths - who obviously have a vested financial interest in destroying small companies before they become competitors. The problem is that our political leaders haven't yet worked out what is happening. Leaders in other EU countries simply refuse to accept new EU legislation which they believe would be damaging to their industries.

5

Now that unions have far too much power it is increasingly easy for a small group of selfish workers to hold the country to ransom. Around 2,000 greedy tanker drivers who can, more readily than almost any other small group of greedy extremists hold the country to ransom, were in the spring of 2012 threatening to go on strike. These semi-skilled workers were being paid £45,000 a year to drive trucks with round bodies. That's about twice the amount paid to a driver who looks after a truck with a flat-sided body. And, like all overpaid, greedy dastards, they wanted yet more money. There are 8,000 petrol stations and 2,000 drivers. All these fellows have to do is to remember to drive from one petrol station to the next. There is no heavy furniture to unload. Just deliver the petrol, have a good lunch and remember to go home at the end of the day. Why didn't the Government announce that they would allow the companies concerned to sack all the drivers and hire replacements? It was agreed that it would take no more than a week to hire new drivers (there would be no shortage of applicants) and the new ones would be unlikely to go on strike when they realised how easy it was to do the work. (And just for fun I would, after firing the idiots print the names and addresses of all the dastardly tanker drivers threatening to hold the country to ransom.) But instead of acting firmly, and telling people to stay calm, the Government did nothing but encourage drivers to rush out and fill up containers with petrol. (They always do the same thing whenever there is the faintest whiff of a terrorist attack; they panic.)

I was particularly depressed by the activity of the trade unions in all this threatening behaviour. Unions weren't created to look after pampered lorry drivers taking home more than twice as much as a highly-trained ambulance driver. Unions were created to look after the oppressed. Unions seem to me to have no place in our society.

16

English workers no longer go to work if they want to watch a football match or enjoy a television programme or sit out in the sunshine. This is not surprising. Even the leader of the Labour Party recently chose to sneak off work to watch a football match.

17

In the bad old days shops employed assistants who helped customers and provided cheery smiles and words about the weather for the elderly and lonely. Those days have gone and more and more shops now have self-service tills where customers are hectored by a computerised voice if their scanning and packing skills fall below the accepted European standards. Even public libraries are introducing these awful scanners. The machines are, of course, introduced because they allow employers to employ less people but the staff who work in these places don't seem to have worked this out and are universally delighted that they can stand around doing nothing. 'Oh there will always be things for us to do,' said a smug librarian as he watched an old lady struggling with the machine that had replaced him. What a stupid sod. If trade unions truly cared about their members they would be fighting this latest takeover by computers, for our supermarkets and high street shops will soon have hardly any staff at all. For a while I used to insist on being served by a person to help preserve their jobs. But the assistants are mostly sullen and uninterested and would clearly prefer that we all use the machines. So in future I will. And they will join the ranks of the unemployed.

8

A friend of the Princess's, who has a job working for a local council, has been told that she must take a 10% cut in her wages. Her income is already low and she told The Princess that the cut means that she will have no holidays and no luxuries and will have to give up her car. Councils everywhere are, it seems, making the public and the lower paid pay for the Brown induced cuts. Meanwhile, so-called executives are giving themselves pay rises, bonuses and increased expense allowances.

9

Most politicians don't understand the problems employers face because most politicians have never run a business and never employed people themselves. Pompous, patronising politicians such as Vince Cable dismiss out of hand the common anxieties of employers, such as not being able to sack lazy and incompetent employees and having to deal with ever more onerous rules about pregnant employees and their husbands.

0

The surly young man in a hoodie who turns up looking unwilling to work can turn into an excited and motivated employee,' said one Government minister, trying to encourage employers to hire hoodies but, to many employers, merely showing just how out of touch a Government minister can be.

Conclusion

Politicians have used a number of tricks to disguise the facts but unemployment has been rising steadily for years. Thanks to the failing economy, the coming global depression and the Internet, unemployment is likely to stay high (and steadily go higher) until there is a revolution.

Chapter 18

Our Creaking Infrastructure

Introduction

Like the worst dictators in the worst slum countries in the world, our leaders (or, more accurately, misleaders) have allowed our nation's infrastructure to fall into appalling disrepair. Our Victorian forefathers (now widely regarded with contempt by young politicians who need to visit You Tube in order to find out how to tie their shoelaces) gave us the world's most impressive infrastructure. English engineers such as Brunel built roads, bridges and railways that were (and still are) the envy of the world.

1

We need to spend at least £500 billion if we are to repair and restore our infrastructure. Much of our current infrastructure was built by the Victorians who did a marvellous job but their needs were rather different to ours. Actually, the truth is that the Victorians did too good a job. Their buildings, railway stations, bridges, sewers and water supply pipes have, by and large, received attention only when they needed repairing. What we should have been doing, of course, was making serious improvements to our infrastructure when we were making oodles of cash as a result of the wonders of all the extra energy provided by oil. That would have been the sensible responsible thing to do. But none of our recent political leaders has been guilty of doing anything sensible or responsible. They've spent the money on sweeties and doughnuts when they should have spent it laying new sewage pipes and building new water treatment works.

2

Our sewers, water pipes, roads, bridges and power stations are all falling apart. Our elderly hospitals and public buildings (such as town halls and libraries) are dignified, spacious and stout but dilapidated and need a little love. We don't need to replace them but we do need to freshen them up. And we need more of them (all apart from the town halls).

Much of our power network will have to shut down by 2019. Our coal-fired power stations will be closed by new EU emission regulations. And our nuclear power plants are reaching the end of their safe and useful lives. It takes a decade to build and commission a new nuclear power station. And the Government, full of people who failed, or should have failed, O level maths, still seems to think it can cram a decade into the years between 2012 and 2019.)

Instead of using the taxes it collects to improve our infrastructure, our governments have, for some considerable time, been busy selling bits of our infrastructure to foreign sovereign funds who won't give a bowl of rice if things don't work properly.

Roughly half of all our essential services (bridges, water supplies, airports, seaports, etc.) now have foreign owners who are not at all concerned about English public opinion and who owe no allegiance to England or the English.

Consider, for example, Scottish Power which supplies gas and electricity throughout England and which is now owned by a Spanish company. Like other energy companies Scottish Power is constantly pushing up its prices. It recently made such vast profits that it was able to lend £800 million to a sister company in America, where it couldn't raise its prices for energy customers because of local regulations. (The American Government, and individual American states, are much tougher on foreign companies than we are.)

England has such weak controls on foreign companies that we have become the first port of call for foreign investors (private or sovereign) looking for a place to invest where big profits can be made without too much trouble from lawmakers or regulators. Our liberal takeover rules, our pliant politicians and our servile media (misled, as always, by the State-run broadcasting service the BBC) have enabled foreign companies to acquire vast amounts of English industry.

In 2009, foreign companies and sovereign funds bought £30 billion worth of English companies. In 2010 they bought just under £55 billion. The Chinese are expected to be spending £400 billion a year on buying big companies. (The Chinese Government already owns 3% of the FTSE 100 and has £2 trillion in cash to invest. Every year. It won't be long before everyone who isn't working for our Government will be working for a foreign one. It has been easy for them to do this. Foreign banks can and do create billions out of nothing and central banks have been printing money with great enthusiasm for years. So our vital utilities have been sold to foreigners using funny money as currency. It wouldn't have been so bad if they'd bought our stuff with gold - which we could have used to replenish our stocks (since Gordon the Moron flogged off the family holdings for a rock bottom price the minute he got control of the keys). Other countries protect their companies and their infrastructure with great enthusiasm. The Americans are very strict about what foreign companies can and cannot do. And foreigners cannot buy oil companies, TV companies, airlines and other essential services. The French don't allow key technologies or companies to fall into foreign hands. The Spanish insist on holding onto their energy companies. And although India has bought English companies such as Land Rover and Jaguar it won't allow English companies to take full control of Indian companies.

There are big problems in all this.

First, foreign owners don't give a toss about what happens to customers in England. All they are concerned about are profits. Costs are cut in order to maximise profits. If you doubt the truth of that just remember that Heathrow is foreign owned.

Second, foreign owners are invariably quick to close English factories and move manufacturing abroad. Executives don't give a damn about their popularity or unpopularity in England. And, in the absence of strict laws, they don't give a damn for what politicians think either. If you doubt the truth of that just think what happened when American baddie Kraft bought iconic English company Cadburys.

The irony is that much of the stuff which foreign companies and sovereign funds own was built with taxpayers' money and so foreigners are now charging us to use facilities which we paid for and maintained. Worse still, most of the new owners are slum landlords and aren't particularly enthusiastic about doing any repairs. Foreign companies (and sovereign investment funds) are buying up England's crumbling infrastructure, and manufacturing companies and will run them into the ground with no regard for the well being of the English people or English workers.

It may or not be because much of it is foreign owned but England is now officially 33rd in the world for the quality of its infrastructure. We are behind Tunisia and Cyprus and alongside Slovenia. And because of union rules, tea breaks and absurd regulations, big civil engineering projects cost 60% more in England than in Germany.

Politicians have been crooked for decades. A politician called Ernest Marples is now largely forgotten but he played a huge part in defining our society and, most significantly, in destroying the railways.

(As an aside it was Englishman Richard Trevithick who devised the first motorised transport. Back in 1802 Trevithick invented the motorcar. Without pausing to take a bow, he then immediately invented the bus. And, because the roads weren't good enough for his new vehicles, he built tracks and invented the train. These days EU regulations and the health and safety people would have stopped him before he sharpened his quill. The first mass production of cars was organised by Thomas Rickett in England in 1860. Karl Benz, the German, was laughably later in 1885 and by the time Henry Ford started experimenting with cars Trevithick's invention was near a century old. Today, most Englishmen and women probably think foreigners invented all these things. This is because foreigners tell us they invented them and, as a nation, we tend to be polite and self-effacing almost to the point of non-existence. But Trevithick was the first. In a single flurry of concentrated genius, he invented the car, the bus and the train.)

Anyway, back down to earth and back to Ernest Marples.

Marples had been a pushy Minister who in the pre-Blair days probably did more to screw up the country than anyone except the utterly repulsive and traitorous Ted Heath. He joined the Government in 1957 as Postmaster General and introduced subscriber trunk dialling which got rid of operators for national telephone calls and, at a stroke, did immeasurable damage to the ability of lonely, middle-aged women to cement their place in society with gossip. He also introduced postcodes and Premium Bonds.

A couple of years later Marples became the Transport Minister and he immediately started making his mark there too. He introduced seat belts, yellow lines and parking meters. And he introduced motorways which quickly became famous for having `Marples Must Go' painted on virtually every bridge. In 1959 Marples opened the first section of the M1 motorway.

Now Marples knew about roads. He had founded Marples-Ridgway, a construction firm that had built many roads, and so he naturally stood to gain enormously from his own enthusiasm for bigger and more expensive roads.

In order to avoid public criticism of a clear conflict of interest, Marples announced that he would sell his controlling interest in Marples-Ridgway and this he duly did. He then not only began furiously building more roads, but also started getting rid of the railways. It was Marples who appointed the notorious and woefully short sighted Dr Beeching who immediately started cutting the best railway service in the world. All requests for money for the railways had to go to Marples. And most were rejected. Marples the road builder destroyed our railways.

Oh, one other thing is worth mentioning.

I mentioned earlier that Marples sold his shareholding in his eponymous road-building company. He did. He sold the shares to his wife, proving that corruption in English politics is no new thing.

Today, thanks to Marples and Beeching, our rail network is a disaster and a disgrace. What a pity no one then or later, had the foresight to realise that with the oil running out the railways are the easiest, most energy efficient, most economical way to move people and goods around the country. What a pity all the rails were ripped up and all the local railway stations sold as holiday cottages. The lunatic Dr Beeching destroyed communities and isolated towns and villages. His short-sighted stupidity resulted in overcrowded roads, and a good deal of pollution

5

Other European countries have fantastic infrastructures. France, for example, has marvellous roads, public buildings, airports and all the rest. The French are now pretty well as broke as we are but when they had some money they spent it wisely. They could have spent all their money on frogs' legs and snails but instead they used some of it on sensible stuff like nuclear power stations. They too spent too much, but they have something to show or their spending.

No other country has copied our experiment with railway privatisation. I'm not surprised. The mess we now have is more complex and confusing (and worse value) than it was when it was called British Rail and we all laughed at the sandwiches. At least in those days you could always take your own sandwiches. These days, the reliability and punctuality record is so poor that, if you want to go anywhere by rail, you really need to take your own train. Taxpayers still pay out as much as when the railways were State-owned, fares are far more expensive and there are more accidents.

Here's another example showing that privatisation may not always be a good idea. In the spring of 2012, it was announced that a hosepipe ban would be introduced into much of England (though not the bits due to host the Olympics, where nice green grass was considered far more important than the growing of potatoes or runner beans). Why was England short of water? Well, the privatised water companies are very good at collecting money but not terribly good at looking after water. Anglian Water, one of the companies introducing a hosepipe ban, made £447 million operating profit in 2011 but spent just £14 million fixing water leaks. Other water companies are much the same. And so, as a result, a quarter of the water sent to customers never arrives at its destination but pours out through mendable leaks.

There's another problem.

You might imagine that if a water company supplying one part of the country had a water shortage then a company supplying another part of the country would help out (for a few million quid, of course). No chance. The water companies (sometimes controlled by people living on the other side of the planet) are focused regionally and they don't see the nation as a whole. So there are no national solutions to water shortage problems.

Anyone who argues that our national infrastructure should remain English will be denounced as jingoistic, nationalistic, racist and someone who probably tucks his shirt into his underpants (if male) or shaves her moustache if female). But England is just about the only country in the world which allows its national infrastructure to be bought and managed by companies and individuals who live thousands of miles away and who care only about profits. It is easy to argue that the utility companies should be privatised. But there have to be controls. And for the controls to work the companies have to be owned by people who at least spend their holidays in England. At the moment much of our infrastructure is owned by businessmen who are intent only on gouging the last penny out of the elderly, the frail and the weak and who don't give a damn what anyone says about them.

9

Successive governments have been criminally incompetent in failing to repair our infrastructure in order to prepare us for the hard times ahead.

In March 2012, it was announced that standpipes would become a regular sight in summers to come. We were encouraged to blame the weather for this (and, presumably, a Christian rather than a Muslim god) but the truth is that for decades governments have failed to plan, organise and pay for proper water storage facilities. They have always assumed that it will rain and that everything will be fine. Proposals for a national water grid were abandoned in the 1970s because it was deemed to be too expensive. Since then we've always had plenty of money to wage illegal wars, and to set up pointless quangos, but we've never had enough money to do something about our creaky water supply infrastructure.

And now we're in a mess.

The shortage of water will lead to higher food prices.

And, as the global supplies of water become scarcer (it is not news that water is in scarce supply and is now the planet's most valuable asset) it is absurd that we waste so much water. Do motorcars have to be washed every Sunday? Are daily baths a real necessity? Does it really help the environment if we all wash out our empty yoghurt cartons?

10

The global shortage of food will, as I forecast some years ago, be exacerbated by the massive increase in the number of Chinese and Indians now eating meat and meat products such as burgers and sausages. The amount of grain used to feed cattle and other animals is so great that if the world became vegetarian or vegan there would be no shortage of food and no starving millions. (And, as a bonus, there would be much less illness.)

1

Our energy supplies are heavily dependent on foreign suppliers. Our existing nuclear power stations are being phased out. Most of our gas and oil comes from the Gulf (hardly the most stable area of the world). The EU is forcing us to abandon our coal-fired power stations. We will soon have regular electricity outages. Politicians haven't yet worked out that it won't be easy for the economy to grow when there isn't any electricity.

2

Our party system has meant that we no longer have national strategies. Everything is short-term. No politicians think more than four or five years ahead. Decisions that should have been taken years ago have been delayed. Politicians refuse to consider `big' issues because they regard the long-term as someone else's problem.

Conclusion

The Victorians found enough money and time to build magnificent hospitals, public buildings, railways, bridges, and railway stations. They built water works and sewage plants and schools galore. What have we produced with all our wealth? Our legacy to the next generation is an outdated and constantly crumbling infrastructure. And our government will continue to do nothing, partly because they cannot now afford to do anything and partly because our politicians are too damned stupid to do anything until the sewage reaches the level of the extractor fan.

Chapter 19

Disappearing Privacy And Lost Freedom

Introduction

Our lives are dominated by people who believe they have a right to control our lives in every conceivable way. They believe they have a right to tell us how to behave and a right to spend our money for us. Busy bodies working for the EU have given themselves the authority to remove our freedom and our liberty and to make all our decisions for us. Economic and social freedom is now just a memory.

The problem with the nanny State (and that's a rather kindly way of referring to the most fascist organisation in human history) is that when you treat adults like children they inevitably start behaving like children. And so we now have a culture built on irresponsibility and entitlement. Millions expect the State to look after their every need, and their daily lives are driven forward not by ambition, determination or the intention to survive but by a sense of constant expectation. And a feeling of grievance when they are occasionally left to make decisions for themselves or, worse still, have to deal with thwarted desires.

The rules and regulations produced with such relentless enthusiasm by the fascist storm troopers in Brussels have created a stagnant society in which too many adults always expect someone else to make their decisions for them, always expect someone else to take all the responsibility and someone else to provide for their every need.

Taking responsibility for your own life isn't easy. Making decisions for yourself is always difficult.

1

There is a State encouraged assumption that anyone who wants to be private must have something to hide. This is nonsense. Even those of us who have no secrets, no hidden skeletons and no shame in our lives like to preserve some privacy. But the State (and its enforcers) don't like the idea of privacy. The State likes to know everything about everyone because knowledge is power and total knowledge is total power.

2

Doctors and lawyers always used to take patient or client confidentiality very seriously. That confidentiality has now gone. Anything you tell your doctor or lawyer is about as private as if you broadcast it on prime time television, or talked about it on your mobile phone. The Government (acting on instructions from Hitler's Bastard Love Child) has made it illegal for members of either profession (and, indeed, other professions) to offer confidentiality as part of their professional service. Moreover, the Government has introduced a law making it illegal for professionals to tell you that they are going to share your secrets with the authorities. Or to even admit that they might.

The only people who can rely on their lives being kept private are senior politicians who rely on people whose wages are paid for by us to provide them with the sort of privacy we would like to enjoy if it had not been taken away by people working for the Government and, again, paid for by us.

Most decent passwords used for the Internet and so on end up being written down because they are impossible to remember. The more passwords we acquire, and the more complex we are encouraged to make them (using a mixture of letters and numbers, upper and lower case and the funny bits from the keyboard) the more we are likely to write them down. But written down is a synonym for insecure. The more complex you make security, the more vulnerable it becomes. I have an employer's account with the HMRC and to operate the account the idiots working there sent me (through the post) an absurdly long password which has to be written down. No one not working as a memory man on the music halls could ever remember such a password. But, then, the people at HMRC are not the folk to whom I would automatically turn for advice on personal security.

'Every man should know that his conversations, his correspondence and his personal life are private.' - Lyndon B. Johnson, forner USA President

Government departments regard privacy as irrelevant - unless it is their privacy that is being discussed. Government buffoon Vince Cable recently apologised for the fact that transparent sackfuls of private mail and confidential documents were dumped outside his constituency office. A resignation letter would have been more acceptable than an apology.

7

All cabs licensed in Oxford will soon have to carry a CCTV camera that will routinely record all discussions in the vehicle. This is, of course, being done `to protect passengers'.

8

`How many of us have paused during conversation in the past (few) years, suddenly aware that we might be eavesdropped on? Probably it was a phone conversation; maybe it was an e-mail or instant-message exchange or a talk in a public place. Maybe the topic was terrorism, politics or Islam. We stop suddenly, momentarily afraid that our words might be taken out of context, then we laugh at our paranoia and go on. But our demeanour has changed, and our words are subtly altered.' - Bruce Schneier

9

The Internet has generated vast stores of information. Much of this material is entirely without value. A good deal of the stored information is dangerously misleading, either by design or through ignorance. A good deal is libellous. Some is useful. The problem is that it is almost impossible for the non-expert user to know which information is of value and which is dangerously misleading. Moreover our growing dependency on the Internet is destroying just about every aspect of our society. Crucially, the Internet is enabling the State (and all international corporations) to deprive us of our individuality, our freedom, our rights and our privacy. Almost every Government department, and every company with whom you and I are likely to come into contact, forces us to conduct our business on the Internet, charges us more if we choose not to, or are unable to use the Internet, will constantly cajole us to visit their damned websites, to ask all our questions on their websites and to manage our businesses on their websites. If we telephone for help or information the accursed `press one, press two...' response will constantly be interrupted by irritating exhortations promoting the damned wonders of the damned website. (The promotion for their website is the second thing they record after the message containing the words `due to a high volume of calls'.) And when you do get to the accursed website (because there is simply no other way to contact anyone) you will usually find something badly designed, incompetently run, littered with annoying, patronising messages and `quite unfit for purpose'.

t has been proven that better lighting is four times better than CCTV cameras at preventing crime in towns and ities. Despite this evidence councils everywhere are turning off the lights and putting up more cameras. Lights elp people. Cameras invade our privacy and help the authorities.

n May 2012, it was announced that the Information Commissioner (someone or something straight out of George)rwell's *1984,* but in this instance perhaps not entirely evil) was investigating allegations that Google used its treet View cars (the ones that wander around taking pictures of everything they see, and then putting the pictures n the Web) to gather personal information from *inside* the houses they were photographing. Google's camera cars ere apparently collecting complete e-mails, texts, Internet passwords, private documents, photographs and online ating searches. They were using wireless connections and specially designed software to steal all this information. oogle was, at the time, already facing a possible anti-trust suit by the European Commission, which was onsidering whether the Google search engine promoted its own products over those of its rivals. (Surely not?) I on't care whether the authorities do or do not decide that Google behaved illegally. In my view they behaved nmorally.

I have repeatedly described Google as being, in my view, one of the most evil companies on the planet. It is orth remembering that whatever you delete from your Google searches isn't really deleted because Google keeps full list of everywhere you go and everything you do. Why? Commercial reasons. What are they going to do with ll that private information? Your guess is as good as mine but if that's not Big Brother in operation I don't know hat is.

ompanies always highlight changes to their privacy policies but how many people read these documents? The erage website privacy policy takes 10 minutes to read and since the average Web user encounters over 1400 rivacy policies in a year that's a lot of small print to read. In fact it would take more than 76 working days to read l those policies and the cost to the economy would be vast.

So, no one can seriously, or realistically, understand what rights they are giving away. Nor can they control their privacy any more.

Companies should be required to adhere to a single, easily read and readily available statement.

13

Some time ago the EU proposed a new right to be forgotten - and to have all personal data removed from Internet sites. This would free many of us from the tyranny of Google et al. Inevitably, nothing has happened and nothing is likely to happen.

14

Facebook has assembled personal data from 850 million people. All these folk have given intimate information away, entirely free of charge, to a ruthless, large American company. The world's largest library of marketing information can now be shared with advertisers, political parties, the CIA and every other commercial and political organisation in the world which has the cash to spend. All the information collected on Facebook is owned by Facebook. (I am not on Facebook by the way, though a site was apparently set up in my name some time ago. I have never visited it.)

15

In early 2012, an international agreement designed to stop online piracy and the theft of intellectual property (books, articles, films and music) was shelved after online campaigns were organised by some of the biggest websites. They used hacking and demonstrations to oppose the legislation which had been planned by the American Government (the *Stop Online Piracy Act* and the *Protect Intellectual Property Act*). In January 2012 Wikipaedia, Google and a bunch of other Web based companies staged a one day protest about these proposed anti-piracy bills which were designed to protect creators and copyright holders.

16

Stores have been trawling their customer databases for years looking for commercial useful information. For example, stores often look through their available information looking for evidence of second trimester pregnancy. (One store recently mailed baby advertising to a teenager before her own father realised she was pregnant.) And political parties and candidates regularly buy data from credit agencies so that they can advertise to specific groups of voters. The electoral register is the most readily available source of private information. (A friend says it isn't difficult to avoid having your name on the register. He suggests you simply tell the authorities that your home is a 'holiday home'. He says that as long as you pay the full council tax they won't care.)

7

Nothing is secure on the Internet. In June 2011, it was revealed that hackers had stolen the entire 2011 census. You might argue that this serves people right for trusting the Government with private information.) A few months earlier, in January 2012 a Web meeting between Scotland Yard and the FBI to discuss hacking was hacked into.

8

Just because you do not take an interest in politics doesn't mean politics won't take an interest in you.' - Pericles 430 BC

9

Our Government is more likely to request details of our Web usage than the authorities in almost any other country. Only Singapore (which has been criticised by Human Rights Watch as an authoritarian state) beats England. And, of course, we have more CCTV cameras than anywhere else in the world. The English are the most spied upon people on the planet.

10

Prisoners are now being hired to do computer work for the Government. It seems safe to assume that they will soon be hired to do call centre work and to manage online banking services. This sort of work should provide all sorts of ideas and possibilities for post-prison employment.

11

Wishing to maintain any degree of confidentiality is now regarded as a crime by the State, and by many who do not understand the value of privacy. 'If you have done nothing wrong you have nothing to fear' is the mantra of the dumb and is the argument against privacy and confidentiality and for snooping by the Government and all its myrmidons.

12

Here are my tips for surviving in our modern world:

a) Always pay cash whenever possible.

b) Assume that everything you write on the Internet, or say on the telephone, will be broadcast on the evening news and published in the daily press.

c) Assume everything is bugged.

d) Know and understand your rights under the Human Rights Act.

e) Don't use the same computer for Internet work and for private work.

23

Your bank probably persists in regarding your birth date as a secure and secret password. But the number of people who know your birth date includes everyone working at HMRC, the DVLA, and every Government department, all insurance companies with whom you have done business, the passport office, all foreign tax organisations with whom you have had encounters, your doctor, your dentist, all the clubs of which you are a member, everyone to whom you are related, everyone who has read any of the reference books and websites which decorate your biography with your date of birth and anyone with access to the Internet.

I doubt if there is a thief on the planet too stupid to find your date of birth within a minute. Even Fred Goodwin could probably find it. Well, perhaps not, but you get the general idea.

And yet your bank still regards your birth date as the fundamental key to your private world.

24

In the spring of 2012, England's newspaper commentators seemed desperately confused when it was announced that the Government was planning to introduce new surveillance laws allowing the police to have real time access to our telephone calls, e-mails and texts. Oh, and also to have details of our entire Internet search histories. The puzzle was that the Tories had opposed exactly the same policy when it had been first suggested by the last Labour Government. At that time the Tories had promised to roll back surveillance legislation. What no one mentioned was that the EU was behind the new laws and so our politicians have no say in whether or not the legislation was introduced. Of the 1,000 plus public bodies already entitled (under existing surveillance laws) to monitor your electronic communications, two thirds are local authorities. Precisely why your council should concern itself with reading your e-mails, listening to your phone calls and looking at your list of Web searches is a mystery. The would, perhaps, be better occupied emptying dustbins and filling in potholes.

5

Here's a thought. Every time I go out of the house I can't help noticing that every other person I see is on the telephone. Where is the Government going to find the 20 million people they will need to monitor all the phone calls being made?

6

'Everyone has the right of freedom of opinions and expression; this right includes freedom to hold opinions without interference and to seek, receive and impart information and ideas through any media and regardless of frontiers.'
United Nations Charter Article 19

7

The Government is planning to store everyone's e-mails and search histories indefinitely. This may appeal to those politicians who believe that freedom and privacy must be sacrificed in the name of protecting our civilised society but when you remove the freedom and privacy there isn't much left of a civilised society.

Freidrich Hayek pointed out that pragmatists are often willing to sacrifice a little liberty here and there for some theoretical advantage but we already have CCTV cameras everywhere, and everything we do is constantly watched and detailed by covert employees of our councils and police forces. At what point will we say `enough'? Hayek's great book was called *The Road to Serfdom* and he was right. We are constantly giving up little bits of freedom and before we know it we will be in a world where the Government does whatever it likes. And we are mere serfs.

Or, perhaps, we are already there.

8

That sanctimonious newspaper the *Guardian* is probably the most establishment newspaper in the country. It is always opposed to anything revolutionary or rebellious. According to an opinion poll published in the *Guardian* an alarming 71% of *Guardian* readers said they thought that compulsory ID cards would be a price worth paying to reduce the threat of terrorism. An astonishing 35% said they would accept a ban on peaceful protests and 22% said they would accept the torture of terror suspects in English jails if it could prevent an attack on our country. What I find particularly scary about all this is that it is the *Guardian* which carries nearly all job advertising for the Government and the BBC and which is, in effect, the house journal for the establishment.

29

The security services, police forces and other agencies made over 500,000 requests to access phone and e-mail records last year. (I hope they found my calls and e-mails edifying.)

30

Part of the problem in our society is that the wrong things are protected by the rules.

Our dentist has a sign up in his waiting room saying that when receptionists are ringing to remind patients of an impending appointment (an annoying habit) receptionists can't share information with patients' relatives about appointments which have been made, might be made or need to be made. They are not allowed to say why they are ringing or to mention the time of any appointment. They are probably not even allowed to say who is ringing. I can imagine the bizarre conversations which might ensue from this nonsense.

Once we get into the surgery, of course, health and safety regulations take over from the Data Protection Act. We have to wear silly spectacles and a plastic bib. There was some consternation when I recently complained that there was no seat belt and that as a result I might fall out of the chair.

31

The USSR and the Eastern Bloc countries maintained power over their citizens by encouraging them to report on one another - creating nations of spies and informers. England has done the same. The Government now actively encourages people to report their neighbours or family to the authorities if they suspect they are claiming benefit to which they are not entitled, avoiding taxes they should pay or are driving a motorcar without a valid road tax licence.

32

`No man hath power over my rights and liberties and I over no man's.' - Richard Overton (political activist in the time of Oliver Cromwell)

33

Drug companies and firms which do animal testing are to be given private, personal medical records. This means hat they will be able to access the home addresses and telephone numbers of those who have publicly opposed nimal experimentation.

4

recently visited a mobile phone shop. I wanted to buy a Pay as You Go telephone with cash. They refused to sell me the telephone unless I showed them a copy of a recent bank statement.

5

Ve recently registered with a new doctor. A receptionist told us that we must provide a passport, driving licence with photograph), utility bill and heaven knows what else. We took along the paperwork they required (minus assports) but when they tried to take them away to photocopy I gently demurred. `You don't have the right to do nat,' I told the woman, politely. `You've seen the documents. That's all you're entitled to do.'

And so there are no photocopies.

We were, as always, the only people to protest about this nonsense.

And so, at every doctor's surgery up and down the land there are photocopies of several thousand passports nd utility bills - quite enough paperwork for an identity thief to have fun for years.

(If you are pushed into a corner and cannot avoid allowing someone to photocopy a potentially sensitive ocument then I suggest that you at least insist on writing the date, and the purpose for which the copy has been nade, across a corner of the photocopy. This may provide you with a little protection against future fraud.)

6

Then we want to travel abroad we must be inspected, pawed, groped, humiliated, hassled and shouted at to prepare s for the round ups, interrogations, disappearances and camps on the Isle of Wight.

And yet the whole damned `security' apparatus is a wild and pointless nonsense. It was recently reported at airport face scanners can't tell the difference between Osama bin Laden and the actress Winona Ryder. Ms yder would be well advised to stay at home. Actually, so, indeed would the rest of us. Flying has become angerous. Wheezing, crippled, 90-year-old Episcopalians making a last pilgrimage to their favourite holiday resort e groped by minimum wage penknife thieves and people quiver and shake as non-English customs men shout at em in badly broken English. Shoes off, pockets empty, belt undone, jacket off, hat off, scarf off. At airports (and, these days, even at Eurostar stations) the immigration police seem to spend ages looking at passports. Why? To build up the queues? Or to make innocent old ladies worry whether the man looking at their passport knows that they put their rubbish out a day early three months ago or, horror of horrors, put a folded cornflake packet into the rubbish instead of the recycling. Complain about the nonsense and you are trouble. A sign says 'Jokes or inappropriate remarks regarding security could lead to your arrest.' Everyone takes this nonsense as normal. It's the new normal. All the rudeness is accepted. I dare not fly. Not because of what they will do but because of what they will do to me when I complain about them doing what they will do. Most people have worked out that the only way to survive is to lower their profile to that of a snake. Sadly, I have yet to learn that lesson.

The problem is that I know that the whole demeaning experience is a farce. Have metal detectors airports ever found anything? No. And they are clearly a waste of time and money since guns, ammunition and explosive are available in non-metallic materials which don't go 'ping' or show up on scanners. The whole process, so enjoyed by the minimum wage granny gropers and the voyeurs, is designed solely to humiliate and frighten us; to put us in our places and to keep us there. Airport security is nothing to do with stopping terrorists but everything to do with making us realise who's in charge. That, indeed, seems to be the sole purpose of much modern legislation.

37

The aggressive silliness at airports and international railway stations is, of course, part of the utterly nonsensical war on terror.

The war on terrorism is a misnomer for we are at war only with the terrorists we dislike. There are many terrorists who have been accepted into polite society (think of the IRA, Nelson Mandela and many historic figures in Israel). Terrorism is, in reality, very successful. Governments refuse to give in to hijackers or kidnappers but if the terrorists' activities are extensive enough, and long lasting, the results can be enormously successful. Look at the success Mandela had in South Africa (terrorist to saint within one lifetime). In Israel, former terrorists do very well indeed. And, former IRA members are today regarded as members of the political establishment.

38

The Princess and I recently went through a Customs checkpoint using each other's passports. Worse still the passport officer examined both passports and allowed us through. It was, I promise you, an honest mistake on our art. But if customs officers can't tell the difference between a balding, male pensioner and a bright, beautiful

oung princess with long hair then there isn't much point in them being there.

9

has recently become known that customs officers now deliberately search white passengers in order to make sure

1at they meet their race quotas. And so, for every sweaty, bearded Muslim in a bomber jacket, with a haversack on

is back, they harass an old, white lady with a white stick and a hearing aid. Brilliant.

0

1 America, travellers must produce two examples of personal paperwork containing photo identification. Who the

ell travels with two photographs of themselves? My guess is that the only people who do so are terrorists. And so

1e authorities should immediately arrest anyone who has the required paperwork.

1

has become illegal for Christians to oppose, or even criticise, social eccentricities such as gay marriage. England

supposed to be liberal, tolerant and forward looking but we are more repressive than ever before. You can now

et arrested in England just for thinking or saying the wrong things. We have thought crimes and a politically

orrect culture. An evangelist who held up a poster saying 'Stop homosexuality. Stop lesbianism. Jesus is Lord'

as attacked by members of the public; politically correct thugs poured soil and water over him. Naturally, the

olice arrested the evangelist and not his attackers. The attackers had merely been guilty of physical abuse. The

vangelist had been guilty of a thought crime.

Pensioners were visited by the police for daring to ask their council if they could distribute Christian

aflets alongside gay rights leaflets. Write or say something which isn't approved by the thought police and you

o could be in trouble. Offering advice which is regarded as offensive is a hate crime.

I think it all started to go wrong when it was decided that a white man raping a black woman is a more

rious crime than a black man raping a white woman. Anyone who questions the wisdom of the EU, or the

ientific validity of vaccination, vivisection or genetic engineering is regarded as dangerous and will probably be

ported to the authorities. Anyone who questions immigration must be a racist. The validity of the global warming

gument is accepted by the scientific establishment and anyone who still questions the value of the argument is regarded as akin to a Holocaust denier. Questioning multiculturalism, positive discrimination, feminism and other tenets of a dogmatic, dangerous and oppressive tyranny is a dangerous business. In our Stalinistic world dissent must be stifled because, well, because the establishment can stifle it and so they will. 'We don't agree with what they are saying so they must not be allowed to say it.' A white, Christian heterosexual male who thinks immigration has got out of control, who wants England to leave the EU, who is sceptical about global warming and who doesn't want his children to be given 30 vaccinations is regarded as a dangerous heretic and likely to be a police target.

42

I am fed up with being bullied. Even banks no longer ask us to do something, they tell us what we must do. There are no longer any requests, just orders. Institutionalised bullying has filtered down from the top with the result that threats now come from every quarter; there are bullies everywhere and bullying has become the official national pastime of civil servants and employees of all national companies.

Conclusion

What is left of our privacy is disappearing rapidly. Our freedom and our traditional rights of free speech are also disappearing. Our politicians take the blame for all the oppressive new legislation being introduced (they have no choice, the rules are that no one can 'blame' the EU for anything) and they claim that the new laws are necessary to protect us from terrorists and moneylaunderers. This argument is nonsensical to say the least since none of the legislation has any effect whatsoever on either of these groups. (Ironically, London is, along with New York, one of the official moneylaundering centres of the planet.) The new laws are being brought in for one purpose only: to spy on us, to prevent dissent and to keep us quiet and docile. None of these laws will be removed and nothing will improve until we leave the European Union and elect an independent bunch of MPs to represent us in the Mother of all Parliaments. That will take some time. Meanwhile, all these intrusions (and the delays they create) dramatically reduce productivity and affect England's attractiveness to businessmen and tourists alike. Even more importantly, people who are oppressed quickly lose their courage, initiative and imagination.

Epilogue

The harder the conflict, the more glorious the triumph. What we obtain too cheap we esteem too lightly. Tis dearness only that gives everything its value.' - Thomas Paine, Englishman

sometimes suspect that I have spent too many hours, days, weeks, months and years of my life hurling myself at windmills and barricades and battering myself senseless against unprincipled bastions of cruelty and wickedness, when the sensible course of action would have been to make a detour, go home, settle down on the sofa with a mug of hot cocoa, draw the curtains and watch Coronation Street, Newsnight or some other trivial, eye numbing light entertainment.

But I have always had a burning yearning to conquer injustices and at the same time I have always been conscious that if you don't fight any battles, you don't win any wars. And so these Sisyphean labours have been part of my life.

However, I am constantly dispirited not just by what has happened to our world (and by what is happening now) but also by the fact that so many good people are now suffocated by their own apathy, and terrified into silence by the justified suspicion that anyone who sticks a nose above the parapet is likely to have it shot off.

The hoodies and the feral youths who roam our streets in increasing numbers are not frightened, of course. They don't give a damn about anything or anyone. They are not cowed by tradition, uniform, expectation or duty. But they aren't interested in making things better or righting wrongs either. They just want short-term joys and excitement. They don't think about next week, let alone next year. They are driven by a pure and toxic mixture of hedonism, selfishness, materialism and by a sense of entitlement.

Sadly, many of the citizens who are sensitive, educated and knowledgable, and who might be expected to do a little windmill tilting of their own, have had the get up and go knocked out of them. Their lives, hopes and aspirations have been overwhelmed by survival induced exhaustion. By the time they are old enough to have acquired the wit and cunning to do something about the ideals they had when they were young, they have become too busy, too beholden, too fearful and too cautious. They have been persuaded (probably unwillingly and almost certainly against their better judgement) to trust those in authority. They are exhausted by the constant demands of the trivial problems and endless unnecessary changes which decimate our days and tear the heart out of weeks (None of the trivial problems appears trivial when they are confronted, of course. Our bureaucratic masters have a way of imbuing every order and every demand with a sense of urgency and importance.) And, eventually, they will have probably forgotten the ideals which burnt into their hearts when they were young and they will have lost the passion that fed them.

The result is that there are no intellectual radicals around these days. Where are our Paines, Bunyans, Cobbetts or Wilkes? Where, for heaven's sake, are our Shelleys or our Byrons? I have no doubt that they exist but they have been silenced. They certainly will not have been given any airtime by the BBC or any column inches by our broadsheets. They self-publish books, booklets, magazines and newsletters. They have been marginalised by the State-controlled media aristocracy.

But all is not lost. I have no doubt that eventually the people will have had enough. There will be anger at the public graft and private plunder; anger at the greed of the bankers and the corporate bosses who bleed their companies dry; anger at the pension fund managers whose investment style is simple smash and grab; anger at the extent of public graft; anger at wasteful government spending; anger at the absurdity of the pensions given to public sector workers; anger at the demands of the scroungers; anger at the extent of corruption in our society; anger at the ever growing taxes; and anger at the all invasive bureaucracy. The anger will result in a demand for change and some sort of revolution will be inevitable.

So, in the end there will be changes. The anger at the bureaucratic fascism of the European Union will lead to a resurgence of strong bordered nationalism. The anger at a combination of unreasonably high taxes and unreasonably low services will lead to mass tax avoidance and evasion and the bankruptcy of State after State around Europe. The European Union will implode and collapse. The United States of America will be bankrupted by its massive debts to China. Globalisation will lead us remorselessly into a global slowdown that will last for decades. (With Europe and America broken and impoverished who will buy all those Chinese television sets?)

But, that's for the future. Meanwhile, there is a good deal more pain to come before we get where we are going.

In the short and medium term we face a bleak future. Governments will spend less and tax more. People will work more but have less to spend. Nationalism and racism will rise in popularity; often with unpleasant and violent consequences. The anger directed at bankers will lead to renewed bouts of anti-Jewish activity. Enthusiasm for globalisation will disappear and be replaced by isolationism and protectionism. As the EU collapses the bureaucrats will, in desperation, demand (and take) more and more power. Inflation will soar, bringing back memories of German citizens buying loaves of bread with wheelbarrows full of money. Growth and productivity will plummet. There will be more wars and revolutions.

Our society is broken; we are controlled by fascist overseers and living in a foreign land. Within England there is not one Government department which is fit for purpose. We have not been led, we have been misled. We are persecuted and harassed by greedy, corrupt, petty, mean and incompetent bureaucrats (largely foreign) who spend their days and our money devising an endless array of pointless, damaging new laws designed for their benefit not ours. Our society is so grotesquely mismanaged that it is possible to argue that it is now immoral to pay tax, immoral to obey the law and immoral to support anyone boasting membership of one of the three main parties. It is possible to argue that in our world, the only true patriots are revolutionary anarchists who know that before we can rebuild our society we must break down the corrupt structure which exists.

So, where is the hope?

With our more thoughtful citizens oppressed and suppressed by police-state broadcasters, fascist politicians and heavily booted forces of law and order the future lies in the hands of the middle classes and the revolution that ferments will not be a peaceful one.

All revolutions are started by middle class people. It isn't the unemployed or the privileged classes who start revolutions. The former are too busy hunting for scraps. The latter are too busy running super-yachts and premier league football clubs. It has always been the same. It is hard-working individuals who realise that things

319

could and should be better. Most of the rebellions and nearly all the reforms which occurred in English history were backed by individuals who were not themselves suffering from the grievances they worked to remove. This is true philanthropy (not the modern kind, which involves a tax dodge, a publicity stunt and a cheque which never actually arrives). Among England's greatest reformers were William Wilberforce, John Howard, Elizabeth Fry and Florence Nightingale. Their reforms changed the world, not just England, and they all relied upon changing public opinion. Revolutionary social ideas were popularised by great artists such as Milton in the 17th century, Blake and Shelley in the early part of the 19th century and, in the later part of the century John Ruskin and William Morris. The world has only ever been changed by small groups of dedicated and determined people, naturally irreverent and uneasy with authority (the sort of behaviour that is banned these days and likely to get you into a lot of trouble.) Tomorrow's revolutionaries will have to work hard and it will, I suspect, be the old-fashioned printing press, rather than the computer or the Internet or the mobile telephone, which will give them power.

And the violence?

Well, there is plenty of historical evidence to show that revolutionary violence works while peaceful forms of protest are easily suppressed. And when violent revolutions work the leaders quickly become the new establishment. Nelson Mandela, the most famous and successful terrorist of the 20th century, is now revered by the fascist establishment as some sort of god-like figure.

So, the bottom, bottom line is that the medium term is bleak. Life for our children, our children's children and their children too, will be dark and hard.

But the long-term...well, the long-term will be what tomorrow's revolutionaries choose to make it.

Vernon Coleman, Summer 2012

The Author

Vernon Coleman qualified as a doctor in 1970 and has worked both in hospitals and as a GP. He is (for now) still registered and licensed to practise as a GP principal. He has founded and organised many campaigns concerning iatrogenesis, drug addiction and the abuse of animals and has given evidence to committees at the House of Commons and the House of Lords. Dr Coleman's campaigns have often proved successful. For example, after a 15 year campaign (which started in 1973) he eventually persuaded the British Government to introduce stricter controls governing the prescribing of benzodiazepine tranquillisers. 'Dr Vernon Coleman's articles, to which I refer with approval, raised concern about these important matters,' said the Parliamentary Secretary for Health in the House of Commons in 1988.

He has worked as a columnist for numerous national newspapers including *The Sun, The Daily Star, The Sunday Express* and *The People*. He once wrote three columns at the same time for national papers (he wrote them under three different names, Dr Duncan Scott in *The Sunday People*, Dr James in *The Sun* and Dr Vernon Coleman in the *Daily Star*). At the same time he was also writing weekly columns for the *Evening Times* in Glasgow and for the *Sunday Scot*. His syndicated columns have appeared in over 50 regional newspapers. His columns and articles have appeared in newspapers and magazines around the world and he has contributed articles and stories to hundreds of other publications including *The Sunday Times, Observer, Guardian, Daily Telegraph, Sunday Telegraph, Daily Express, Daily Mail, Mail on Sunday, Daily Mirror, Sunday Mirror, Punch, Woman, Woman's Own, The Lady, Spectator* and *British Medical Journal*. He was the founding editor of the *British Clinical Journal*.

For many years he wrote a monthly newsletter. He has worked with the Open University and lectured doctors and nurses on a variety of medical matters.

He has presented numerous programmes on television and radio and was the original breakfast television doctor. He was television's first agony uncle (on BBC1's *The Afternoon Show*) and presented three TV series based on his bestselling book *Bodypower*. In the now long-gone days when producers and editors were less wary of annoying the establishment he was a regular broadcaster on radio and television.

In recent years he has worried many parts of the establishment and today he is widely banned from television and radio and his books are no longer reviewed in newspapers where editors hope to be remembered in the honours lists.

In the 1980s he wrote the algorithms for the first computerised health programmes - which sold around the world to those far-sighted individuals who had bought the world's first home computers.

His books have been published in the UK *by Arrow, Pan, Penguin, Corgi, Mandarin, Star, Piatkus, RKF Thames and Hudson, Sidgwick and Jackson, Macmillan* and many other leading publishing houses and translated into 25 languages. English language versions sell in the USA, Australia, Canada and South Africa as well as the UK. Several of his books have appeared on both the *Sunday Times* and *Bookseller* bestseller lists. Altogether, he has written over 100 books which have, together, sold over two million copies in the UK alone. His novel *Mr Caldicot's Cabbage War* has been filmed and is, like many of his other novels, available in an audio version. He has co-written four books with his wife, Donna Antoinette Coleman. He has, in addition, written numerous articles (and some books) under a vast variety of pennames (many of which he has now forgotten). When he feels tired (which happens with increasing frequency) the Princess reminds him of all this and he sometimes feels better for a little while.

He has never had a proper job (in the sense of working for someone else in regular, paid employment, with a cheque or pay packet at the end of the week or month) but he has had freelance and temporary employment in many forms. He has, for example, had paid employment as: magician's assistant, postman, fish delivery van driver, production line worker, chemical laboratory assistant, author, publisher, draughtsman, meals on wheels driver, feature writer, drama critic, book reviewer, columnist, surgeon, police surgeon, industrial medical officer, social worker, night club operator, property developer, magazine editor, general practitioner, private doctor, television presenter, radio presenter, agony aunt, university lecturer, casualty doctor and care home assistant.

Today, he likes books, films and writing. He writes, reads and collects books and has a larger library than most towns. A list of his favourite authors would require another book. He has never been much of an athlete though he once won a certificate for swimming a width of the public baths in Walsall (which was, at the time, in Staffordshire but has now, apparently, been moved elsewhere). He no longer cherishes hopes of being called upon to play cricket for England and is resigned to the fact that he will now never drive a Formula 1 racing car in anger.

He doesn't like yappy dogs, big snarly dogs with saliva dripping from their fangs or people who think that wearing a uniform automatically gives them status and rights over everyone else. He likes trains, dislikes planes and used to like cars until spoilsports invented speed cameras, bus lanes and car parks where the spaces are so narrow that only the slimmest, and tinniest of vehicles will fit in.

He is inordinately fond of cats, likes pens and notebooks and used to enjoy watching cricket until the authorities sold out and allowed people to paint slogans on the grass. His interests and hobbies include animals, books, photography, drawing, chess, backgammon, cinema, philately, billiards, sitting in cafés and on benches and collecting Napoleana and old books that were written and published before dustwrappers were invented. He likes log fires and bonfires, motor racing and music by Beethoven, Mozart and Mahler and dislikes politicians, bureaucrats and cauliflower cheese. He likes videos but loathes DVDs.

Vernon Coleman lives in the delightful if isolated village of Bilbury in Devon where he and his wife have designed for themselves a unique world to sustain and nourish them in these dark and difficult times. He enjoys malt whisky, toasted muffins and old films. He is devoted to Donna Antoinette who is the kindest, sweetest, most sensitive woman a man could hope to meet and who, as an undeserved but welcome bonus, makes the very best roast parsnips on the planet. He says that gourmands and gourmets would come from far and wide if they knew what they were missing but admits that since he and his pal Thumper Robinson took down the road signs (in order to discourage American tourists travelling to Bilbury on coaches) the village where he lives has become exceedingly difficult to find.

Reference Articles referring to Vernon Coleman

'Volunteer for Kirkby'

The Guardian, 14.5.1965

(Article re VC's work in Kirkby, Liverpool as a Community Service Volunteer in 1964-5)

'Bumbledom forced me to leave the NHS'

Pulse, 28.11.1981

Vernon Coleman resigns as a GP after refusing to disclose confidential information on sick note forms.

'Medicine Becomes Computerised: Plug In Your Doctor.'

The Times, 29.3.1983

Sample quote: 'When the children have finished playing the games on your Sinclair or Commodore Vic 2 computer, you can turn it to more practical purposes. For what is probably Britain's first home doctor programm for computers is now available. 'Dr Vernon Coleman, one of the country's leading medical authors, has prepare the text for a remarkable set of six cassettes called *The Home Doctor Series.* Dr Coleman, author of the new boo *Bodypower,* which is a new self-help approach to medicine, has turned his attention to computers.'

'Computer aided decision making in medicine'

British Medical Journal, 8.9.1984 and 27.10.1984

Editorial (and subsequent letter) discussing Vernon Coleman's computer software.

'Doctor with the Common Touch.'

Birmingham Post, 9.10.1984

Sample quote: 'Dr Coleman has the golden gift of being able to sweeten the bitter pill of knowledge with a coatir of humour, and of presenting revolutionary concepts in words everyone can understand.'

'Sacred Cows Beware: Vernon Coleman publishing again.'

The Scotsman, 6.12.1984

Sample quote: 'Vernon Coleman's books combine straightforward advice with stern criticism of techniques, products or services which he believes to be a waste of time and money or which may cause actual harm.'

'I'm Addicted To The Star'

The Star, 10.3.1988

Sample quote: 'Dr Coleman has consistently called for rethinking on the drugs known as benzodiazepines. Now the Government's Committee on Safety of Medicines has reacted to Dr Coleman's campaign. They have issued stringent guidelines for the prescribing of the drugs. Mrs Currie (Health Minister) told a Commons standing committee that the Government acted because of Dr Coleman's columns in *The Star.* She said 'Dr Coleman's articles, to which I refer with approval, raised concern about these important matters and I sent them to the appropriate bodies.'

'Our Doctor Coleman Is Mustard'

The Sun, 29.6.1988

Sample quote: 'Dr Coleman cuts like a scalpel through all the jargon to bring you fresh information on the medical matters that mean most to you...Dr Coleman's controversial views have often rocked the medical profession but that has never stopped him saying what he thinks.'

'The Sun's Medic reveals his all.'

UP, 12.7.1991

Sample quote: 'He clearly believes what he writes and nobody 'not the editor of *The Sun* or anyone else' tells him what stance to take. And once he gets his teeth into an issue he will campaign in partisan and highly effective style.'

`Reading the mind between the lines.'

BMA News Review, November 1991

Sample quote: `Not someone to mince his words.'

Doctors' Firsts

BMA News Review, 21.2.1996

Interview with VC.

`The big league of self publishing.'

Daily Telegraph, 17.8.1996

Sample quote: `Dr Coleman is one of a growing band of go-it-alone novelists who have taken the risk of publishin

their own books. Dr Coleman's books are published in 22 languages and he was published for many years b

mainstream publishers like *Penguin, Reed* and *Harper Collins,* before going it alone.'

`Doctoring the books'

Independent, 16.3.1999

Sample quote: `He says there are three things in life worth doing: trying to change the world, trying to have fun an

trying to make money. If you can do all three things at the same time then that's fantastic.'

`Conscientious Objectors'

Financial Times magazine, 9.8.2003

Interview with VC after he resigned from The People.

`Sick Practices'

Ode Magazine, July/August 2003

Sample quote: `Dr Vernon Coleman has made it his life's work to teach us about our self-healing abilities. Th erudite Englishman wrote over 90 books on the subject.'

You have been warned, Mr Blair.'

Spectator, 6.3.2004 and 20.3.2004

Sample quote: `He doesn't have an agent, a publisher, a distributor or a heap of remaindered copies reminding him he never earned out his advance, because he does all these jobs himself. As a result our doctor is completely independent, and can afford to stick two fingers up not only at medicine and mainstream publishing but also at Bush, Blair, Lord Hutton, those who want to surrender British sovereignty to a European superstate, the pharmaceutical industry, animal experimenters, Dr Atkins, Uncle Tom Cobley and everyone who eats meat.'

Food for thought with a real live Maverick.'

Western Daily Press, 5.9.2006

Sample quote: `Simply a very good and genial individual and it's a great pity there aren't more like him.'

The doctor will see you now'

Independent, 14.5.2008

Sample quote: `He's frank, fearless and prolific. He's outrageous, outspoken and iconoclastic. A Vernon Coleman book will change your life...and may even save your life.'

Note 1: Vernon Coleman gave evidence to the *House of Lords Select Committee on Animals in Scientific Procedures* (2001-2) on Tuesday 12.2.02

Note 2: Significant interviews with Vernon Coleman have appeared in *Devon Life* (`Vernon Coleman Scourge of the BMA.'), *National Health Executive,* (`An interview with Vernon Coleman'), *The Therapist* (`Vernon Coleman - the doctor's dilemma.' and *The Flag* (`Interview with Dr Vernon Coleman')

Printed in Great Britain
by Amazon

48511708R00194